RUSSIA'S
TRANSFORMATION

RUSSIA'S
TRANSFORMATION

SNAPSHOTS OF A CRUMBLING SYSTEM

ROBERT V. DANIELS

ROWMAN & LITTLEFIELD
Lanham • Boulder • New York • Oxford

ROWMAN & LITTLEFIELD PUBLISHERS, INC.

Published in the United States of America
by Rowman & Littlefield Publishers, Inc.
4720 Boston Way, Lanham, Maryland 20706

12 Hid's Copse Road
Cummor Hill, Oxford OX2, 9JJ, England

British Library Cataloguing in Publication Information Available

Library of Congress Cataloging-in-Publication Data

Daniels, Robert Vincent.
    Russia's transformation : snapshots of a crumbling system / Robert V. Daniels.
      p. cm.
    Includes bibliographical references and index.
    ISBN 0-8476-8708-2 (cloth : alk. paper)—ISBN 0-8476-8709-0 (pbk. alk. paper)
    1. Soviet Union—Politics and government—1985–1991. 2. Russia (Federation)—
Politics and government—1991– I. Title.
DK288.D36   1997
947.085'4—dc21   97-36039
                                                  CIP

ISBN 0-8476-8708-2 (cloth : alk. paper)
ISBN 0-8476-8709-0 (pbk. : alk. paper)

Printed in the United States of America

♾ ™ The paper used in this publication meets the minimum requirements of American
National Standard for Information Sciences—Permanence of Paper for Printed Library
Materials, ANSI Z39.48–1984.

Contents

PART IV
THE CRISIS AND COLLAPSE OF PERESTROIKA, 1990–1991

PART V
RUSSIA SEEKS SALVATION, 1992–1995

PREFACE

This book is a collection of observations on Soviet and Russian politics, mainly since the beginning of reform under Mikhail Gorbachev in 1985, and extending to the consolidation of power by Boris Yeltsin. My aim in bringing these articles together is to provide a moving picture of the system as it appeared from moment to moment, and thus show what could be known or anticipated at the time of the actual events as the history of Russia's extraordinary transformation unfolded.

The focus of these articles is top-level politics in Moscow. This is not to denigrate the significance of social, economic, and cultural issues, or of foreign affairs, or the importance of regional life or the national minorities, but simply reflects my interest. However, in the Soviet system and to a degree for its successor, politics at the center has been unusually decisive in shaping the problems and possibilities in other locations and in other aspects of public life.

In republishing these articles no attempt has been made to correct or update their content; rather, the intention has been to preserve the view of the Soviet/Russian scene just as it appeared at the time of each successive observation. The materials have been lightly edited to remove repetitious or extraneous material, or improve readability. Where the editing of published versions diverged from my original manuscripts, I have generally adhered to the latter. The individual articles appear in the chronological sequence of their composition, except for a couple of instances where the chronology of the subject matter invites a different order.

The preparation of this collection has been a collaborative effort with my wife, Alice M. Daniels; without her contribution it could never have been accomplished. I am also indebted to Abraham Brumberg for his editorial suggestions and critiques. I am grateful to Susan McEachern of Rowman and Littlefield for her constant support and encouragement, and I especially wish to thank Myron Kolatch, executive editor of *The New Leader*, for his kind permission to reprint a number of my articles which first appeared there.

ACKNOWLEDGMENTS

Chapter 1 was first published in Martine Godet, ed., *De Russie et d'ailleurs: Feux croisés de l'histoire* (Paris: Institut d'Études Slaves, 1995), 213–23; slightly abridged here. Reprinted by permission.

Chapter 2 was first published in John W. Strong, ed., *The Soviet Union under Brezhnev and Kosygin* (New York: Van Nostrand Reinhold, © 1971), 16–25. Reprinted by permission of Wadsworth Publishing Co.

Chapter 3 was first published in Norton T. Dodge, ed., *Analysis of the USSR's 24th Party Congress and 9th Five-Year Plan* (Mechanicsville, Md.: Cremona Foundation, 1971), 75–79. Reprinted by permission.

Chapter 4 was published in French in *Le Monde Diplomatique*, July 1977, 10–11; the author's translation is published here, by permission.

Chapters 5–11, 13, 14, 22–24, 26, 28, 30, and 34 first appeared in *The New Leader*, 29 Nov. 1982; 24 Jan. 1983; 20 Feb. 1984; 11 March 1985; 24 Feb. 1986; 19 Oct. 1987; 11 July and 31 Oct. 1988; 28 Jan. and 30 Dec. 1991; 14–28 Feb. 1994; 9–23 Sept. 1991; 29 June 1992; and 8 March and 4–18 Oct. 1993. Reprinted by permission.

Chapters 12, 15, and 17–21 were published in Italian in *Rinascita*, 25 June 1988; 8 April 1989; 22 March, 29 April, 22 July, and 2 Dec. 1990; and 20 Jan. 1991.

Chapter 25 is an abridged version of a chapter published in James E. Hickey and Alexej Ugrinsky, eds., *Government Structures in the USA and the Sovereign States of the Former USSR* (Westport, Conn.: Greenwood Press, an imprint of Greenwood Publishing Group, Inc., 1996), 31–40. Reprinted by permission.

Chapter 29 was published in Italian in *L'Unità*, 28 Oct. 1992; the author's translation appears here.

Chapters 32, 36, and 38 are abridged versions of articles that appeared in *Dissent*, fall 1993, 489–96; winter 1994, 32–34; and summer 1995, pp. 307–12. Reprinted by permission.

Chapter 33 was published in Italian in *Politica ed Economia* 24, no. 3 (Nov.–Dec. 1993), 9–14.

Chapter 37 is an abridged version of a chapter published in Michael Kraus and Ronald Liebowitz, eds., *Russia and Eastern Europe after Communism: The Search for New Political, Economic, and Security Systems* (Boulder, Colo.: Westview Press, © 1996), 51–64. Reprinted by permission of Westview Press.

Chapter 39 appeared in Michael Cox, ed., *The End of the USSR and the Collapse of Soviet Studies* (London: Pinter, 1997). Reprinted by permission.

Chapters 16, 27, 31, and 35 have not been previously published.

CHRONOLOGY OF EVENTS

1917	February Revolution (in March, by the Western calendar); fall of Tsar Nicholas II; Provisional Government
	October (November) Revolution: Bolsheviks led by Lenin establish Soviet Republic
1918–1921	Civil War and "War Communism"
1921–1928	New Economic Policy (NEP)
1922 (Mar.)	Stalin made General Secretary of the Communist Party
1924 (Jan.)	USSR established
	Death of Lenin
1928–1929	Stalin becomes dictator; Stalin Revolution with five-year plans and collectivization begins
1931	Gorbachev and Yeltsin born
1936–1938	Purges
1941–1945	World War II
1953 (Mar.)	Death of Stalin
1956 (Feb.)	"De-Stalinization" under Khrushchev
1964 (Oct.)	Fall of Khrushchev, Brezhnev General Secretary
1982 (Nov.)	Death of Brezhnev; Andropov General Secretary
1984 (Feb.)	Death of Andropov; Chernenko General Secretary
1985 (Mar.)	Death of Chernenko; Gorbachev General Secretary, begins *perestroika*
(Nov.)	Geneva Summit (Gorbachev and Reagan)
1986 (Feb.)	Twenty-Seventh Party Congress
(Apr.)	Chernobyl disaster; Gorbachev begins *glasnost*
(Oct.)	Reykjavik Summit (Gorbachev and Reagan)
1987 (Jan.)	Central Committee plenum: Gorbachev begins democratization
(summer)	Gorbachev writes *Perestroika*
(Nov.)	Gorbachev's anniversary speech
(Dec.)	Washington Summit (Gorbachev and Reagan; INF treaty signed)
1988 (Jan.)	Law on State Enterprises
(Mar.)	"Andreyeva letter"; conservative threat
(Apr.)	Geneva Agreement on Afghanistan
(June–July)	Nineteenth Party Conference
(Sept.)	"September Revolution"—defeat of conserva-

	tives; Gorbachev chairman of Supreme Soviet; constitution democratized
1989 (Mar.)	Election of Congress of People's Deputies
(Apr.)	Tbilisi massacre
(May)	Congress convenes, elects new Supreme Soviet
(Oct.–Dec.)	Anti-Communist revolutions in Eastern Europe
(Dec.)	Malta Summit (Gorbachev and Bush; Cold War ended)
1990 (Feb.)	Party gives up monopoly
(Mar.)	Gorbachev elected president by Supreme Soviet
	Election of republic parliaments; Popular Front victories
(Mar.–May)	Baltic republics declare independence
(May)	Yeltsin chairman of Supreme Soviet of Russia
(July)	Twenty-Eighth Party Congress; Yeltsin quits Communist Party
(Aug.–Sept.)	500 Days economic reform plan
(Dec.)	Gorbachev appoints conservatives; Shevardnadze resigns
1991 (Jan.)	Vilnius massacre
(Mar.)	Democracy demonstration; Gorbachev rejects repression
(Apr.)	Novo-Ogarevo Agreements on Union Treaty
(June)	Yeltsin elected president of Russia
(July)	Last Central Committee plenum; new party program
	Moscow Summit (Gorbachev and Bush; START treaty signed)
(Aug. 19–21)	Attempted coup; Communist Party leadership dissolved
(Nov.)	Yeltsin gets emergency powers, starts economic decontrol
(Dec.)	Belovezhsk Agreement: Soviet Union dissolved, Commonwealth of Independent States proclaimed; Gorbachev resigns
1992 (Jan.)	Yeltsin decontrols prices; inflation accelerates
(June)	Washington Summit (Yeltsin and Bush)
(Dec.)	Gaidar replaced by Chernomyrdin as prime minister
1993 (Mar.)	Yeltsin threatens to dissolve parliament, escapes impeachment
(Apr.)	Yeltsin wins referendum
(Sept.–Oct.)	Yeltsin dissolves Russian parliament, suppresses resistance

(Dec.)	Election: new constitution adopted; Duma—Communist and nationalist comeback
1994 (Mar.)	Duma votes amnesty
1995 (Dec.)	Duma election—Communists gain
1996 (June–July)	Yeltsin reelected president

Introduction

Rarely in history, short of defeat and occupation or a bloody revolution, does a nation go through such a rapid and at the same time profound transformation as Russia/the Soviet Union has experienced since the mid-1980s. Some, including the reform chief Mikhail Gorbachev himself, call this time of intense change a revolution, though it hardly reached that extreme; indeed, it was more nearly the end of a long and often agonizing process of revolution that began in 1917 or even in 1905. This perspective helps explain why the Communist system did not undergo a broadly violent convulsion in its death throes, and ended with a whimper, not a bang.

Nevertheless, Russia's transformation as Communism came to its demise was far-reaching and unsettling. Psychologically and economically, the progression from dictatorial order to the chaos of free-market experiment was as disruptive as any literal revolution. Why, then, was such a cataclysmic event not more explicitly anticipated and understood by those outside the Communist realm—academics, journalists, government experts—whose profession it was to observe and interpret the Soviet Union and its sphere? The answer, contrary to the common impression, is that the collapse of Communism was indeed anticipated, at least in an incremental sort of way, as events unfolded and evidence accumulated. No stage of Russia's transformation was altogether surprising to people who were aware of the immediate background of events, though the details of the ultimate outcome were beyond the scope of initial prediction. History is buffeted by too many indeterminacies, and events may be as surprising to the political actors themselves as to those who observe them.

Certain interpretive themes have advanced or receded in their applicability as Russia underwent its transformation; others have remained consistently prominent. Russia has been constantly caught in the tension between a modernizing society on the one hand, and on the other, governments, both Soviet and post-Soviet, that have tried to evade the implications of modern social and economic reality through recourse to one form or another of utopian rhetoric. The politics of insider rivalries and power struggles have gone on shaping public policy under diverse regimes and rationales. An enduring political culture, comprising habits of both dominance and submission, of long-suffering apathy and bouts of impassioned defiance, underlay events throughout the transformation.

In other respects, the pre-Gorbachev, Gorbachev, and Yeltsin eras make very different calls upon their interpreters. The prereform Soviet system, whatever else may be said about it, was much more orderly and rule-governed than what came after, even if some of the rules—the status system in the Communist leadership, the "circular flow of power," the peculiar pluralism of "participatory bureaucracy"—were unacknowledged and accessible only through the inference practiced by "kremlinology." Hindsight, of course, makes the Soviet system seem clearer. As Tolstoy pointed out, it is easier to discern (or imagine) regularities and reason in events, the further back one looks.

Prereform Russian government, being more stable, became with the passage of time a unique gerontocracy. Conflict among generations was a hallmark of the Gorbachev period, while the post-Soviet system became an arena for youthful egoism, both in politics and in economic life. Each era was distinguished by a dominant personality, in a distinct progression from the rigidity of Leonid Brezhnev through the incremental boldness of Mikhail Gorbachev to the mercurial radicalism and self-justification of Boris Yeltsin. Decisions by individual leaders, and conflicts among them, notably the duel between Gorbachev and Yeltsin, added a high measure of unpredictability in a country where the will of the top man had an inordinate importance whatever the kind of regime he headed.

Understanding Russia through all the surprising phases of its transformation has been a daunting challenge to specialists in the West, whether academic or governmental, even though they have made it their business to follow and interpret developments in that enigmatic country. Theories have come and gone with the kaleidoscope of events, and the immensity of the whole transformation of the 1980s and 1990s seemed to the laity to call into question the entire enterprise of Soviet/Russian studies. Yet as the transformation unfolded, the experts understood more than the popular media credited them with, and the need for such expert understanding did not cease with the official demise of Communism. While the successor regime is more open, it is also less orderly and more paradoxical. Russia is still far from becoming what its people long for, a "normal country."

PART ONE

THE SETTING

CHAPTER ONE

The Revolutionary Process, the Moderate Revolutionary Revivial, and Post-Communist Russia (1994)

The decline, fall, and replacement of the Soviet system has been a historical process of epochally complex proportions. Its adequate understanding requires a perspective that can relate this startling experience to the Soviet past as a whole. This end is served by a comparative theory of revolution that can connect events in Russia from 1917 to the present time in a dynamic framework of successive causes and effects, culminating in a series of disruptive efforts to shed decades of postrevolutionary dictatorship and return to some form of historic hopefulness.

The startling series of events in Russia since the advent of Mikhail Gorbachev and *perestroika* in 1985 has generated a multitude of interpretations from every political direction. A new revolution, as Gorbachev himself maintained? A counterrevolution, as the few die-hard Communists allege? A "transition to democracy" on the Latin American model, as Western aid-givers hope? Or a new "Time of Troubles" opening the way to a new authoritarianism and a new tsar, as pessimistic Russian liberals suggest? Generally these theories rely on facile historical analogies chosen to suit the political inclinations of the individual observer. Hardly anyone analyzes realistically the processes in Russian society that set the stage for this chaotic era, or puts these developments in a proper perspective of world history.

I propose to argue that the kaleidoscopic record of Russian politics since 1985 cannot be fully understood without placing it in the context of the country's tortuous revolutionary experience ever since 1917. In turn, to extract its full explanatory relevance, the Russian Revolution has to be seen in a comparative framework, as one instance of a complex but intelligible phenomenon that has erupted in the history of many different countries at various points in time.

❖   ❖   ❖

To begin with, a convulsion such as the Russian Revolution is not a momentary event but a long process, where one event or set of circumstances leads to another in a recognizable, in part even predictable, chain of cause and effect. True revolutions like the upheaval in Russia cannot be explained merely as the work of revolutionaries, for good or for ill; they are the violent expression of a deep crisis in the historical development of the society in question. As the Emperor Napoleon remarked in exile, "A revolution can be neither made nor stopped."[1]

The revolutionary process has a characteristic shape, manifested one way or another in all the great revolutions of history. They break out when the tension between a changing, modernizing society can no longer be sustained. Shaken by some triggering event such as defeat in war or a financial crisis, the Old Regime yields to liberal reformers, who hope to cure the country's ills by legal and nonviolent means. But radicalism grows, with the political mobilization of broader strata of the population and the expression of popular demands that have long gone unmet. At the same time, the liberals are challenged by counterrevolutionaries trying to preserve the old authoritarian order, even at the price of civil war. By civil war or by coup d'état, radical leadership takes over and sets a course of violent utopianism, often accompanied by terror. Finally, of its own volition or by force of another coup, the revolutionary government is adjusted to the need to retreat from its extreme goals, and experiences the "Thermidorean reaction," on the model of the downfall of Maximilien Robespierre in 1794.

This pattern of upward and downward curves in the revolutionary process has been noted by many writers. Shortly before his expulsion from the Communist Party, Leon Trotsky warned,

> In the Great French Revolution there were two great chapters, of which one went like this [points upward] and the other like that [points downward].
>   . . . When the chapter headed like this—upwards—the French Jacobins, the Bolsheviks of that time, guillotined the Royalists and the Girondists. We, too, have had a similar great chapter when we . . . shot the White Guards and exiled the Girondists [i.e., the Mensheviks and SRs]. And then there began another chapter in France, when the French Ustrialovs and semi-Ustrialovs—the Thermidoreans and Bonapartists from among the right-wing Jacobins—began exiling and shooting the Left Jacobins—the Bolsheviks of the time.[2]

The American historian Crane Brinton used a medical image of the process, likening the revolutionary society to a patient suffering from a fever that rises up to a point of crisis, and then subsides.[3] However, Brinton and most others had little to say about the path a country might follow after the Thermidorean Reaction had moderated the revolution's excesses. Generally this period witnesses the reassertion of authority by an individual—sometimes the radical leader, more often someone else—who accomplishes a synthesis of old methods and new rhetoric, and launches revolutionary war against foreign powers or against his own people.

This characteristic stage I call "postrevolutionary dictatorship." The term is designedly broad, so as not to limit its applicability by naming it after one particular practitioner such as Bonaparte or Stalin, or by connecting it exclusively either to the revolutionaries or the counterrevolutionaries.

❖   ❖   ❖

Time does not stand still, and the revolutionary process does not end with the postrevolutionary dictatorship or even with monarchical restoration. Typically there comes a point—it was the Glorious Revolution of 1688 in Restoration England, and the Revolution of 1830 in Restoration France—when postrevolutionary authoritarianism is thrown off. A similar purgation can be observed in countries where the revolution had come to grief in avowedly counterrevolutionary dictatorships, notably in West Germany after 1945 and in Spain after the death of Francisco Franco in 1975. Seeking a new beginning at this point, the nation turns back to the principles of the earliest, liberal stage of its revolution, with emphasis on personal liberty and representative government. This final stage of the revolutionary process I therefore term the "moderate revolutionary revival." It takes place when a country manages to start its revolution over again, so to speak, without the fanaticism and polarization that undermined the original attempt at reform and drove the process on to dictatorship and civil war.

The English, when asked about their revolution, usually prefer to think of 1688, a very moderate, bloodless, properly English sort of event, while they push to the back of their consciousness the far more profound, violent, truly revolutionary—and un-English—events of 1640 to 1660. There is a reason for this historical preference: 1688 was indeed more moderate than the 1640s and 1650s because it was the end of a revolutionary process, not the high point, and our English contemporaries are the heirs of the settlement of 1688. 1688 restored the constitutional balance between the crown and the legislative branch (soon to evolve into parliamentary supremacy), along with religious toleration, leaving intact the symbolic traditions of the monarchy and the church hierarchy. Rejected in 1688 were the aims both of the extreme revolutionaries—the republican regicides and religious libertarians of 1649—and of the counterrevolutionaries—the restorationists of 1660 and especially the partisans of royal absolutism supporting King James II.

The French revolutionary experience differed significantly from the English, particularly in involving the urban and rural masses as historical actors. Nevertheless, the basic shape of the revolutionary process commencing in 1789 bore remarkable resemblances to its cross-Channel predecessor: a relatively moderate beginning, again, as the new representative bodies challenged the power of the monarchy and the Church; an eruption of escalating extremism in 1792, with localized manifestations of civil war; two episodes of dictatorship, revolutionary under Robespierre and postrevolutionary under Bonaparte (whereas Oliver Cromwell's regime evolved from the one to the other); and monarchist restoration. Then came the reaction to the reaction, as in England, when the partisans of constitutional government overturned the Bourbon dynasty in July 1830 and instituted a limited monarchy resembling the constitution of 1791.

With Germany we come to a very different kind of revolutionary experience, one not usually recognized in comparative studies of the phenomenon. I would nevertheless suggest that many of the essential features of the Anglo-French type of revolutionary process can be identified in Germany. The November Revolution of 1918, though it removed the monarchy, was contained within moderate channels—so much so that the moderate phase was prolonged throughout the 1920s, despite assaults on the Weimar Republic from both the Left and the Right. The distinctive difference in Germany was that the moderate regime fell victim to an extremist mass movement not of the Left, with its slogans of democracy and equality, but to an extremist mass movement of the Right, distinguished by its avowed authoritarianism and aggressive nationalism.

Adolf Hitler's revolution of the Right, from the standpoint of the process analysis, combined features of the classic extremist phase, of the postrevolutionary dictatorship, and of conservative counterrevolution. Like Bonaparte's postrevolutionary regime, it ended in complete military defeat, but in this instance the conquerors sponsored not a restoration of the Wilhelmian Empire but regimes more in their own images. In the new West Germany the Western powers set up what was in effect a revived Weimar republic, in other words the moderate revolutionary revival by courtesy of the occupation forces. The process went by quite a different route in the Soviet zone of Germany, where the representatives of the victors fashioned a clone of the postrevolutionary dictatorship prevailing in the Soviet Union.

An outcome similar to Germany's can be observed in Spain, following the moderate revolution of 1931 against the monarchy, the extremist eruption of 1936, the victory of counterrevolution in the Civil War, and the long dictatorship of General Franco, a restored monarchy without a monarch. This time it was simply the death of the dictator that opened the way for the moderate revolutionary revival and democratic government, facilitated by the restoration of the actual monarchy on a constitutional and largely symbolic basis (a concession to tradition that the liberals of 1931 had rejected).

While these parallels may be persuasive, the concept of the moderate revolutionary revival requires some kind of explanation in terms of the social forces underlying the revolutionary process and the political legacy that it bequeaths. Generally, every great revolution, as a developmental crisis, unleashes aspirations for social change that run ahead of what the given country's level of development or degree of modernization can sustain for long—hence the inevitability of retreat and consolidation, whether under revolutionary or counterrevolutionary auspices. But eventually social development again overtakes the political synthesis of postrevolutionary rule, as in the original revolutionary instance, though less intensely. Further, the eventual failure of the French experiment of 1830 suggests that if the moderate revival tries to turn the clock back too far—to 1789 instead of 1792 in this case—its chances of success are diminished. This could be a lesson for Boris Yeltsin's Russia.

❖   ❖   ❖

In its early years the process of revolution in Russia conformed closely to the Anglo-French model—a moderate phase represented first by the abortive revolution of 1905 and then by the February Revolution and the Provisional Government, and an extremist phase initiated by Vladimir Lenin's October Revolution and pursued through the years of the Civil War and War Communism. Thereafter, the actual course of events in Russia took an unusual turn. By introducing the New Economic Policy in 1921, Lenin opted for a strategic retreat from the party's revolutionary goals, and thus the Russian revolutionaries were able to cling to power by carrying out their own Thermidorean reaction. However, the survival of the one-party dictatorship and the centralist legacy of the War Communism period, along with "the disintegration of societal life, . . . cynicism, dual morality, and loss of faith," to cite Gorbachev's lieutenant Alexander Yakovlev,[4] created the opportunity for an aspiring postrevolutionary dictator.

Joseph Stalin was the man to seize this opportunity, after Lenin made him General Secretary of the party and then fell ill too soon to correct his mistake. Building upon an apparatus of personal power within the party, Stalin achieved the functional analogue of Bonaparte's command of the revolutionary army. The party was the instrument that enabled him to bid successfully for the role of postrevolutionary dictator, and to launch his "revolution from above."

Stalin naturally claimed full continuity with Lenin, and in mood and method he seemed at first to be reviving the era of War Communism. Yet he subjected the country to a more oppressive and exploitative regime than anything it had suffered under tsarism, and with the aid of the bureaucratic hierarchy amassed total power in his own hands. Thus, in the terms of the process model of revolution, Stalin brought the Soviet Union into the phase of postrevolutionary dictatorship, where an opportunistic egomaniac, mastering the main levers of power, proceeds to combine old autocratic methods of rule with the revolutionary mythology and to declare war on the nation's alleged enemies. In Stalin's case, up to World War II, they were internal foes—the bourgeois specialists, the "petty-bourgeois" peasants, former Communist rivals, and finally the men of his own political apparatus.

The USSR did not, of course, move on from the "Bonapartist" phase of postrevolutionary dictatorship to an outright monarchical restoration like England or France. One can imagine something on this order if Hitler had waged political warfare in 1941 as astutely as he waged the Blitzkrieg militarily, and had sponsored a counterrevolutionary government to get Russia out of the war. But even though this did not materialize, assessment of the real character of Stalin's political and social system, including his sweeping reversal of most of the libertarian and egalitarian social policies and cultural standards that had been introduced or encouraged by the revolution, along with the new nationalistic symbolism that he sponsored during and after the war, could support a description of the later years of Stalinism as the functional equivalent of a monarchical restoration.

❖   ❖   ❖

Naturally the Russian Revolution differed from its predecessors in the political details of each phase, thanks to the many accidents of leadership, timing, and circumstances. But there was a greater difference of a programmatic and ideological nature, a difference of basic social values, that distinguished the revolution in Russia from its "bourgeois" predecessors. The Russian Revolution was the first of its kind to be animated by the mission of transforming the economic order to realize the values of economic equality and community, in other words, socialism in its broadest sense.

Socialism was central to the self-righteous militancy of the Bolsheviks and to the compulsive self-justification of every succeeding form of Communist rule whether in Russia or anywhere else. It was not lightly to be given up even when perestroika dawned in the 1980s: The limiting condition in Gorbachev's reformist mindset was the retention of some form of economic framework that he could continue to call socialist. "I have retained my loyalty and devotion to the socialist idea," he told a meeting of miners' representatives as late as April 1991.[5]

When Stalin broke with the NEP in 1928–1929 in the course of disposing of his rivals within the party leadership, he committed the country to a particular new model of socialism, based on the totally nationalized or collectivized economy, centrally planned and bureaucratically administered. Differing from the War Communism model of socialism in its scope (it included the peasantry by way of collectivization) and in its rejection of egalitarianism in favor of a frank inequality of authority and rewards, it corresponded directly to the phase of postrevolutionary dictatorship. If this was "barracks socialism," it was barracks socialism complete with the hierarchy of military-style rank and privilege, and complemented with huge disciplinary battalions for the misfits. This was the end of the old revolutionary ideal and its honest believers.

Thanks to the durability of the Stalinist model of socialism and the intensity of propaganda identifying it with the revolutionary goal, for much of the outside world the identity of Stalinism and socialism became axiomatic. This was equally true for adherents of the socialist ideal for whom Stalinism was thereby prettified, and for enemies of socialism for whom Stalinism was proof of its iniquity. The international Left was divided and confused, while up to World War II the international Right thrived on the Communist menace. Continuing assumptions about the identity of the Stalinist model and the socialist ideal eventually caused the collapse of the one to carry the other down with it. "We ourselves," says Yakovlev, "did a great deal to deform the image and values of socialism."[6] It can well be said that its historic identification with the Russian Revolution and the tragic burden of that tortuous experience was the worst thing that could have happened to socialism.

❖   ❖   ❖

From Stalin's time until the advent of perestroika Soviet Russia seemed not to experience any further fundamental change. In effect, the revolutionary process was frozen at the stage of postrevolutionary dictatorship with restorationist trappings, thawed only slightly during Nikita Khrushchev's years of limited and erratic reform. Reaction under Brezhnev appeared to confirm the common theory of irreducible totalitarianism. Yet consideration of the parallel processes of other revolutions should have raised the question, even before 1985, whether the Russian Revolution like the others would eventually come to the stage of the moderate revolutionary revival.[7]

Now that we have some perspective, we can see that the era of perestroika does indeed fall into place as the concluding phase of the revolutionary process in Russia. By 1987, something of this nature was obviously developing.[8] As in Spain, the opportunity for change in Russia was the death of the postrevolutionary dictator—actually, of three old men in quick succession. Backed by a younger generation of administrators and determined to rouse the country out of its "era of stagnation," the eventual successor Gorbachev commenced a journey back in time to dismantle the postrevolutionary regime, piece by piece. He challenged the Stalinist centrally-planned economic system, questioned the whole history of the Five-Year Plans and collectivization, and tried to devise a sort of market socialism on the lines that had facilitated the country's economic recovery in the 1920s. Pushing further back, he questioned the primal Leninist bias against petty-bourgeois enterprise, especially in services and in agriculture, the nationalization of which has been universally inappropriate and counterproductive. He held out for the ideal of socialism and the sanctity of Lenin, but he allowed socialism to be redefined very loosely, and extolled the very un-Leninist Lenin of the last, deathbed writings of 1923.

By 1987, Gorbachev found himself compelled by bureaucratic resistance to challenge the power of the Stalinist party apparatus. This led him to call into question the essence of Lenin's political system, the monolithic discipline of the Communist Party and its controls over all other institutions in Soviet society. To do battle with the apparatus conservatives, Gorbachev had to abandon the principle of unity that Lenin had imposed on the party with the 1921 ban on organized factions. Rejecting the party's direct domination over the civil government of the soviets, and inviting non-party organizations to engage in pluralistic dialogue with the party instead of serving as mere "transmission belts" of the party's will, he went against the power arrangements that had prevailed ever since the Russian Civil War.[9]

Other steps taken by Gorbachev in 1989 and 1990 ran counter to the Bolshevik Revolution itself. Toleration of organized opposition groups in the 1989 elections, and the abdication of the Communist Party's constitutional leading role in 1990, carried Soviet politics all the way back to 1917 and the democratic election of the ill-fated Constituent Assembly, before the infant Soviet regime became a strictly one-party affair. Yakovlev took the occasion of the two-hundredth anniversary of the French Revolution to compare the Bolsheviks with the Jacobins: "It must be said that the idealization of terror made itself sharply apparent in the October Revolution." The great mistake was

> to use the means of terror not only to put an end to counterrevolutionary activities, but also to stimulate the processes involved in building a new society. A cruel price had to be paid for these mistakes, for the immorality of pseudorevolutionary behavior.[10]

With these sentiments against revolutionary extremism, the Gorbachevian reformers had definitely embraced the moderate revolutionary revival. Gorbachev told the Twenty-Eighth Party Congress, "The Stalinist model of socialism is being replaced by a civic society of free people. . . . The atmosphere of ideological *diktat* has been replaced by free thinking, *glasnost*, and the openness of society to information."[11]

❖   ❖   ❖

One obvious difficulty in applying the concept of the moderate revolutionary revival to the Gorbachev era is the great span of elapsed time under the postrevolutionary dictatorship. But this is not such a puzzle if we consider the Khrushchev years as an incomplete, irresolute, and eventually abortive attempt to bring about the moderate revolutionary revival thirty years earlier. Possibly, perestroika would have been distinguished by more idealism and less cynicism if it had been successfully implemented in Khrushchev's time. Khrushchev's failure and the ensuing delay in fundamental reform can be explained partly as a failure of leadership, partly by the sheer immobility of the Stalinist bureaucratic system, and partly with reference to the deep roots that the Stalinist and neo-Stalinist regimes were able to put down in the authoritarian soil of Russian politi cal culture. Then, recognizing the inordinately long sway of postrevolutionary dictatorship in the Soviet Union, we can better appreciate the growing contradictions of modernizing society and rigid government that undermined the Brezhnev regime.

The moderate revolutionary revival does not immediately guarantee a stable outcome of freedom and democracy, nor does it determine exactly what mix of goals and values from the original moderate phase of the revolution will be recovered and preserved. England went through years of political infighting between crown and parliament—generating the first two-party system of pro-king Tories and pro-parliament Whigs—until parliamentary supremacy was achieved in the first half of the eighteenth century. Meanwhile periodic plots and uprisings of the absolutist Jacobites had to be fought off. France experienced a particularly chaotic sequel to its moderate revolutionary revival, when unresolved class conflict erupted in the Revolution of 1848, followed by a complete new revolutionary cycle taking the path under Louis Napoleon Bonaparte of a revolution of the Right, presaging the development of twentieth-century Germany and Spain. The end came only in the violence of the Paris Commune, before a new moderate revolutionary revival was arrived at in the form of the Third Republic. By contrast, in Germany and Spain, in the aftermath of revolutions of the Right and the demise of counterrevolutionary dictators, moderate revolutionary revival came easily and without serious dissention, if we leave out of consideration the comic-opera putsch of right-wingers among the Spanish military in 1978.

The course of the moderate revolutionary revival in Russia has not been smooth. Gorbachev's experiment in reform, proceeding step by step to the introduction of semi-constitutional government in 1989, was fatally destabilized by economic crisis and ethnic separatism. The attempted coup of August 1991 was more serious than were reactionary efforts in any other country's experience at the corresponding stage. Even so, there was and is no real prospect of restoring "Communism," i.e. neo-Stalinism, after the shattering effect of the moderate revolutionary revival upon the old beliefs.

The August Putsch had the paradoxical effect of displacing Russia's moderate revival back to the path of an earlier sub-phase of the original revolutionary process. Gorbachev had addressed the bankruptcy of the postrevolutionary dictatorship gradually, and had worked his way back to the turning point of October 1917 in terms of democracy and decentralist socialism. His successor Boris Yeltsin took his cue for more drastic reforms from the turning point of February 1917 or perhaps even from the post-1905 era, repudiating all expressions of socialism and endorsing unfettered capitalism with a government at best of guided democracy. Conceivably the swing of Russia's moderate revolutionary revival back to such an early and relatively conservative reference point is related to the peculiarities of the postrevolutionary, Stalinist phase of the revolutionary experience. It was inordinately long, but all the while masked by ideological links to the original revolution. Consequently, in many minds now the only way to exorcise the successive traumas of Leninism and Stalinism is to repudiate any institutions and policies even verbally associated with them, including any hint of socialism and even the simple Russian name of "soviet" for a local council.

In any case, the Yeltsin regime is not likely to end the political perturbations and pendulum swings as Russia seeks a normal, non-revolutionary form of existence. In the best case, the Yeltsin government could mellow into a presidential democracy on Gaullist lines. In the worst case, we may retrospectively see that Gorbachev's moderate revolutionary revival merely set the stage for a new cycle of revolutionary turmoil, as in France in 1848, where Yeltsin becomes the new Napoleon III and the country must await a new crisis and a new essay at ultimate democratic stability.

PART TWO

FROM IMMOBILITY TO CRISIS, 1968–1984

CHAPTER TWO

SOVIET POLITICS AFTER KHRUSHCHEV (1968)

The years under the leadership of Leonid Brezhnev, 1964–1982, known to his successors as the "era of stagnation," represented the longest stretch of political stability, without wars or leadership crises, that Russia had experienced since the beginning of this century. To preserve its power monopoly, the Soviet regime maintained the Stalinist habits of secrecy and official unanimity, but the techniques of "kremlinology" made it possible to explain events such as the fall of Khrushchev, and to infer much about the system's problems and evolutionary possibilities.

The investigation of Soviet politics is beset by peculiar problems. It is the study of a system which is based on a commitment to a dogmatic ideology, but which manipulates this ideology to conceal rather than advertise its fundamental political realities. Soviet practice has been at variance with Soviet theory almost since the Revolution itself—viz., the ultra-democratic classless ideal and the totalitarian bureaucratic actuality. Official Soviet statements and studies, which are the main sources we have to go by, are no direct reflection of Soviet reality. Therefore Soviet politics has to be studied indirectly, by inference and conjecture from the contrived statements and bits of information that reach the outside student. This art of educated guesswork is what goes by the evocative term "kremlinology," an art which this chapter will undertake to defend.

Kremlinology may be defined as the occult science of deducing what is going on in the Kremlin from whatever scraps of evidence may come to light. It has its margin of error. For example, the order in which the Soviet dignitaries parade themselves on top of Lenin's tomb is a distinctly unlaughable way of getting at the hierarchy of influence among them. On 7 November, 1967, the new Defense Minister Marshal Grechko appeared alongside General Secretary Brezhnev and Premier Kosygin. Aha! The military are rising in influence. But no—someone notes that the military chief has always had a place of prominence at the anniversary review—so, nothing is proven. On the same occasion one member of the Politburo, P. Y. Shelest, was absent altogether. Had he fallen? No, he was reviewing the troops in Kiev; he happens to be the only representative of a non-Russian minority on the Politburo, and he went home to the Ukraine for the November celebration. But there was an earlier and memorable occasion when an absence proved to be of more significance—the evening in

June 1953 when Lavrenty Beria failed to show up at the opera with his colleagues, and gave the world the first hint that he had been purged.

It is clear, despite the inevitable percentage of miscalculations, that the Soviets' profound rank-consciousness and passion for the proper precedence order among their officials can be a constantly revealing source about relationships and attitudes inside the Kremlin. When a number of Soviet officials are named at some function, the practice is to list those at each rank in alphabetical order, starting with the members of the Politburo even if their membership in that body is not mentioned. Candidates to the Politburo come next, then members of the Secretariat who do not belong to the Politburo, then other officials. When *Pravda* on 8 November 1967 listed Yuri Andropov at the beginning of the second alphabetical series, discerning readers were alerted to the fact that this party secretary, recently put in charge of the secret police, had now been accorded the status of candidate member of the Politburo, even though no such overt announcement was made.

At the cost of considerable labor in collecting details, significant inferences can be made about the status of lesser officials and about diverse political priorities. One odd Soviet custom is to list in detail, with full titles, every member of an official group of foreign leaders. The importance attributed to the foreign country, both in magnitude and in particular emphasis, can be deduced from the composition of the counterpart Soviet delegation. The travels to the airport to meet the incoming Communist delegations on the eve of the November 1967 anniversary were particularly interesting, because so many arrivals were crowded into one day's time. Eight such meetings were reported in *Pravda* on 2 November, each in a separate story in the style of the following (translated here verbatim and in its entirety):

> On 1 November, at the invitation of the CC of the CPSU, the Presidium of the Supreme Soviet of the USSR, and the Council of Ministers of the USSR, there arrived in Moscow for the celebration of the 50th anniversary of the Great October Socialist Revolution a party and governmental delegation from the Czechoslovak Socialist Republic headed by First Secretary of the Central Committee of the Communist Party of Czechoslovakia and President of the Czechoslovak Socialist Republic Comrade A. Novotny. The delegation included Member of the Presidium of the CC of the CPCz and Chairman of the Government of the CzSR Com. J. Lenart, Member of the Presidium of the CC of the CPCz and Chairman of the National Assembly of the CzSR Com. B. Lastovická, Member of the Presidium of the CC of the CPCz and Chairman of the Slovak National Council Com. M. Chudik, and Secretary of the CC of the CPCz Com. V. Kouchy.

At the Vnukovo Airport the Czechoslovak comrades were met by: General Secretary of the CC of the CPSU Com. L. I. Brezhnev, Member of the Politburo of the CC of the CPSU and Chairman of the Council of Ministers of the USSR Com. A. N. Kosygin, Member of the Politburo of the CC of the CPSU and Chairman of the Presidium of the Supreme Soviet of the USSR Com. N. V. Podgorny, Member of the Politburo of the CC of the CPSU and First Deputy Chairman of the Council of Ministers of the USSR Com. K. T. Mazurov, Member of the CC of the CPSU and Deputy Chairman of the Council of Ministers of the USSR Com. L. V. Smirnov, Member of the CC of the CPSU and USSR Minister of Heavy, Power, and Transport Machine Construction Com. V. F. Zhigalin, Member of the CC of the CPSU and Chief Editor of the Newspaper "Pravda" Com. M. V. Zimianin, Member of the CC of the CPSU and USSR Deputy Minister of Defense Marshal of the Soviet Union Com. N. I. Krylov, Candidate Member of the CC of the CPSU and Head of a Department in the CC of the CPSU Com. P. K. Sizov, Member of the Central Auditing Commission of the CPSU and First Deputy Head of a Department in the CC of the CPSU Com. K. V. Rusakov, USSR Deputy Minister of Foreign Affairs Com. L. F. Ilyichev, and others. The delegation was also met by officials of the Embassy of the CzSR in the USSR.

The report on the Polish delegation followed on the same page and in the same form, together with this passage on the group meeting it:

At the Vnukovo airport the Polish comrades were met by: General Secretary of the CC of the CPSU Com. L. I. Brezhnev, Member of the Politburo of the CC of the CPSU and Chairman of the Council of Ministers of the USSR Com. A. N. Kosygin, Member of the Politburo of the CC of the CPSU and Chairman of the Presidium of the Supreme Soviet of the USSR Com. N. V. Podgorny, Member of the Politburo of the CC of the CPSU and First Deputy Chairman of the Council of Ministers of the USSR Com. D. S. Poliansky, Member of the CC of the CPSU and Deputy Chairman of the Council of Ministers of the USSR Com. I. T. Novikov, Member of the CC of the CPSU and USSR Minister of Transport Construction Com. E. F. Kozhevnikov, Member of the CC of the CPSU and First Deputy Minister of Defense Marshal of the Soviet Union Com. I. I. Yakubovsky, Candidate Member of the CC of the CPSU and USSR Minister of Civil Aviation Marshal of Aviation E. F. Loginov, Candidate Member of the CC of the CPSU and USSR Deputy Minister of Foreign Affairs Com. V. S. Semenov, Member of the Central Auditing Commission of the CPSU and First Deputy Head of a Department in the CC of the CPSU Com. K. V. Rusakov, First Deputy Head of a Department in the CC of the CPSU Com. I. P. Yastrebov, and others.

   The delegation was also met by officials of the Embassy of the Polish Peoples Republic in the USSR.

The ritual went on and on, with similar reports on the arrivals of the Bulgarians, the Rumanians, the Yugoslavs, the Mongolians, the North Koreans, and the Hungarians. (The North Vietnamese came the day before; the Albanians were not invited; the Chinese refused to come; and the Cubans failed to send a top-level delegation.) *Pravda's* odd practice of reporting each encounter with everyone's full name and title, without reference to the other reports involving the same Soviet personalities on the same page, makes it apparent that the Soviet press is not concerned here with news so much as a sort of journalistic ceremony, to give each Soviet leader and each satellite government just the proper amount and emphasis of prestige in print.

   It is clear, of course, that all the satellite governments rated the presence of Brezhnev and Kosygin on the welcoming committee. (Whether Brezhnev and Kosygin trooped out to the airport for each separate arrival or sat out there to meet everyone as they arrived is not revealed.) Each committee had military representation, though it was rotated so that no marshal could claim the limelight. Each committee included a cabinet minister for some economic activity, carefully chosen to reflect that industry of the respective satellite which the Soviets judged most distinctive, such as the Rumanians' oil and the North Koreans' fisheries. One obscure man, "First Deputy Head of a Department in the CC of the CPSU Com. K. V. Rusakov," turned up at every one of the meetings, conveying to us the significant unpublished information that Rusakov was one of the leading functionaries in the office for relations with bloc Communist parties.[1]

   There are always hazards, of course, in the inferences made from such information. When Defense Minister Malinovsky failed to meet his counterparts from the satellites arriving for a conference in 1966, I decided that he was going to be sacked; the unfortunate man was merely sick, and died a few months later. Whenever conjecture is used—as it must be—it must always be labelled for what it is and discounted to the proper extent. Some overenthusiastic commentators write as if they had personally bugged the conference room of the Politburo and can report every word that passed among its members. This is irresponsible, but since conjecture, recognized as such, is under Soviet conditions of news control the nearest thing we have to knowledge, we cannot help depending on it.

If we recognize that most of what passes for knowledge about Soviet politics is only conjecture, it is not surprising that there is so much disagreement among the experts. There are two main schools of speculation. Carl Linden calls the two views the "totalitarian model" and the "conflict model."[2] The totalitarian model of Soviet politics assumes that power is stable and undivided once a new leader has firmly succeeded to the top position in the Communist Party. The conflict model presumes the continuance of factional in-fighting among liberal and conservative bureaucratic cliques behind the façade of Communist Party discipline.

Both positions have their merits. It happens that each model is more convincing for a particular epoch: the totalitarian model, of course, under Stalin, and the conflict model during the last years of Khrushchev. A fairly convincing case can be made for the existence of a strong anti-Khrushchev conservative faction under party secretary Frol Kozlov from 1960 to 1963. The main trouble with this view is that the faction did not come forth to claim the spoils of victory when Khrushchev fell in 1964.

To work toward a more realistic view of Soviet politics I favor a third model, which I term the "circular flow of power." Ever since Stalin's rise to power in the 1920s, political power in the USSR has been based on the hierarchy of Communist Party secretaries, nominally elected by the provincial and local organizations of the party, but actually appointed by the central party Secretariat. The provincial and local secretaries dictate the actions of their respective organizations and control the selection of representatives to the higher echelons and to the All-Union Party Congress, itself made up mostly of secretaries. When the congress formally elects the Central Committee, it actually confirms a list made up mostly of central and provincial party secretaries plus ministers in the central government. Finally, as the Central Committee elects the Politburo, the party Secretariat, and the First Secretary, the circuit is closed: The First Secretary is confirmed in office by a circular process that ultimately he himself controls—or can control.

The circular basis of power in the CPSU was established by Stalin during the course of his rise to power in the 1920s. At the time he became General Secretary in 1922 he found the practice well established of the central party leadership "recommending" individuals to the provincial organizations to serve as their secretaries. Stalin simply took over control of this activity and made the assignment of provincial secretaries virtually a matter of his own personal appointment, with a powerful patronage-based political machine resulting. By the spring of 1923, when the Twelfth Party Congress was convening, Stalin was able, through his secretaries, to dominate the selection of delegates to the congress, and at the congress itself he was able to expand the Central Committee and to control the selection of new members for it. In 1925, when his rivalries with Trotsky and Zinoviev had broken out into the open, Stalin began to use his power in the Central Committee to remove oppositionists from that body and from the Politburo. By 1930, after his victory over Nikolai Bukharin and the Right Opposition, Stalin had completed the process and perfected a party machine entirely of his own choosing. He controlled the body that nominally elected him, and was in a position to use all the instruments of political control, from ideological manipulation to police terror, to maintain himself in power until his death.

Since Stalin's power was never juridically embodied in a supreme office, his demise in 1953 removed the master switch from the circuit of power. It was necessary for the entire process of building personal control around the circle to be repeated by someone else, if Stalin's system were to be restored.

In the succession arrangement of March 1953, Khrushchev got the same position that Stalin had had in 1922, now under the title of First Secretary. Like Stalin thirty years before, Khrushchev was a party organization professional, and inconspicuous enough not to appear a threat to his colleagues in the collective leadership. He climbed to the top in almost exactly the same way. Between 1953 and 1955 he obtained a firm personal grip on the central party Secretariat, and began replacing provincial secretaries with his own men. In 1955 and early 1956 he stepped up the transfers of provincial secretaries, and had firm control of a majority of the delegates at the Twentieth Party Congress (February–March 1956) when he launched his celebrated de-Stalinization campaign. Khrushchev evidently dictated the selection of new Central Committee members, so that when the crisis of open opposition in the party Presidium came in 1957, he was able to take his appeal down to the Central Committee and overrule the Presidium. His enemies at the top level were removed, and Khrushchev found himself in nearly the same position of individual leadership that Stalin had achieved by the late 1920s.

Here the parallel ceases to be so exact. While Khrushchev clearly made himself the country's number-one leader (especially when he assumed the prime ministership in 1958 along with the party secretaryship), he never had full control at all points of the circuit of power. There is considerable evidence (mostly derived from kremlinological inference, to be sure) that a minority in the Presidium and the Central Committee continued to oppose Khrushchev, in the form of a neo-Stalinist "conservative" faction led by Mikhail Suslov and/or Frol Kozlov in the late 1950s and early 1960s, with their differences subtly appearing in the wording of their statements on such issues as steel versus chemicals or the degree of sin borne by the Molotov-Malenkov opposition of 1957. A more tangible clue of renewed seismic activity inside the Soviet political monolith was offered by a new rise in the turnover rate among provincial secretaries in the period from late 1959 to mid-1961. At the time the phenomenon was not even recognized, let alone explained, but numerous observers took the fall of Khrushchev's lieutenants A. I. Kirichenko and N. I. Beliaev as a sign that the opposition challenge was stiffening. In retrospect, it appears that an opposition group had broken into the political circuit at the level of the Secretariat and was using the power of appointment against Khrushchev, in the same way he himself had used it earlier. Thanks to replacements and expansion, the Central Committee elected by the Twenty-Second Party Congress in October 1961 consisted of over half new people (107, including twenty-six promoted from candidate member, out of 175). The revealing thing is that the new appointees practically all survived the fall of Khrushchev in 1964 and were confirmed in the Central Committee by the Twenty-Third Congress in 1966. They are clearly the adherents of the new group who wrested the key appointment power away from Khrushchev in 1959 and 1960.

The top-level shakeup of May 1960 (simultaneous with the U-2 incident) was evidently the first open sign of the shift against Khrushchev. There followed a period of rather tense and unstable jockeying, when the opposition had enough influence to curb Khrushchev but not enough, presumably, to challenge his formal leadership. Khrushchev evidently retained prime influence in foreign policy and ideological matters, and seems to have tried to manipulate the issues in an apparently arbitrary and erratic manner to keep the opposition politically off balance. This uneasy political situation may help explain the impulsive vagaries of Khrushchev's foreign policy from 1960 to 1963, veering as it did from the Berlin ultimatum and the Cuban missile gambit to the Nuclear Test Ban Treaty and the open break with the Chinese. Khrushchev's ideological ventures in the 1961 Party Program and his bizarre experiments in party organization in 1962 may be similarly explained. The latter measures were undone forthwith by his successors in 1964.

Khrushchev's removal, coming, presumably, as soon as the opposition had mobilized the strength and the determination to depose him, marks a fundamental watershed in the history of Soviet politics. This was the first time in the entire history of Russia since Prince Riurik that the established leader of the country was removed by the rules of representative procedure. Since the leader was removed, it follows naturally that he was and had been *removable*, and it follows equally that the successor leadership is removable in the same way. A basic change has occurred in the circuit of power in the Soviet system: Real control does not pass to the top leader, but flows instead from the top collective bodies around through the party organization. The top leader is only a representative of the group, at best first among equals, and his tenure of leadership depends on the support of that group.

By making succession to the leadership depend on the confidence of the Central Committee, Soviet political practice has taken a long step toward a sort of miniature parliamentary system at the top of the great bureaucratic pyramid of the party. The Central Committee can be likened to a parliament, the Politburo to the cabinet, and the General Secretary to the prime minister (not to be confused with the actual governmental prime minister who is only second-in-command in the party). There are of course vast differences as against a real parliamentary system: Issues and procedures are beclouded by the mask of public unanimity, and the "parliament" is not responsible to an electorate, but is de facto appointed by the "prime minister" or the "cabinet." Nevertheless, as this system continues to operate, it seems to permit change further down in the political system, as each participant in the parliamentarism of the Central Committee seeks support below him among his "constituents" to enhance his own power. Conceivably the parliamentary practice can spread to regional and local party committees, and the party may become more and more a forum for the plurality of interests among the complex Soviet bureaucracy.

What appears to be evolving in the Soviet Union is a new kind of politics, "participatory bureaucracy." Actually this is familiar to anyone with experience in a Western government or corporation or university, though it is not recognized in political theory as a model for the political system as a whole. Conventionally a bureaucratic structure is seen as a system where influence is transmitted only from the top down, whereas influence from the bottom up is assumed to operate only in the democratic party system. But in any complex modern bureaucratic organization, it is impossible to function purely from the top down: All manner of influence—information, advice, recommendations, problems, complaints—must flow upwards, or else the top leadership cannot make the informed decisions on which the life of the entity depends. The problems of managing a complex economy and technology have made it abundantly clear to the Soviet leadership that they must allow this reverse stream of influence to flow freely, and their main concern is that the flow be kept within the organizational structure of the Communist Party.

The power of the party and its monopoly position in the Soviet power structure is the major limitation on the free extension of bureaucratic representativeness within Soviet society. The party bureaucracy—however they share power among themselves—are clearly determined to perpetuate their power as an institution, and by extension, the power of the country they rule. In reality the power of the party apparatus does not exist for any higher purpose: It is an end in itself. Even where and when it becomes economically or technologically dysfunctional, the control function of the party continues to be asserted as the first political absolute: The controllers must maintain control in order that they continue to be controllers.

As a body primarily oriented toward the maintenance of control for the controllers' sake, the party apparatus tends to attract a particular kind of person—energetic and ambitious, not the most intelligent, not too principled—who is willing to conform in order to share in the exercise of power. The apparatus is still dominated by men born between 1905 and the Revolution, who rose from humble beginnings and filled the top slots after Stalin's purges. Typically, they are anti-intellectual, nominally puritanical, and rigidly philistine in their views. They retain all the Stalinist habits of ideological manipulation to justify their own regime, imposing conformity on the rank and file and assuming the pose of official unanimity themselves. They pretend to represent the world's highest form of democracy; they give the appearance of monolithic totalitarianism; their actual relationships within the leadership group are somewhere in the middle.

Between the party apparatus and certain segments of the Soviet populace, mainly the intelligentsia in its broad sense, there exists a sharp distinction and a recognized and growing tension. Like tsarist Russia, the Soviet regime has to contend with a profoundly disaffected opposition among the young educated class, as expressed mainly by the writers. But there is a newer type of recruit to the opposition, the young scientist, exemplified by Maxim Litvinov's physicist grandson Pavel. Thanks to the dead hand of party control in the humanities and social sciences, the most intelligent, creative, and sensitive people have gravitated to the natural sciences. Almost invariably foreign students studying in the Soviet Union, regardless of their own fields, find their most congenial friends among the Soviet students of natural science, where the best Soviet minds have found a haven of relative freedom and privilege.

Obviously the scientific and technical intelligentsia is of the utmost importance to the party leadership in its aspirations to build the international influence of the Soviet Union. Unlike the Tsarist regime, the Soviet government depends heavily on the intelligentsia for the progress of sophisticated industry and science, and must treat the scientists and engineers with commensurate circumspection. The Soviet intelligentsia, in short, has become the kind of social force singled out by J. K. Galbraith as the key power in modern society, the "technostructure," i.e., the organized intelligence that is replacing land and capital as the crucial factor in contemporary economic life everywhere.[3]

The party apparatus is psychologically as remote from the technostructure as the tsarist bureaucracy was from Ivan Turgenev's nihilists, if not more so. The party bureaucracy, existing to keep control for the controllers' sake, is functionally an anachronism. It needs to cultivate and use the intelligentsia, but cannot accord them freedom and power: It encourages them and then frustrates them. This is the new Soviet class struggle; it is the stuff revolutions are made of.

Khrushchev's answer to this contradiction was to elaborate and accentuate the role of the party organization. Consistently he promoted the authority of the party controllers over the governmental and industrial administrators as well as over the creative intelligentsia. This might be the practical significance of his reviving the doctrine of the "withering-away of the state" in 1961. The state might wither, but the party never would, and the only prospect Khrushchev offered was perpetual domination of Soviet life by the professional secretaries. This was too much even for his successors in the party, who quickly repealed the economic functionalism that Khrushchev had introduced into the party organization, and silenced talk of the withering-away of the state.

The group of Communist leaders who unseated Khrushchev in 1964 have so far managed to provide the country with remarkably stable leadership. Of the eleven men in the Politburo at the end of the Khrushchev era, seven are still in office at this writing. One member died (Kozlov) and two retired with honors (Anastas Mikoyan and N. M. Shvernik); only Khrushchev himself has been removed. In the Central Committee, as noted earlier, there has been relatively little change; turnover at the Twenty-Third Congress in 1966 was much lower (only forty-six new members out of 195) than at the Twenty-Second in 1961, or at the Twentieth in 1956 (fifty-three new members out of 133; the Twenty-First in 1959 did not elect a new Central Committee).

In the party Secretariat there have been some changes of potential significance. At the time Brezhnev took over from Khrushchev as First Secretary (now again called General Secretary as in Stalin's day), Podgorny was kicked upstairs to become Chief of State. A little later Alexander Shelepin was kicked downstairs to head the trade unions. The number-two man in the party organization now appears to be Alexei Kirilenko, a close associate of Brezhnev in the Ukraine in the 1940s and early 1950s. All these points contribute to a picture of strengthened control in the hands of General Secretary Brezhnev, at least for the time being. The 1967 shake-up in the KGB, replacing Shelepin's protégé Semichastny with party secretary Andropov, reinforces the view that Brezhnev, through the party apparatus, is in a firm position of leadership.

The greater questions about the Soviet future lie in the more distant future. Can party bureaucracy hang on after outliving its usefulness, as the barons of medieval feudalism perpetuated their control as a parasitic ruling class for centuries after their initial service of defense had lapsed? Or will the tendency toward participatory bureaucracy necessarily admit segments of the administrative and intellectual class into the decision-making and controlling process, and thus permit a pluralistic evolution? Conflicts are inevitable, between aspirants for leadership who link up with different elements in the technostructure that take different positions on the issues, and between the party structure as a whole and the aspirations of the entire technostructure as a whole for a freer and more effective voice in the destinies of the country. There appear to be two main possibilities: The party bureaucracy can hang on by reaffirming its political monopoly and going back to Stalinist terror, at great cost in national progress and morale; or it can leave the door open to a sort of creeping constitutionalism that may gradually but profoundly transform the Soviet system as we know it.

CHAPTER THREE

PARTICIPATORY BUREAUCRACY (1971)

Behind its appearances of totalitarianism and continuity, the Soviet system under Brezhnev was becoming steadily more complex and in its own way pluralistic. Analysis of the Central Committee of the Communist Party shows it to have become the capstone of this process, whereby functional and regional entities within the bureaucratic hierarchy could promote their interests. Though it was limited by the qualities of the leadership trained under Stalin, the system had enough flexibility to survive for years until a new generation could introduce change.

For the last two decades, at least, Western studies of Soviet politics have been dominated by a presumption of continuity. Continuity in the political order regardless of the evolution of public opinion or material circumstances is prescribed rigorously by the model of totalitarianism, which until recently has been taken as a point of departure by most students of the Soviet system.

Quest for New Models

A quest presently appears to be under way in Soviet studies for a new model to replace the concept of totalitarianism as the basic principle of Soviet politics. Among various alternatives, the interest-group approach to politics has attracted considerable attention in its applicability to the Soviet system.[1] A variant of the interest-group approach, the so-called "conflict model" of top-level Soviet politics, has been popular for some time, vindicated as it appeared to be by the fall of Khrushchev.

Generally these newer approaches posit some form of dynamic interplay that permits or even generates change and therefore diminishes continuity. The shift of interest from the totalitarian model to the newer group-tension models itself is a reflection of changes in the Soviet system: Totalitarianism was a reasonable representation of the Stalin era, but less satisfactory in describing the more mobile politics of the succession era.

There remain, nevertheless, substantial limitations in the group-tension approach as applied to Soviet politics. Continuity, as the Brezhnev era has amply demonstrated, still outweighs change rather heavily. Even if the Soviet system can no longer be accurately described as totalitarian, it has characteristics which make the interest-group model quite unrealistic. Fundamentally, the fact which makes the Soviet system un-reachable by conventional interest-group analysis is the institution of the party and its system of pervasive controls over all aspects of life. What has changed from the old totalitarian style, I suggest, is not the power of the party but the distribution of power within the party. The party as an institution is the reconciler and balancer and shaper of individual ambi-tions and group interests, such that the Soviet system may now have achieved—for the time being—a greater degree of stability and continuity than it has ever known since the Revolution.

Participatory Bureaucracy

To take cognizance of the changes in Soviet politics since Stalin, while recognizing the fundamental institutional basis of the regime, I propose an alternative model of Soviet politics. This is the model of participatory bureaucracy.

The notion of participatory bureaucracy is based on recognition of the complex character of large organizations and the interplay of individual influences, upwards as well as downwards, that can take place within such entities. There is an extensive literature on the sociology of modern organizations underscoring the manifold constraints that complexity places on the leaders of the organization, the power enjoyed by experts and specialists by virtue of their expertise, and the ultimate requirements of autonomy for the branches of an organization if it is to meet the test of survival.[2] All of us are familiar with participatory bureaucracy in Amer-ican universities and government agencies. The organization does not run just on decrees from the top down, any more than the nervous system of an animal could function without sensory input. The organization, and its responsible officials at every level, are dependent on information, ad-vice, and suggestions from below—it is humanly impossible to operate otherwise—and along with this input come the inevitable complaints and conflicts among the subordinates that the organization must respond to if it is to maintain reasonable efficiency and effectiveness.

The peculiar sclerosis of Stalinism was its unwillingness to delegate responsibility and to accept accurate information, endeavoring instead to compensate for these deficiencies by force and terror. No truly modern organization can operate this way. If for reasons of economic success alone, it is clear that the USSR cannot go back to these Stalinist methods.

To the extent that the model of participatory bureaucracy is accurate, it means that the Soviet policy-making process is complex and open-ended. It means that experts and officials have a substantial degree of security as well as influence. It means that the ranks of the bureaucracy enjoy a certain amount of power as against the top leadership—or at least that the vulnerability is mutual. It suggests that there are openings in the bureaucratic structure for the exercise of influence by all manner of individual and group interests. I will try to explore each of these propositions, aiming the analysis particularly at the bureaucratic level of the Central Committee of the CPSU.

Key Role of the Central Committee

Viewed in the context of the model of participatory bureaucracy, the Central Committee of the CPSU is the keystone of the entire Soviet system. In its make-up it represents all the constituent elements of the Soviet power structure, both functionally and geographically. Its sessions provide the country's only continuing broad-based policy forum. Finally, it constitutes the primary institutional counterweight to individual bureaucratic dictation in the Stalinist fashion. In short, it is the Central Committee that allows the bureaucracy to be participatory.

The composition of the Central Committee has some rather obvious implications for its participatory functions. To begin with, membership in the Central Committee is enjoyed almost exclusively by individuals holding leading positions in one or another of the country's bureaucratic structures, primarily the party apparatus, then the government, the military, and miscellaneous institutions ranging from the trade unions to the Academy of Sciences. Every significant institution is represented, represented moreover in close proportion to the importance accorded that institution in the Soviet scheme of things. Thus, in the Central Committee elected by the Twenty-Fourth Congress, 41 percent of the full members are officials of the central and local party apparatus; 39 percent come from the government, mainly heads of key ministries and prime ministers of union republics; 9 percent are military; 1 percent are trade-union officials. A small number—3 percent—are rank-and-filers, token representatives of the masses, distributed by social category and not usually reelected. A very few individuals are members in their own right—elder statesmen like Mikoyan, or semi-retired party officials serving out their time in a diplomatic pasture.

The evidence of congress after congress shows very clearly that Central Committee membership is not a matter of individual selection. The Central Committee is basically a collection of job slots—now the two hundred or more most important jobs in the country, followed by the one hundred fifty or so next most important jobs carrying the rank of candidate member, and seventy or eighty lesser jobs carrying the rank of member of the Central Auditing Commission (which is in its make-up really an honorable-mention category for job-holders who do not quite make the Central Committee). Membership in the Central Committee, at the appropriate rank, is automatically conferred on the holder of a job that carries Central Committee rank. This is a rule of Soviet politics that is invariably observed.

It follows from this unwritten but nonetheless stringent rule of Central Committee composition that a man who is secure in his job will be secure in his Central Committee membership, and that he cannot be removed from the Central Committee without being removed from his Central Committee-level job. Correspondingly, a man who loses his job and does not move to another at the Central Committee level will almost always be dropped from the Central Committee at the next congress, unless an especially honorable retirement is intended for him. In general, the association of the job and Central Committee rank makes it difficult for higher authority to reshuffle and pack the Central Committee at random, without causing a commensurate disturbance in the agencies—party, government, or whatever—whose leadership is affected. While individuals can always be shifted by the authority of the central Secretariat, mass changes would appear to be increasingly difficult, and the tenure of any given Central Committee member is therefore likely to be reasonably secure.

Growing Entrenchment of the Central Committee

The decline in the vulnerability of the individual Central Committee member has been one of the distinctive developments of the past decade, at the same time that the removal of Khrushchev demonstrated the vulnerability of the top leader. During his rise to power, following Stalin's pattern of the 1920s, Khrushchev was able to reshuffle the hierarchy to the extent that only seventy-nine of Stalin's 1952 Central Committee of one hundred twenty-five survived in 1956, for a holdover rate of 63 percent. Between 1956 and 1961, the combined casualties of Khrushchev's consolidation and the early moves of the anti-Khrushchev faction left only sixty-six holdovers out of one hundred thirty-three, for a rate of 55 percent. By contrast, the solidarity of the Soviet hierarchy in the transition from Khrushchev to Brezhnev is attested by a survival figure of one hundred thirty-nine out of one hundred seventy-four, or 80 percent, between 1961 and 1966. Nor has there been any substantial shake-up subsequently that would indicate Brezhnev was rebuilding a personal machine; one hundred fifty-three out of one hundred ninety-five Central Committee members were held over from 1966 to 1971, a rate of 78 percent. Among those dropped this time the median age was sixty-four, indicating that retirement rather than political infighting was the main consideration. The trend from congress to congress in terms of the Central Committee member's security is marked: 63 percent and 50 percent under Khrushchev, 80 percent and 78 percent under Brezhnev. The stability and continuity of the post-Khrushchev leadership at the Politburo level is fully complemented by this evidence of stability and continuity at the Central Committee level. Such continuity is distinctly a contrast to the factional struggles and leadership shake-ups that followed the deaths of both Lenin and Stalin. Brezhnev has not imposed himself on the Soviet leadership in the Stalin and Khrushchev manner; rather, he has worked with the existing material, allowing himself—perhaps by force of necessity—to be the representative and the reflection of the existing bureaucratic hierarchy rather than the architect of a new political machine designed in his own image.

There has, of course, been some opportunity for leadership influence in the expansion of the Central Committee membership carried out at each congress, and particularly at the latest. However, the opportunity for personal manipulation has been limited even in this respect, since the expansion has been accomplished mainly by upgrading candidate-status jobs and their tenants with them. Among these people also there has been growing stability. The percentage of candidate members either promoted or held over fell from 53 percent in 1956 to 48 percent in 1961, but rose to 64 percent in 1966 and to 67 percent this year.

Increased Vulnerability at the Top

Since the 1950s, two trends in the Soviet bureaucratic structure have combined to produce what may conceivably turn out to be a fundamental shift in the locus of political power. I have noted the growing security and declining vulnerability of the individual Central Committee member vis-à-vis the top leadership. On the other hand, Khrushchev's career, with his near-defeat in 1957, his evident difficulties after 1960, and his ultimate demise at the hands of his own bureaucratic subordinates, demonstrates the growing vulnerability of the top leadership vis-à-vis the Central Committee. The removal of Khrushchev is absolute proof that the top leader is removable.

What of Brezhnev? Is he equally removable, or has he found a more secure power base? There is no evidence that anything has happened to change the balance of forces that manifested itself in 1964. The Central Committee, as we have seen, has become more solidly entrenched than it ever was before. Brezhnev has taken no obvious steps to impose himself, presumably because he was not able to do so in the face of the established power of the Central Committee. It follows that the power of the top leader is definitely circumscribed by the bureaucratic body of which he is merely the choice and the representative.

Individual members of the Central Committee are still vulnerable to some extent, of course, to the Secretariat's power of transfer or demotion from their Central Committee-rank jobs. On the other hand, the General Secretary is highly vulnerable to any concerted opposition within the Central Committee. If he started to use his power of removal to threaten any substantial number of Central Committee members all at once, he would in all probability provoke a general rebellion of the body which could seriously endanger his own tenure of office. In other words, Central Committee member and General Secretary are mutually vulnerable and mutually dependent.

Responsiveness to Interest Groups

Given the element of independent power enjoyed by the Central Committee, it follows that the discussion and decision of key issues among the members of that body must involve a great deal more give-and-take and head-counting than meets the public eye. The reality of the Soviet policy-making process probably lies somewhere between the official claims of democratic centralism and the official appearances of monolithic conformity. Within the Central Committee, consequently, there must be at least some opportunity for the representation of the views and interests of all those constituencies whose chiefs hold Central Committee rank.

The relation between the Central Committee member and his own regional or functional constituency, may, in the light of this analysis, bear some similarity to the relation of the top leadership and the Central Committee. The regional secretary or cabinet minister works with committees and hierarchies of lesser functionaries, whose confidence and co-operation he needs in order to make a success of his job and thus minimize his vulnerability to intervention from the top. He will therefore be inclined to represent the views, interests, recommendations, and complaints of these subordinates in the deliberations of the Central Committee. These expressions of interest from below can include not only party views but the positions of all the diverse institutions—governmental, industrial, military, trade union, educational, etc.—that are represented in the provincial and local party committee structure. Conceivably this participatory process may be opening up well down in the party hierarchy, such that the party bureaucracy may come to serve as a fairly effective channel for the transmission of all manner of ideas and desires from below upwards.

How far this participatory bureaucracy may actually have developed is, of course, only a matter of speculation. What is less uncertain is that it is a factor at the top level and that it is a force for continuity, allowing gradual change in response to the needs that are felt lower in the power structure, while maintaining a relatively stable leadership group from congress to congress.

The Future of Participatory Bureaucracy

Participatory bureaucracy in the Soviet system is not, it should be noted, synonymous with liberalism. The attitudes that prevail among the Central Committee membership do not appear to leave much room, for example, for accommodation with the forces of dissent among the intelligentsia. The mentality of the Soviet power elite might be described as Stalinist without Stalin and without Stalinism, in the sense of the capricious and terroristic rule associated with the late dictator, but perpetuating the narrowly pragmatic, suspicious, and anti-intellectual values of the Stalin regime.

This is hardly surprising. The bulk of the present leadership were well launched on their political careers before Stalin died, and had gone through the selection process of reliability and conformity characteristic of that era. Those in their sixties, including the leading members of the Politburo, are still the direct heirs of the purges of the 1930s.

There are obviously certain forces that may change this state of mind. The present leadership cannot live forever. Since 1952 the average age of the Central Committee has increased at each congress; renewal has not kept pace with the passage of time nor involved enough sufficiently younger men. The Soviet leadership are tending to grow old all together.

It is therefore a safe prediction that the rate of turnover in the Soviet leadership will increase at the next couple of congresses, and particularly at the Politburo level. What is less certain is the liberality of attitudes that newer and younger leaders may bring with them. So far, by all accounts, the people born in the 1920s and now reaching Central Committee eligibility are no better than their elders, but even these people presently in their forties were well along in the Komsomol experience, at least, by the time of Stalin's death. It may take another decade for much of the truly post-Stalin influence to work its way up the party hierarchy.

The more immediate question is how the channels of participatory bureaucracy may reflect and accommodate the currents of new opinion among the post-Stalin generation and in the intelligentsia as a whole. The door may open gradually, perhaps only enough to ease the pressure and reassure the continuity of the present party system.

CHAPTER FOUR

THE FALL OF PODGORNY AND THE SOVIET GERONTOCRACY (1977)

The most notable disturbance of the Soviet political equilibrium under Brezhnev came in 1977, with the ouster of President and Politburo member Nikolai Podgorny. Brezhnev's power was strengthened all the more, and major concessions by the aging Soviet leadership to the younger officialdom and the problems they confronted were put off until new leadership could take over.

The fall of the Chief of State of the Soviet Union, Nikolai Podgorny, announced on 24 May 1977, and his replacement in this capacity by Mr. Brezhnev, open the succession crisis in Moscow. We are now suddenly confronted with new and complicated questions concerning Soviet political life. Has Podgorny been removed because of his advanced age, or rather to make room for the ambition of his colleague, younger than he but senior career-wise? Was it done to benefit one of the tired old leaders—Kosygin, Suslov, or Kirilenko—or was it for one of the rising *apparatchiki*? Does the introduction of the new constitution presage deeper changes in the political structure of the USSR?

It is worthwhile, to begin with, to review the history of the singular position of Chief of State in the USSR. Recognized by Soviet constitutions since 1918 as the Chairman of the Presidium of the Supreme Soviet (formerly the Central Executive Committee of the Soviets), the post has long been occupied by individuals who have played an exclusively ceremonial role—Mikhail Kalinin (1919–1946) and Nikolai Shvernik (1946–1953). Shvernik was not even a member of the Politburo (except for his last five months, when this organ was enlarged to become the party Presidium in 1952–1953). Kliment Voroshilov, former commissar of war, was already seventy-one years old in 1953 when he began his seven years in the presidency, which he made a sort of retirement home.

It was another matter in 1960, after Voroshilov was removed by Khrushchev because of his relations with the "Anti-Party Group" of 1957. He was replaced by none other than Brezhnev. This time the presidency of the Republic fell to a man who was still dynamic and not too old (he was then fifty-four), who showed himself to be a real candidate for power. A member of the party Secretariat since 1956 and of the party Presidium since 1957, Brezhnev probably owed this promotion to Secretary Frol Kozlov, the strong man in the apparatus from 1960 until his heart attack in 1963. After jointly holding his functions in the party Presidium and in the chairmanship of the Presidium of the Supreme Soviet, Brezhnev took back his post in the Secretariat when Kozlov fell ill. Anastas Mikoyan, former minister of trade and elder statesman, succeeded him as Chief of State, in a position of semiretirement comparable to that of Voroshilov. Finally, in 1965, Mikoyan was retired de jure and replaced by Podgorny.

Podgorny, a long-time member of the apparatus, joined the Secretariat in 1963 with Brezhnev, which made him also figure as a possible candidate for supreme power. At first number-three in the post-Khrushchev troika, along with the new Secretary General Brezhnev and Prime Minister Kosygin, Podgorny rose more recently to the number-two position in Communist protocol, after Brezhnev but ahead of Kosygin. Overall, this history indicates that the post of President of the Republic, long a merely honorary one, has acquired growing importance and influence in the Communist hierarchy.

One may note at the same time that half of the People's Democracies have gone further in this respect: they have modified their constitutional practice by combining the functions of Chief of the party and Chief of State. This is what has occurred in Romania (Nicolae Ceauşescu), in Bulgaria (Todor Zhivkov), and in Czechoslovakia (Gustáv Husák), as well as in Yugoslavia (Josip Broz Tito).

Most commentators have foreseen such a development in the USSR. For them, the fall of Podgorny is a preliminary step permitting Brezhnev to become President in name as well as actual boss. The text of the new constitution actually suggests that the post of "First Vice-Chairman" of the Presidium of the Supreme Soviet was created in order to assist the President-General Secretary in duties of protocol. *Pravda* has noted an influence of theory from the constitutional experience of the countries of Eastern Europe, making an apparent allusion to the joining of the headships of the party and of the State. Further, in reporting Brezhnev's meeting with the Bulgarian chief Zhivkov, the Soviet daily juxtaposed the formulas "Secretary General of the CC of the CPSU L. I. Brezhnev" and "First Secretary of the CC of the CPB, President of the State Council of the People's Republic of Bulgaria Todor Zhivkov." This procedure was employed in two articles on page one on May 31, and four times on June 1. On the latter date *Pravda* published the text of Zhivkov's greeting, notably characterizing Brezhnev as "leader of the CPSU and of the Soviet State."

The decision to remove Podgorny appears to have surprised him as much as the rest of the world. The Central Committee was considering the draft of the constitution, when it heard a proposal by Donets Province secretary B. V. Kachura to give Brezhnev the title of Chief of State. The Leningrad secretary Grigory Romanov then proposed to remove Podgorny from the Politburo, as an "opportune measure." The Central Committee immediately voted for Romanov's proposal. Caught completely unawares by this well-orchestrated coup, Podgorny got up from his seat on the platform and silently descended to sit among the ordinary members.[1]

Although the Central Committee had only removed him from the position of member of the Politburo, Podgorny's name immediately disappeared from official bulletins and from documents ordinarily signed by the President. The newspapers of May 25 announced the fall of Podgorny by one line in the communiqué released at the end of the Central Committee session. The same day *Pravda* reported a meeting of Brezhnev, Podgorny, and Kosygin (in that order) with the President of Finland, Urho Kekkonen; this was the last mention of Podgorny. After May 26 he became an "unperson." No reference, no official explanation, not even any denunciations, up to the present time.

The successful coup against Podgorny demonstrates that Brezhnev now holds the power to remove anyone from the Soviet leadership, even the number-two man. Podgorny had pursued a career in the apparatus almost paralleling Brezhnev's, though he had moved up a little later relative to his age. Born in 1903, three years before Brezhnev, he attained the post of first secretary of Kharkov Province under Stalin, in 1950, at a time when Brezhnev was already first secretary of a republic (Moldavia). Podgorny's rise continued under Khrushchev: He became second secretary of the Ukraine in 1953, then first secretary of the Ukraine four years later, which by custom gave him the right to be elected to the Party Presidium. He became a candidate member in 1958 and a full member in 1960, while Brezhnev had become a member of the central Secretariat in 1956 and a member of the Presidium in 1957.

In 1963, after the illness of Secretary Kozlov, Podgorny was called to Moscow to be a member of the Secretariat, at the same time that Brezhnev rejoined it. The relations between the two men remain difficult to determine. The sovietologist Myron Rush suggests that Podgorny was promoted by Khrushchev as a "counter-heir" to counterbalance the influence of the "heir-apparent," Brezhnev.[2] Michel Tatu, for his part, believes that Podgorny did not take part in the conspiracy by Brezhnev and Mikhail Suslov aiming to get rid of Khrushchev, and that he was not notified about it until the last minute.[3]

In any case, after October 1964 Podgorny was the highest generalist in the Secretariat next to Brezhnev himself, while the other members specialized in ideology, industry, etc. Thus there were only two attitudes that Podgorny could take towards Brezhnev: to be his second-in-command or his principal rival. Apparently it was mainly the rival that Brezhnev saw in him. In December 1965, after consolidating his own position, Brezhnev applied the treatment that he had experienced from Kozlov five years before, and moved Podgorny from the Secretariat to the post of Chairman of the Presidium of the Supreme Soviet. Why not remove him completely? Perhaps because Brezhnev, recalling the fate of Khrushchev, did not yet dare to threaten a colleague in the "collective leadership" too overtly. Podgorny remained Chief of State and number-three or number-two in the Politburo for more than eleven years, treated with every attention and honor until Brezhnev felt ready to satisfy his own ambition more openly. It was said in Moscow that Podgorny had opposed the policy of détente and even the improvement of consumer-goods supplies. These were undoubtedly explanations after the fact which did not reflect the real reasons for his removal.

After the fall of Khrushchev, Brezhnev appeared at first to be a solid man of the bureaucracy, the first among equals and no more. But he has assumed a more and more prominent role, in both foreign and domestic policy. Last year [1976] he had himself made a Marshal of the Soviet Union and a war hero. The propaganda associated with the Twenty-Fifth Party Congress represented him as the genius of national reconstruction. (In Moscow people jokingly called his program of industrial efficiency "the Marshal Plan".) Now Brezhnev has sacrificed one of his closest collaborators, the fourth in length of service in the Politburo and one of the five members surviving from the Khrushchev era, in order to insure his own place in world history and in protocol at foreign airports. Such are the limits of personal loyalty within the Soviet leadership. One may then ask: Who will remain loyal to Brezhnev's memory after his passage to the next world?

The median age of the Central Committee and of the Politburo has been growing over time, despite a partial replacement of leading personnel after each party congress. In essence the generation of Stalinist apparatchiki, thrust into positions of power in the course of the Great Purge of the thirties, has been growing old in office. In 1939 the median age of the Politburo was forty-five; in 1953, fifty-seven; in 1966, fifty-nine; in 1976, sixty-seven.

This progression will come to an end, sooner or later, if only for biological reasons. It is already possible to discern at the level of regional party secretaries a rejuvenation resulting from appointments made during the seventies. The removal of Podgorny frees up one of the seats on the Politburo for one of these sharp-toothed young apparatchiki and opens up the prospect of a number of replacements of the same sort in the years to come.

To whom will power go after Brezhnev? The question is still open. Brezhnev himself is no doubt aware that the USSR, as foreign sovietologists have emphasized, has no established procedure to designate a successor and the transfer of power. After Lenin, after Stalin, after (or rather under) Khrushchev, it was necessary to have recourse to conspiracy behind the scenes to win the leadership of the party. If Brezhnev leaves behind a collective leadership of geriatrics, one can expect that conspiracies will resume. The other possibility is to get rid of all the powerful old men of the Politburo and to create a mechanism allowing the designation of a single successor, anointed ahead of time. This is what Stalin tried to do during the last months of his life, for the benefit of Georgi Malenkov, but we know that this arrangement and a possible purge were interrupted by the timely death of the old *khoziain.*

CHAPTER FIVE

MOVING THE IMMOVABLE: THE
LEGACY OF BREZHNEVISM
(JANUARY 1982)

By the time Brezhnev died in November 1982 the contemporary Soviet social order had been exhaustively studied by Western specialists. The condition of the Soviet Union was a subject of much controversy within the American government, when CIA estimates of Soviet economic power were challenged as overly generous by a "Team B" of outside analysts. Whatever the quantitative arguments, however, the qualitative deficiencies in the Soviet system were obvious to almost all observers: The regime was at the point of profound crisis because of the contradiction between social and economic change and a rigid political order, while the aging leadership was about to give way to new blood.

One prediction that can be made with assurance about the near political future of the Soviet Union is the inevitable death of the present gerontocracy and its replacement with a younger cadre of leaders. The immobilism of the Brezhnev years is destined to yield to a new generation whose personal political consciousness no longer embraces the experience of Stalin's purges nor even, for many, the Great Patriotic War. What change this renovation may bring to the world's most powerful political system is a matter of intense concern to every other government on earth. However, the nature of the change can only be inferred by projecting from current pressures and movements in the Soviet system insofar as we can observe them.

Western scholarship on the Soviet system in the various social science disciplines has reached a high level of sophistication and has yielded a plethora of empirical, bountifully documented studies on the various facets of the Soviet phenomenon. Current work on the Soviet government, economy, and social system has established a broad but firm consensus. No longer have we emotional debates or terminological hairsplitting over whether the Soviet Union is revolutionary or conservative, totalitarian or pluralistic. Practically all scholars recognize what T. Harry Rigby calls the "mono-organizational system," in which the leading and controlling role is reserved for the apparatus of the Communist Party.[1] At the same time, most agree that the image of a completely centralized totalitarian despotism, rigidly imposing its orders on everyone, is outdated. Most also stress that the distinctive characteristics of the Brezhnev regime of the last fifteen years have been pragmatic conservatism and gradualist rationality, within which the imperatives of a complex modern society can be at least partially contained. None encourage expectations of any sudden and fundamental change even after the Old Guard leaves the political scene.

❖   ❖   ❖

The impetus to change comes, ironically, from the socioeconomic base, that is, from the growing technological sophistication of the industrial economy and from a more affluent (or less impoverished) population which aspires to self-fulfillment in everything from consumer goods and services to literary expression and professional accomplishment. The superstructure of political power and control institutionalized in the party is thereby confronted with a chronic dilemma, to which it responds with an equally chronic ambivalence. How derive advantages from high technology and educated manpower in the form of economic and military power, without making concessions with respect to decentralization of initiative or special-interest values that might compromise the essential principle of control and goal-setting from the top? This dilemma lies at the heart of what is variously perceived as the "immobilism," "inertia," or "incrementalism" of the Brezhnev era, and it will clearly require that the successor leadership formulate some coherent policy to move the system off dead center.

Economically the Soviet system has come to be threatened by the implications of its own success. One might argue that in building a tremendous modern industrial plant and resource base and in avidly espousing the "scientific-technological revolution," the Communist regime that Stalin bequeathed to his successors has sown the seeds of its own destruction, or, at least discomfiture. In a wide range of endeavors the Soviet economy has reached a level of complexity, diversification, and scientific refinement which cannot be properly accommodated and taken advantage of by the traditional Stalinist model of centralized administration and directed planning.

The continuing use of quantitative output norms constitutes a drag on the upgrading of industrial quality, while wasteful overinvestment leaves resources short for incentives in the consumption sector. To be sure, there has been steady progress until recently in wage levels and in the supply of consumer goods and services, such as health and housing, though these accomplishments have always fallen short of the rising expectations of the Soviet populace, not to mention Western standards. But the country has of late been overtaken (no less than the West) by a growth rate crisis, as the possibilities for development within the constraints of the Soviet administrative structure become progressively narrower. In classic Marxian terms, the Soviet system of "relations of production" has become a "fetter upon the mode of production," and one anticipates the time when "this integument is burst asunder."[2]

There is no easy way out of the impasse. Further gains entail greater costs; the marginal return to increased investment drops; and the economic trade-offs become more agonizing. Even the natural riches of Siberia pose increasing obstacles of cost to their economical exploitation. Soviet agriculture, as the world well knows, has been particularly disappointing despite the shift under Brezhnev from squeezing the peasants to providing them with costly subsidies; giantism and centralism in agriculture seem to be, at least under Soviet conditions, counterproductive. People in the middle management and professional class are particularly irritated by the inadequacy of material incentives and the contrast of relative opulence visible in their frequent visits to Hungary, Czechoslovakia, or East Germany.

The potential for technological innovation and its effective application requires, more than ever, the devolution of responsibility and initiative to the local level and the enterprise manager, but the system balks at such an alteration in its principles. One of the probable reasons for Soviet interest in détente with the West and circumspection toward dissenters is the importing of technological innovations which its own system frustrates. Yet for the same reason it is doubtful that such imports are effectively utilized. Similarly, the subtleties of environmental protection break down because of the lack of low-level responsibility and commitment to the observance of safeguards.

Law has also emerged as a visible indicator of the Soviet Union's systemic dilemma. Traditionally subordinated to the leadership's insistence on total and arbitrary decision-making power (under Khrushchev as well as under Stalin), law has begun to come into its own as a reflection of the need for a rational and consistent structure of rules and expectations within which local authorities can begin to exercise some initiative. Soviet experts and political scientists have begun to find that they are taken seriously when they address the petrifaction of the administrative system. But a real change in principle in the force of law has yet to win acceptance.

In some facets of life the authorities have retreated in the face of complexities that they cannot master, notably the trends in family life toward fewer children and more divorces. They have no effective answer for the perennial nationality problem or for the demographic erosion of Great-Russian dominance. Repression and manipulation are failing to guarantee conformity even in the area of religion. Overall, one is struck again and again by evidence of an anachronistic political system muddling through its social and economic difficulties with a minimum of concessions in its traditional style of rule.

❖   ❖   ❖

Western scholarship perceives the Brezhnev regime as conservative, if such be possible for the presumed heirs of a revolution. It is elephantine, glacial, leaden. It is not averse to pragmatic improvements of a material sort, but it can hardly move under its own weight. The bureaucratic system built by Stalin (or recreated from the ruins of the old Russian state) could, in his day, be moved to all manner of revolutionary actions by a leader strong enough. Khrushchev was still able to throw the bureaucratic establishment off balance with his erratic initiatives and his appeal to a populist spirit. The Brezhnev style, immanent in that bureaucratic establishment which now sets de facto limits to the leader's power, is to avoid the big issues and undertake only incrementalism of the most practical and unthreatening sort.

This fear of change has incurred its greatest potential cost in the realm of economic reform. The new Brezhnev regime, evidently cognizant of all the logical reasons for decentralizing industrial decision-making, nevertheless backed away in the late 1960s from such a drastic change in the familiar way of doing business. Its apprehensions seemed to confirm Alec Nove's reasoning that the central plan requires the party dictatorship, and the party dictatorship requires the central plan—the economic price for a political principle.[3]

Still, the spirit of the dictatorship in the Brezhnev era has changed to a "substantive rationality," in Rigby's words, so that personalist fanaticism has yielded to "the natural caution of entrenched elites."[4] Ideology has not lost its importance, but its function is legitimation rather than guidance. Wherever the doctrinal cloak has fit too tightly, it has been retailored. The latest alteration is the proposition of "developed socialism" as a historic stage of indefinite duration in which the Soviet system now professes to find itself—a notion which seems to make the leadership more comfortable in entertaining pragmatic policy suggestions from the experts. There is now considerable evidence to support Jerry Hough's initially controversial argument that the regime tolerates and even invites empirical policy studies and professional controversy to a far greater degree than formerly, as long as they do not overtly question official claims to Marxist legitimacy.[5] According to Roy Medvedev, the demurrers of loyal intellectuals sufficed to deflect the proposed rehabilitation of Stalin in 1969.[6] Open dissent may still be firmly curbed, much to the detriment of the quality of cultural life, but with respect to the inner circles of the specialists the regime appears not to be bothered so much by what they say as by how they may say it.

❖   ❖   ❖

The confluence of socioeconomic modernization and political-administrative immobilism has given a distinctive form to the evolving

Soviet system, though it is hard to categorize. It is neither despotic nor free, neither totalitarian nor pluralistic, but a curious amalgam of functional interests and technical imperatives embedded in a commitment to the monopoly of power. In its very rigidity the system has become more rational, more routinized, more rule-bound than it has ever been since the days of the tsars. Laws and regulations, within which everyone knows his permitted scope, operate with a high degree of predictability. According to Max Weber's typology of authority, as Rigby observes, Russia has passed from the "traditional" to the "charismatic" and then through the "routinization of charisma" to the "rational-legal" model—although Rigby prefers to call it "goal-rational"—now approximated in the Soviet bureaucracy.[7]

Within this context, two conclusions emerge which to a degree vindicate the adherents of both totalitarian and interest-group models of the Soviet system. The party continues to dominate the scene as a supreme bureaucracy, integrating all other political and social functions through the hierarchical personnel controls of its *nomenklatura* system. But it does not obliterate the identity or the responsibility of the manifold functional and geographical entities that make up the institutional structure of the nation. These, in turn, are differentiated by a multitude of organizational interests and specialized perspectives. They pursue their diverse functions and needs with whatever latitude the party center has accorded them, and vigorously compete with one another for resources, influence, and turf. Darrell Hammer cites Jerry Hough's phrase, "institutional pluralism," and my own term, "participatory bureaucracy," as possible conceptualizations for a complex hierarchy which contributes policy inputs by its information and advice, and plays an even more influential role in policy outputs by shaping or impeding implementation.[8] Perhaps the leadership attempts so little in the way of grand initiatives because it is not sure of its own power to drive a major innovation through the bureaucratic jungle.

❖   ❖   ❖

What choices, burdens, and opportunities does all this mean for the prospective new leadership of the Soviet Union? When the irresistible force of socioeconomic change meets the immovable object of autocratic government, one has the makings of a revolutionary situation. Will the new leadership be of such a mind as to entertain the more fundamental reforms that seem essential in order to avert such a potential collision? Little is really known, unfortunately, about the inclinations of the middle-aged individuals who are likely to emerge from the party apparatus when the day of the succession arrives. But it must be kept in mind that the current upper echelon still represents the Stalinist post-purge leadership generation who have collectively grown old in office for more than four decades. We know that the new leadership will not carry the direct burden of the Stalinist experience, and is therefore likely to have a greater level of confidence about the stability of the Soviet system and its place in the world. To this extent they may be freer to consider the big decisions, the basic reforms, which Western empirical studies have underscored as logical necessities for the Soviet system. A dramatic new departure is at least conceivable even within the mono-organizational structure of Communist rule. After all, there is the example of the "Prague Spring" and "Socialism with a Human Face," which were brought about by the frustrated lower echelons of the Communist Party in 1968 Czechoslovakia. Such an initiative had been unthinkable until it actually took place.

The limits and deterrents to such a rosy resolution of the Soviet Union's quandaries are most likely to be found in the deeper continuities of Soviet life. One may mention, among other factors, the bent toward hierarchy and centralism in the old Russian political culture; the consolidation of the New Class with its perquisites and privileges; the reaffirmation of Russian nationalism, at the expense of greater friction with the minorities; the profound and increasing militarization of the Soviet system and its priorities. It is at least open to question whether the people who benefit from the system really want to change anything unless circumstances compel them to do so. But the USSR may nonetheless face a fateful parting of the roads leading to liberal reform or to naked reactionary chauvinism.

CHAPTER SIX

BREZHNEV'S TWO FACES
(NOVEMBER 1982)

By the time General Secretary Brezhnev died in November 1982, the contradictions in the Soviet system had become more and more obvious, even if official growth figures were exaggerated. This was all the more so in the second stage of Brezhnev's administration, after 1975, when adventurism abroad against economic stagnation at home created strains that his successors were obliged to address.

Since 1917 the Soviet Union has known only four long-term leaders. Each of the latter three distinguished himself by reacting against the excesses of the previous era: Stalin against the factionalism and controversy that marked the Communists' first ten years under Lenin and his entourage; Khrushchev against Stalin's terror; Brezhnev against Khrushchev's "hare-brained schemes."

Brezhnev, whose eighteen-year rule ended with his death on 10 November, is rightly regarded as the most conservative leader the Soviet Union has had. He gave the country stability, if nothing else, even though it was the stability of the police state. Both domestically and up to a point internationally, his reign was marked by no great initiatives, no really new ideas, no sensational purges, no interesting controversy that we know of. Once he had cancelled his predecessor's disruptive innovations in administration and in culture, the watchword for Brezhnev was the status quo.

Yet change did not grind to a halt under Brezhnev. The great paradox of his years was a regime that preferred to avoid or suppress issues, but that nevertheless achieved steady growth in the Soviet Union's potential as a modern society and as a military power. The contradiction between what the Soviet Union was and what it could be became obvious.

During the Brezhnev era, or more exactly, from the census of 1959 to the census of 1979, the Soviet Union grew in population from 209 million to 262 million, an increase of 25 percent (compared with U.S. growth of 27 percent, from 179 million to 227 million, in the same period). The entire net growth was channelled into the urban sector, which for the first time in Russia exceeded 50 percent and approached the two-thirds mark. Industrial development, still guided by the planners' penchant for heavy industry, proceeded apace and in certain basic categories actually surpassed the United States. Steel output, for example, rose from 85 million metric tons in 1964 to 149 million metric tons in 1981, while American production was fluctuating between 100 million and 130 million depending on the business cycle. Coal rose from nearly the American figure of 500 million tons annually to half again as much, and the Soviets more than doubled their extraction of petroleum and became the world's largest producer. By the end of the Tenth Five-Year Plan of 1976–80 the Soviet GNP reached about 60 percent of the American level, and net current investment was actually greater in absolute terms.

Given facts such as these, how explain the conventional rhetoric about the failure of the centrally planned Soviet economic system? The answer is that it is a failure, or at least does not deliver according to its potential, in certain specific sectors—in agriculture, in consumer goods, and in high technology. These failures are only relative, in the inability to keep up with the needs of a population that is larger, more urban, more educated, and more demanding, and with the requirements of the military establishment for the last word in technological sophistication.

These deficiencies were pragmatically recognized by the Brezhnev team, even if they were not prepared to deal with them radically. Agriculture, always the stepchild since Stalin's time, began to receive heavy investments; ultimately the peasants were being subsidized rather than exploited. The Soviet Union became, surprisingly, the world's number-one wheat producer, and had no problem with the bread supply. Where it fell down was in the animal feed necessary to supply the population with the meat it wanted, as well as in the ability to market the broad variety of food that Westerners take for granted. The weather, always undependable at high latitudes, contributed to repeated bad harvests in the last few years. All this led the leadership to announce a grandiose "food program" last spring, still without openly attacking the systematic limitations of an overcentralized economic system.

As the basic answer to his problems, Brezhnev embraced with enthusiasm the so-called "scientific-technical revolution," though he was incapable of allowing the lower-level initiatives and incentives requisite for taking full advantage of the movement. He steadily expanded technical and specialized education, created dozens of new provincial universities and institutes, and saw the total number of Soviet citizens with some higher education more than double. But this progress had its dialectical counterpart in the growth of a sophisticated class of experts who could not forever be treated with the mindlessness of party ideology and denied the right to live in adult dignity. The restlessness of educated Soviet youth and their obsession with all things Western has been confirmed by countless observers.

In foreign policy as in domestic, the early Brezhnev approach was cautious promotion of the status quo. This entailed the pursuit of détente with the United States in the teeth of the Vietnam War; a long freeze with

China; low-risk endorsement of "national liberation" to woo allies in the Third World; firm action to keep the European satellites in the Soviet security zone; and steady enhancement of military power by committing 10 to 12 percent of the annual GNP to the armed forces and military-oriented industry.

Military progress gave the Soviets the confidence of strategic equality. Détente finally was consummated in 1972, so this writer was later told by officials of the Institute of World Economy & International Relations, when the Nixon Administration acknowledged the Soviet Union's right to nuclear parity. Eventually the Brezhnev regime pushed its advantage too far; of this, more below.

Politically Brezhnev's era saw none of the open struggles and purges that had punctuated the rule of his predecessors. Brezhnev himself came to power under circumstances unprecedented in the entire history of Russia, when the established leader was removed constitutionally by vote of a supposedly rubber-stamp body, the Central Committee of the party. By all appearances, the succession to Khrushchev was prearranged among the leading members of the Politburo (or party Presidium, as it was called at that time), and this impression is confirmed by the unbroken tenure of Brezhnev's top associates until death or infirmity weeded them out in recent months. Kosygin, assuming Khrushchev's office of Prime Minister at the same time that Brezhnev became First Secretary of the party, functioned in that capacity until his death in 1980. Suslov, kingmaker and high priest of the state religion, likewise held his Politburo seat and presumably his influence until he died last spring. Kirilenko served with Brezhnev as the number-two party organization man until illness— medical or political—took him out of the top rank only days before Brezhnev himself died. Podgorny, a potential rival to Brezhnev shunted to the function of Chief of State in 1965, held that office for twelve years until Brezhnev decided to claim the honor for himself in 1977.

Other changes made by Brezhnev in the leadership lower down proceeded much more slowly and selectively than under Khrushchev, not to mention Stalin, and without the rhetoric of purge or denunciation. Two old-timers in Khrushchev's Presidium, Mikoyan and Shvernik, were retired forthwith, and three others (Shelest, G. I. Voronov, D. S. Poliansky) were eased out in the early 1970s. Replacements for these people were loyal bureaucrats who had worked their way up the party hierarchy, plus the heads of the key arms of governmental power—the military (Grechko and now Dmitri Ustinov), the police (Andropov), and the foreign office (Andrei Gromyko). More and more, Politburo participation came to be expected on the basis of bureaucratic entitlement.

One top-level change attracting more than the usual attention was the case of the relatively youthful and potentially threatening party secretary

Shelepin, former head of the Communist Youth and the KGB. He had been advanced to the Presidium as part of the post-Khrushchev deal in 1964, but three years later he suddenly found himself removed from the Secretariat and consigned to head the trade unions. There he lingered until 1975, when he was finally dropped from the leadership altogether.

Down below, among the provincial party secretaries and other offices of Central Committee rank, the rate of turnover registered in the twenty years before Brezhnev slowed down dramatically. The entire party and governmental apparatus proceeded to grow old together in relatively quiet stability, with only occasional youngsters winning advancement as death and debility created openings. The Minister of Railways, B. P. Beshchev, to take an extreme example, served from 1948 until he retired in 1977 at the age of seventy-three; A. Y. Snechkus headed the Communist Party in Latvia from the time of the Soviet takeover in 1940 until he died in office in 1974 at the age of seventy. Of the 219 members of the Central Committee elected in 1981, ninety-five had held office at that rank or just below (candidate member or Central Auditing Commission) at least since 1961, and fifty-five more had been members of this elite since Brezhnev's first party congress in 1966.

What has been said here of the successful conservatism of the Brezhnev administration is truer for its early years than its later ones. In fact, one can distinguish two Brezhnev eras, very different in character and in problems. The first, extending from his takeover in 1964 up to 1975, conforms to the picture of status quo leadership, building the economy, pursuing détente, and maintaining political equilibrium at home. The second phase, from 1975 to the end just now, contrasts in almost every way.

To begin with, economic growth began to falter, and agriculture repeatedly fell short. Labor productivity ceased to grow despite the material and educational investment that the regime was putting into the economy, and the plan as often as not went unfulfilled. This problem came on top of a labor shortage resulting from low birth rates in European Russia during and since World War II, coupled with the social malaise reflected in rising alcoholism and infant mortality. At the same time, the Russians found themselves about to become a minority in their own country, as the high birth rate among Central Asian Moslems pushed the total of all non-Russian nationalities in the Soviet Union close to the 50 percent mark.

In the face of all these warning signs, the Brezhnev regime shifted from pragmatism to egocentrism, as the leader began to claim the honors of the personal power that he had up to then foregone. In 1976 he had himself made a Marshal of the Soviet Union and a retroactive war hero. In 1977, removing Podgorny, he had himself designated Chief of State and gave his name to the revision of the Soviet Constitution. Meanwhile he stepped up the campaign to silence the dissident movement and harass Jews attempting to emigrate, with the arrests and deportations that so disturbed opinion abroad.

Brezhnev's foreign policy acquired a new tone about the same time. The double-pronged turning point was the fall of South Vietnam and the clash of rival independence movements in Angola in 1975. Evidently sensing American weariness with the role of world policeman, and assuming the worst about American-Chinese rapprochement, the Brezhnev leadership gambled with detente and embarked on a course of bold exploitation of political opportunities in the Third World. But there was a price to be paid: These moves in pursuit of immediate Soviet advantage undercut the whole point of Brezhnev's previous policy of détente, and destroyed the possibility of a fundamental accord with the most peace-loving American president of this century, Jimmy Carter.

Uppermost in Western minds is the legacy of Brezhnev's last half-dozen years, of impasse and oppression, both at home and abroad. Clearly Brezhnev has bequeathed to his successors some awkward situations in dealing with the economy no less than with the resistors in Poland and Afghanistan. But the deeper problem, both a challenge and an opportunity, is the product of Brezhnev's first phase—the growing economy and maturing society confined by an archaic and unbending political and administrative system. In this contradiction the Brezhnev legacy suggests the classic prerevolutionary situation, which, if sparked by major foreign failures or political schism among the leadership, could spell trouble or change of a highly unpredictable sort. The Soviet people no longer have need—if they ever did—of the regime that grips them for the sake of its own self-perpetuation. The successor leadership will have to face the fact that their system has outlived its excuses.

CHAPTER SEVEN

ANDROPOV AND THE NEW SOVIET GENERATION (JANUARY 1983)

Upon Brezhnev's demise the Politburo decided by a narrow margin to pass the torch to the former KGB chief Yuri Andropov, who immediately began an effort to renovate the party leadership. With a call for "acceleration" and incentives, he sought to reinvigorate the Soviet economy and instill a new sense of discipline and sobriety.

Every episode of succession to the supreme power in Soviet Russia has been unique. Lenin's death in 1924 was followed by half a decade of open factional struggle ending in the personal despotism of Joseph Stalin. Stalin's death in 1953 signalled a shorter period of contention and then the reform leadership of Nikita Khrushchev. Khrushchev's overthrow by a neo-Stalinist conspiracy in 1964 ushered in Leonid Brezhnev's rule as Chairman of a more or less collegial Board. Without any relaxation in the rule of the Communist Party, the trend each time has pointed toward a less personal and more collective form of rule by the top bureaucracy.

Andropov's succession to the Soviet leadership when Brezhnev died last November has been distinctive in a new way. What is most striking about this episode is Andropov's quick success in asserting his own personal power. Seemingly the old trend toward more collective leadership has been reversed.

This turn of events became possible thanks to another unique circumstance at the time of Brezhnev's demise. During most of his long tenure of office Brezhnev had shared power with a collective of top leaders who moved in with him when Khrushchev fell: Prime Minister Kosygin, Chief of State Podgorny, party ideologist and presumed kingmaker Suslov, and the number-two party organization man Kirilenko. The persistence of such a stable group around the new chief was itself unique in the annals of Soviet politics, but in the later 1970s, with advancing age and political incapacity, this team began to disintegrate. Podgorny, removed in 1977 at the age of seventy-four to allow Brezhnev the Chief-of-State title, finally died in retirement this month. Kosygin died in 1980 at the age of seventy-six, followed by Suslov in January 1982 at the age of seventy-nine. Just a few days before Brezhnev died, Kirilenko, then aged seventy-six, was relieved of his top posts on the ostensible grounds of ill health.

Thanks to these largely natural developments, there was a partial vac-
uum in the top leadership when Brezhnev left the scene. Leadership responsibilities had fallen to a newer, if not much younger, echelon of
Politburo members who had been promoted during the later Brezhnev
years. These were the men who have waged the quick post-Brezhnev succession game and asserted their places in the current leadership: Andropov himself, a Politburo member since 1973; his rival Konstantin
Chernenko, a member only since 1978; Defense Minister and new kingmaker Dmitri Ustinov, a member since 1976, along with Leningrad party
secretary Grigory Romanov; Moscow party boss Viktor Grishin, Ukrai-
nian chief Vladimir Shcherbitsky, and Kazakhstan leader Dinmukhamed
Kunaev, all dating from 1971.

Both the disintegration of the top Brezhnev collective and the failure
of the second echelon to present themselves as a team are readily under-
standable in terms of a third peculiarity in the Brezhnev-Andropov succession. This is the advanced age attained not only by the previous
leadership group but also by those from the second echelon who have
been waiting for the chance to move up. Andropov at sixty-eight is just
one year younger than Ronald Reagan when he was elected president of
the United States. Grishin is also sixty-eight, Kunaev is seventy, Chernenko is seventy-two, Foreign Minster Andrei Gromyko is seventy-three,
Ustinov seventy-four, Prime Minister Nikolai Tikhonov seventy-seven,
and Party Control chairman Arvid Pelshe eighty-two. (Only Shcherbitsky,
sixty-four, Romanov, fifty-nine, and the agriculture chief Mikhail Gorbachev, fifty-one, are under traditional retirement age.) The age factor inex-
orably rules out any long period of collective rule such as the original
Brezhnev team enjoyed.

We still do not know clearly the political alignments within the post-
Brezhnev Politburo. However, if they had held together as a collective,
presumably rallying around Brezhnev's favorite Chernenko, the best the
party could expect would be a few years of caretaker government. In fact,
it appears that the Politburo split, and that Ustinov played the decisive
card when he threw the support of the military behind Andropov. Still,
the ease of Andropov's trend-upsetting victory demands more explanation than is offered by theories of special-interest military and police support. One factor may be the growing generational spread between the
aging upper crust in the Politburo and the broader power base in the
Central Committee of the party, coupled with frustration among the
younger leaders over the immobilism of the Brezhnev Old Guard.

The Brezhnev generation, the men now in their seventies who are rapidly dying off, has had an unusual history. Their rise to power as a group
goes all the way back to the Great Purge of 1937–38, when Stalin killed
off practically everyone in the Soviet bureaucracy over the age of thirty-

five. This massacre opened the way for the *vydvizhentsy* or "promotees," men who had been plucked from the working class or peasantry and put through crash training programs to prepare them to take over from the Old Bolshevik purge victims. Individuals such as Suslov, Kosygin, and Brezhnev rose meteorically. Ever since, this group has been growing old in office, meanwhile forcing younger people to wait longer and longer for positions to open at the top level. The median age of the Politburo, to take the most obvious indicator, rose from fifty-eight in 1961 (when there were hardly any purge survivors over sixty) to seventy-two after the most recent party congress in 1981. In the Central Committee the median age went up from fifty-three in 1961 to sixty-two in 1981, and the proportion of members over sixty-five rose from a mere 3 percent in 1961 to 39 percent in 1981 as the generation of purge survivors born after 1902 moved on into the senior age bracket. Statistics confirm the impression that the top Soviet leadership has become a creaking gerontocracy.

Nevertheless the self-perpetuation of the post-purge leadership has not precluded all rejuvenation in the party hierarchy. Gradual turnover and enlargement of the Central Committee (now standing at 319 full members) have made room for a substantial number of new middle-aged members, so that the ages of the membership as a whole are spread out much more than they were formerly. While one quarter of the 1981 Central Committee were sixty-eight or over, older than Andropov, another quarter were still under fifty-five. Already there are 130 members of the Central Committee—40 percent—who were under thirty when Stalin died. In the next Central Committee they will assuredly be a majority, as time thins the ranks of the Stalinist functionaries moving on into their seventies.

How different from the present leadership these post-Stalin people may prove to be when they reach the highest offices is still a matter of conjecture. Most reports out of the Soviet Union indicate that they are as tough as their elders in the apparatus. These are not ordinary Soviet citizens, after all, but professionals who have opted for high-pressure careers and have in turn been carefully screened and molded by their Stalinist predecessors. But they are presumed to be more confident, more pragmatic, and more sophisticated, and they are certainly better educated than the over-seventies of the post-purge generation.

Considering the differences of age and background that now exist in the Soviet leadership, it is not unreasonable to surmise that the younger contingent, growing in size, maturity, and experience, may now constitute an effective pressure group within the Central Committee for serious reform, particularly measures that might break the logjam in the Soviet economy. We still do not know how far the Central Committee can operate as an effective political force, but on occasion—in 1957 and in 1964—it has been the critical forum to sustain a threatened leader or to validate the choice of a successor. When Brezhnev's demise became imminent, the new generation was available in strength in the Central Committee to lend support to that one member of the old leadership who seemed most prepared to gamble on change, in other words the candidacy of Andropov.

Whatever the strength to these speculations, the generational spread in the Soviet leadership is a key to Andropov's future, as opportunities arise to replace older people with more of the younger set. At the Politburo level there were three vacancies after Brezhnev died, and at least two other positions seemed ripe for retirement. These openings for replacements put Andropov within easy striking distance of control over the Politburo. Promotions in turn open the way for patronage appointments all down the line, and this circumstance, coupled with the actuarial odds against the oldest third of the Central Committee, sets the stage for the most rapid renovation of the Soviet leadership since Stalin's time, in accordance with the circular flow of power from the General Secretary down through the apparatus and up through the party's conferences and congresses to the Central Committee and the Politburo. To be secure in his power, as Stalin was to his death, and as Khrushchev was briefly, the leader needs time to get his own men into the key party positions and establish a majority that he can control in the Central Committee and the Politburo.

These appointments cannot be made randomly or capriciously, even if the chief has the last word. Over the past thirty years a body of practice and expectation has governed the selection of people to sit on the ruling bodies of the party as an automatic privilege of the particular bureaucratic offices they hold. Both the Politburo on a small scale and the Central Committee on a much larger one are assemblies of representatives of bureaucratic functions, primarily the professional party organization men and the leaders of the civil government and the armed forces. In order to control the Central Committee or the Politburo, one must find or create vacancies among the specific positions that confer Central Committee or Politburo rank, and then be able to dictate who is promoted to fill those vacancies. This is a task that cannot be accomplished overnight, though the aging process will naturally facilitate it.

So far, Andropov has refrained from dramatic moves to rebuild the party leadership, but the early steps he has taken confirm the direction suggested here. Scarcely a week after taking over, he picked Geidar Aliev, fifty-nine, party chief of Azerbaijan and a former colleague of his in the KGB, for the post of first deputy prime minister. This made Aliev heir apparent to Prime Minister Tikhonov and qualified him for promotion to fill one of the vacancies on the Politburo that Andropov had at his disposal. One of the two openings on the ten-member Secretariat, decisive for organizational control of the party, was filled by the fifty-three-year-old economic planning expert Nikolai Ryzhkov. Since then, new men have been appointed to the KGB, to the ministries of railroads and agricultural construction, and to the party propaganda department and the Communist Young League, all positions carrying Central Committee rank.

The tactical pattern suggested by Andropov's early moves is not a sudden housecleaning, but a series of step-by-step appointments of younger men as vacancies arise or are selectively created. However, the age factor alone assures that vacancies in jobs at the Central Committee level will arise in rapid succession from now on. Andropov will automatically have the opportunity to build the power base of younger people that can confirm his own hold on the leadership, even within the limited term that his advanced age allows him. In so doing, he will find himself presiding over a new generational revolution in Soviet politics, whatever this may portend for new directions in dealing either with the Soviet people or with the outside world.

Chapter Eight

Back to Chernenko:
Evading the Inevitable
(March 1984)

The choice of party secretary Konstantin Chernenko to succeed Andropov when the latter's reforming administration was cut short by his death from kidney failure in February 1984, appeared to be a step backward from forthright confrontation with the Soviet Union's needs and problems. Nonetheless, the aging of the Soviet leadership made the advent to power of a new generation and a new outlook more and more imminent, though specific changes in policy direction were hard to predict.

Political power is an elusive substance under any circumstances. In a society as secretive as the Soviet Union the laws governing its allocation and operation are particularly mysterious. Hence the occult science of kremlinology, attempting to discern the lines of influence and policy within the Soviet leadership from such casual clues as who is seen speaking with whom on the platform at Supreme Soviet meetings, or who is included in the delegation to meet a certain foreign dignitary at the airport.

Nothing puts our limited knowledge of Soviet politics to the test as much as the transfer of leadership from one individual to another. How is the successor actually chosen? Is power directly handed on or must it be acquired in other ways? Does the identity of the new leader make any difference? How does the new leader assure his tenure of power? None of these questions have clear and consistent answers.

It was, of course, apparent ever since Andropov failed to show at the celebration of the Bolshevik Revolution last 7 November that medical factors were likely to make the era of his rule as General Secretary of the Communist Party of the Soviet Union the shortest by far in the history of the Soviet state. His illness assured the extension of a trend observable ever since Stalin died in 1953, of a diminution in the personal power of the party leader and his capacity to make memorable changes in the political and social structure of the country. Nevertheless, Kremlin watchers were confounded by the arrangements made by the Politburo, presumably, during the twenty-two hours before Andropov's demise was publicly announced on 10 February, and ratified by the Central Committee three days later. Instead of catering to the impatient younger echelons of the party hierarchy and choosing someone who would continue Andropov's initiatives of reform and discipline, the kingmakers handed the position of honor to the very man he had upstaged in winning power fifteen months ago, the man identified more than anyone else with the superannuated bureaucratic conservatism that had come to mark the later years of the Brezhnev regime.

Konstantin Ustinovich Chernenko was born in Siberia in 1911 to what is plausibly described as a peasant family. Little is known of his life until after World War II, when he surfaced as propaganda chief in the Moldavian Republic, so-called, the old province of Bessarabia which Stalin had taken back from Romania during the war. There he began his three decades of unbroken association with Leonid Brezhnev that led him eventually to the highest rank in the Communist power elite.

The chronology of Chernenko's life permits some interesting interpolations. A party member since 1931, he belonged to the age group of the *vydvizhentsy*—the promising young workers and peasants recruited by Stalin in the late 1920s and early 1930s for crash education programs and rapid promotion. By and large they were a group attracted to power and practical results, impatient with theory except as a means of blanketing doubts, and both ignorant and suspicious of the outside world. As a generation they have dominated the Soviet system ever since, with relatively little infusion of younger blood into the upper ranks. Chernenko, like Brezhnev and Andropov, is a representative of this post-purge generation of Stalinists.

The events preceding and surrounding Brezhnev's death seemed to suggest that the logjam of bureaucratic immobilism and corruption associated with the aging Stalinist cadre was about to be broken. Andropov's initial steps to punish corruption, round up slackers, and sharpen incentives for efficiency and productivity in the sluggish Soviet economy betokened the alliance of military, police, and younger party organization men that presumably backed his successful candidacy for the office of General Secretary.

As to who actually had a voice in the selection of Andropov we know no more definitely than who shared in the choice of Chernenko upon Andropov's death. The sequence of events in each case, particularly the quick designation of the ultimate successor to head the funeral arrangements for his predecessor, indicates that the succession was agreed upon before the Central Committee could convene in Moscow to give its official blessing to the choice. The will of the previous leader does not appear to have counted for much: Brezhnev had obviously tried to set Chernenko up as his successor, to no avail at the moment, and Andropov is thought by most commentators to have preferred Gorbachev, at fifty-two the youngest member of the Politburo. We are left with the presumption that the Politburo, reflecting the pressures of the various constituencies represented in it, made its own choice in each case.

If this is true, as it appears to be, ultimate power in the Soviet Union, expressed at moments of transition, is collective rather than individual. This means that there is an arena of genuine, if behind-the-scenes, politics, where commitments and compromises made to secure the leadership will constrain the leader, at least in the short run, to respect the interests that put him into office. With old leaders, transitions become more frequent, and hence the bureaucratic constituencies gain even more influence and the chance to entrench their resistance to change from without.

The exact composition of the Politburo, fluctuating between eleven and fifteen, is governed more by bureaucratic custom than by rule. Nevertheless, its makeup for years has followed an unwritten law of ticket-balancing: four or five seats for the professional party organization (most recently Andropov as General Secretary; secretaries Chernenko, Romanov, and Gorbachev; and Moscow party boss Viktor Grishin); representing the nominal government, the prime minister (presently Tikhonov) and (if he is not the same as the General Secretary) the titular Chief of State; the Minister of Defense (Ustinov), the Foreign Minister (Gromyko) and the head of the KGB (momentarily Viktor Chebrikov at the lower "candidate" level); and three or four key regional figures, who at present include the party chiefs of the Ukraine (Shcherbitsky) and Kazakhstan (Kunaev) and the governmental leader of the Russian Republic (Vitaly Vorotnikov).

All of these men enjoy their Politburo seats by virtue of their specific office; rarely would they be retained if they lost that office. By the same token, to remove them from the Politburo means removing them from the offices that conferred Politburo rank, a step that is not taken lightly or too often. The result is a virtually locked-in leadership elite that can only be changed slowly—and not as fast as it ages. The median age of the twelve Politburo members is now seventy, and the median length of service at this rank is seven years. In the meantime, the Politburo has a strong and growing voice not only over the choice of the leader but also over the initiatives that he can take. At one remove, the same principles hold for the Central Committee, made up on the same basis of bureaucratic job slots, whose members have a vital role in the success or failure of the leader's programs.

Considering the entrenched character of the Soviet regime's leading bodies, it was remarkable that Andropov with his police background was able to make himself acceptable to a majority of the Politburo and then to the Central Committee. Conceivably some of his colleagues saw him as a compromise between the need to tighten up, and the fear of a younger man with a long tenure in prospect who could gradually get his own people into the key jobs and shake the entire Old Guard out of their positions. But Andropov's rival Chernenko, far from being thrust aside, kept the acknowledged number-two slot as party secretary in charge of ideology, and remained prominently in view as a champion of ideological rigor and indoctrination. In one of the intriguing indicators of the exact Russian sense of status, Chernenko tied with Prime Minister Tikhonov for second place (naturally following Andropov) in the number of multiple nominations arranged for him in different districts for the Supreme Soviet elections on 4 March.

Andropov's death has again presented the Politburo with the question of age and short-term stability versus youth and renovation. The logical contenders, as in 1982, were restricted to those men in full-time party organization work in the central Secretariat who also enjoyed full Politburo membership. After Andropov there were only three: Chernenko, the also-ran; the youthful Gorbachev; and the sixty-year-old Romanov, the man distinguished by the surname of the late royal family, who had just moved to Moscow last summer from his old post as Leningrad party boss. All of these qualified, incidentally, as members of the dominant Great-Russian nationality. Ruling out Chernenko as a loser and Gorbachev as a kid, the smart betting had to go for Romanov, whose repositioning within the Secretariat was directly reminiscent of Andropov's switch to that body the year before. Romanov would have kept the line of succession within the party apparatus, as it had traditionally been, while signalling the first significant step toward the rejuvenation of the leadership since the fall of Khrushchev.

Chernenko's designation as General Secretary to succeed Andropov confounds all this logical expectation. It can only be explained as the result of a shifting alignment within the Politburo, this time away from Andropov-style reform and rectitude, and back, for the short run, to the bureaucratic business-as-usual represented by Brezhnev. Whose moves accounted for this retrograde step cannot be guessed at the present time, though most speculation centers on Defense Minister Ustinov as the putative kingmaker.

What is certain about the selection of Chernenko as General Secretary is that it only postpones, and probably not for long, the day of reckoning when real generational change comes to the Soviet leadership. At seventy-two, Chernenko is older than any leader the Soviet Union has ever operated under since the Revolution, except for Stalin in the last year of his life. He will immediately have the problem as well as the opportunity of replacing elderly cabinet ministers and provincial party leaders as death, illness, or incapacity overtake them, a process obviously accelerating during the recent months of Andropov's illness (when Chernenko was perhaps already influencing the choice of new officials by virtue of his position in the Secretariat). These circumstances allow Chernenko to build personal influence in the traditional Soviet manner, but at the same time they contribute to the generational shift building up against the Old Guard. It does not seem conceivable that after Chernenko the leading role could be kept again within his age group.

There have been some indications that Chernenko might be inclined to take an approach to the country's internal and external problems somewhat less confrontational and more accommodating than Andropov. One American authority finds reason to expect of him "a heightened interest in arms control with the West, some efforts to slow defense spending, an increasing emphasis on consumer production, economic reform, and an expansion of democratic practices both within the party and in the country as a whole."[1] If this seems too much to hope for, it may at least give reason to expect that the moves in the opposite direction associated with Andropov are to be restrained.

Looking ahead, one can anticipate another relatively short administration, and another succession once again reinforcing the power of the top party collective, but this time going to Romanov or some younger party organization man who can establish the confidence of his colleagues and the institutions and interests they represent. One to watch along with Gorbachev is Vladimir Dolgikh, fifty-nine, the heavy industry specialist on the Secretariat who became a candidate member of the Politburo following Brezhnev's death. Beyond these possibilities, the sudden emergence of a dark horse is unlikely; the promotion patterns through the party hierarchy on the basis of job status have been far too consistent to allow any exception at this juncture.

What difference will the age and identity of Chernenko's successor make? Here only the loosest sort of guesswork and projection are possible. Age is important because the difference in years means a different educational and political experience—typically a genuine higher educational background (if only in engineering) and a political career commencing in earnest only after the death of Stalin. By most accounts of Soviet citizens and émigrés, members of this younger generation coming up in the leadership may be just as tough and illiberal as the elders who selected them, but are at least more sophisticated and more flexible as they undertake to deal with the Soviet Union's problems both internal and external.

Certainly neither the accession of Chernenko nor his likely successors portend any easy breakthrough in Western dealings with the Soviet government. In Chernenko one can anticipate neither the ability nor the inclination to alter the primary reliance on military power and its projection abroad that marked the last half-dozen years of the Brezhnev era. Nothing suggests a diminution in the police regime internally, or a curb on the emotional drift toward heightened Russian nationalism and anti-Semitism. The major question is whether the leadership will shift their attention from chimerical schemes and fears abroad to the crying problems of economic reform at home. For this to occur in any substantial way we will undoubtedly have to wait for the post-Chernenko generation.

Part Three

The Progress of Perestroika, 1985–1989

Chapter Nine

Gorbachev — The End of the Transition? (March 1985)

Before Chernenko expired on 10 March 1985, Mikhail Gorbachev had already established himself as the number-two man in the Kremlin's lineup. As was reported later, however, he won the succession over Moscow party boss Viktor Grishin only by a narrow margin in the Politburo. As a representative of the new leadership generation, finally, Gorbachev resumed Andropov's campaign for acceleration and sobriety, and put the circular flow of power into play to shore up his newly-bestowed authority.

Last years's most popular joke in Moscow may no longer be heard for quite a while. A Soviet citizen was trying to get into Red Square for Andropov's funeral. At the police checkpoint he was asked for his pass. "Pass? I don't need a pass. I have a subscription ticket."

Transitions at the top in the Kremlin have seemingly become a routine event, but the latest passage of power, from Chernenko to Gorbachev, has the potential of being something very different. It is not only a matter of the new leader's relative youthfulness and probable tenure. He opens up the prospect of an epochal change in generational styles of rule.

Gorbachev's expeditious selection to succeed Chernenko in the office of General Secretary of the Communist Party came as no surprise. Very quickly after the already ailing Chernenko was picked to replace Andropov barely a year ago, Gorbachev was de facto accorded the number-two position as Second Secretary and chief ideological guru of the party. There was reason to surmise that the titular leadership of the party was given to Chernenko as part of a deal between the Old Guard and the Young Turks who had rallied around Andropov and Gorbachev. The arrangement would allow one more member of the older generation to enjoy the limelight in his time, while the prospective leader of the new wave prepared for the real transition.

In April of last year, Chernenko was extended the additional honor of the presidency of the USSR ("Chairman of the Presidium of the Supreme Soviet"), in proceedings broadcast by Moscow television. When the acting chair of the Supreme Soviet called for nominations to fill the vacancy left by Andropov, Gorbachev stepped forth by prearrangement with a fifteen-minute nominating speech on Chernenko's behalf. Gorbachev was smooth, firm, a compelling speaker, clearly acting like the man in charge.

After Gorbachev spoke, according to protocol, the Chair called for other nominations. Silence. "I now put it to a vote. All in favor of Konstantin Ustinovich Chernenko?" As though the puppetmaster had pulled one string, all right hands in the hall went up in unison. "Opposed?" No surprises. "Abstentions?" No one moved. "I therefore proclaim Comrade Chernenko elected Chairman of the Presidium."

To thunderous applause Chernenko staggered to his feet to give his acceptance speech. The emphysema was telling on him already; he mumbled his words three or four at a time, then gasped for breath. Definitely no charismatic leader here. To the chagrin of Soviet citizens of every political view whose hopes had been raised by the vigor of Andropov's few months of action, the Kremlin seemed to be turning into a nursing home for the next leader's tenure of office. One anguished institute scholar was seen banging his head against a wall when he heard the news of Chernenko's election.

This latest time around, however, the circles who determine the identity of the next Soviet chief appear to have had enough of the improvisations of geriatric leadership, and have demonstrated their readiness to go with the vigor of youth and the renovation of the whole political structure. Not only is Gorbachev at fifty-four twenty years younger than Chernenko, and in fact the youngest member of the Politburo; he will be the first Soviet leader who commenced his political career after the shadow of Stalin had passed. His is the new generation of university-trained executives, enjoying a very different formative experience from the Brezhnev-Chernenko generation of workers and peasants suddenly promoted in the late 1930s to fill the shoes of Stalin's purge victims.

How Gorbachev will specifically approach the Soviet Union's great questions of economic growth and military security can only be known as his actions unfold in the months to come. His speech to the Central Committee accepting designation as General Secretary referred to the "strategic line worked out with the vigorous participation of Yuri Vladimirovich Andropov and Konstantin Ustinovich Chernenko" (conspicuously leaving Brezhnev unmentioned). He identified himself with the recent economic reform movement by calling for "a decisive turn in transferring the national economy to the tracks of intensive development" and "enhancing the independence of enterprises, raising their interest in the end product of their work." He professed complete continuity with the foreign policy of his predecessors—negotiations on the one hand, and on the other maintenance of the power to deal "a crushing retaliatory strike."

But Gorbachev's personal predilections will not alone determine Soviet policy, either foreign or domestic. Ever since Stalin's demise, the movement in Soviet politics has been away from the commanding individual and toward the bureaucratic collective. Lately this trend has been strengthened by incapacity and turnover in the topmost job. The question for Gorbachev, therefore, is how he will deal with the apparatus and leading organs of the party to try to consolidate his own leadership vis-à-vis the residue of the Old Guard and younger people who may wish to challenge him.

The two key power-wielding bodies in the Soviet political structure are both, of course, in the party rather than in the nominal government—the Politburo for policy decisions and the Secretariat for organizational control. Both are a bit short-handed now, due to the death rate among the old Stalinists. Normally the Secretariat includes four or five men who are members of the Politburo and a couple more who have candidate rank in that body, plus three or four others of lesser status. But at the moment, in the key group of Secretariat members who have full rank in the Politburo, there are only two individuals—Gorbachev himself, and the man who by every calculation has to be considered his rival, Grigory Romanov.

Two years ago, under Andropov, Romanov looked like the man most likely to succeed. The tough, sixtyish boss of Leningrad had just had himself made a member of the Secretariat in Moscow, and is thought to have acquired primary responsibility for industry and the military. Exactly what his role was and how he was kept on the sidelines when Andropov died and again when Chernenko left the scene are simply unknown. In any case, Romanov's institutional position now makes him inevitably the first challenge that Gorbachev must reckon with.

Gorbachev has the opportunity of fleshing out the Politburo and the Secretariat to their normal complement, which means that he will dominate those bodies with his own people if he can control the appointments. The most crucial step will be the promotion or transfers to give at least two new people full membership in both the Politburo and the Secretariat, and thereby neutralize Romanov. Here the key figures are Dolgikh, a Secretary who already holds candidate rank in the Politburo, and Vorotnikov, the head of government in the Russian Federation and a Politburo member, who is known to be an Andropovite reformer. Conferring Politburo candidate rank on the recently appointed Secretariat members Nikolai Ryzhkov or Yegor Ligachev could further strengthen Gorbachev's hold.

A crucial role could be played here by Moscow party boss and Politburo member Viktor Grishin, seventy, who appeared prominently during Chernenko's last weeks and at the funeral, and could readily assume the function of a central Secretary. If Grishin and Dolgikh, say, were to team up with Romanov to protect the old Brezhnev crew and keep Gorbachev's power from getting out of bounds, we could see an extended period of unstable or compromise leadership that could well disappoint the hopes of Soviets and foreigners alike for a really new look in the Kremlin.

The natural target in any of these maneuvers is control of the preparations for the next party congress, the Twenty-Seventh, which according to the rules is due to be held in the spring of 1986. The congress will install a new Central Committee in office, which in turn must ratify the composition of the top party organs and the tenure of the General Secretary. In this procedure the key people are the provincial secretaries of the party, who arrange the choice of delegates to the congress and who, by what has become an automatic tradition, themselves qualify for placement on the slate of members to be elected to the next Central Committee. Under Andropov, a major shakeup of the party apparatus was set in motion, and around 20 percent of the provincial secretaries were replaced (and hence rendered de facto ineligible for the new Central Committee). If Gorbachev, through control of the central Secretariat, should be able to continue this work of bureaucratic renovation, he could put together a new Central Committee largely of his own choosing or at least of his own inclination.

Only at this point, when Gorbachev has a new personal machine in place within the party organization, are we likely to see broad and overt moves to unburden the country's top leadership of the superannuated Stalinists who still dominate it. Such a development at the level of the Politburo would in turn smooth the way for reforms in economics and in other policy areas that finally would accord with the taste of the rising technocratic generation. Then, for better or worse, we could expect the Soviet Union to put on a distinctly new face.

CHAPTER TEN

GORBACHEV CONSOLIDATES
(FEBRUARY 1986)

Immediately upon his accession to the Soviet leadership, Gorbachev put the circular flow of power into motion again. When the Twenty-Seventh Congress of the Communist Party convened in February 1986 he was able to lock in substantial personnel changes in the country's power-wielding bodies and secure the predominance of the post-Stalin generation. On this basis he turned more realistically than any of his predecessors to address the stagnation of the national economy and the impasse in relations with the West. The risk was that new opposition might arise even among Gorbachev's cadre of new officials.

A party congress in Moscow bears little resemblance to a congress or convention of a political party in a democratic country, other than the mere fact of periodically bringing together a few thousand local political activists from around the country. Congresses of the Communist Party of the Soviet Union do not make decisions or choose leaders: They ratify them, with set speeches and unanimous votes, all by prearrangement. Needless to say, they are not called upon to prepare political campaigns against the opposition. If there is a political enemy in sight it is the party's own past and the "shortcomings and slip-ups" of its dead or deposed leaders of yesteryear, always excepting the canonized cult figure of the founder, Lenin.

The Twenty-Seventh Congress of the CPSU was a predictable triumph for General Secretary Gorbachev. He has secured formal endorsement both of his policies of reform and détente, and of the sweeping renovation of the party and governmental officialdom that has been under way for the past three years.

Though he has held the number-one position for barely a year, Gorbachev has already put a strong stamp on public life in the Soviet Union as well as on the personal makeup of its top leadership. When Chernenko died last year there was still strong resistance to this Young Turk. If the rumors are to be credited, there was a challenge in the Politburo as Gorbachev's rival Romanov nominated Grishin; Gorbachev reportedly squeaked through by one vote. In any case, he then moved with surprising speed and apparent ease to dispose of his senior opponents, ousting Romanov from the Politburo in May 1985, and Grishin in January of this year, not to mention the eighty-year-old prime minister Tikhonov, who retired last December. If there really was a serious opposition alignment, it collapsed ignominiously.

At the congress, perhaps as a concession to coopt the Romanov crowd in Leningrad, Gorbachev rounded out the Politburo by bringing in the man who had been following in Romanov's footsteps, party secretary L. N. Zaikov. The presumed supervisor of the military and of defense industry, Zaikov has thus become number three in the party hierarchy. Now, apart from himself, his patron Gromyko, and the holdover bosses of the Ukraine and Kazakhstan, Gorbachev has a Politburo which dates entirely from the post-Brezhnev era.

The net effect of the leadership changes put through in the last three and a half years, primarily under Andropov and under Gorbachev, has been a dramatic arrest of the Kremlin's creeping senility. Between 1981 and 1986 the average age of the Politburo was brought down almost by a decade, from seventy-two in 1981 to sixty-four now. But Gorbachev himself, at fifty-four, remains the youngster of the group.

At the Twenty-Seventh Congress Gorbachev made even sharper changes at the second level of the Soviet hierarchy, among the candidate members of the Politburo and in the Secretariat. Three members of the eleven-member Secretariat, all in their seventies or eighties, were replaced by an unusual new crew, including Ambassador Anatoly Dobrynin to head international work for the party, along with former Ambassador to Ottawa A. N. Yalovlev as propaganda chief, and the first woman to join the Secretariat since the early 1930s, the trade-union official Alexandra Biryukova.

These shifts have been mirrored on a broader scale by the renovation of the Central Committee accomplished since Brezhnev's death and registered officially by the Twenty-Seventh Congress. Since Andropov took over from Brezhnev in late 1982, office-holders of Central Committee rank have been ousted from their posts in a steady stream, usually for reasons of "health" or "retirement on pension," and replaced by people a generation younger. The tempo of renovation was stepped up when Gorbachev finally took over personally, to the point that over 35 percent of the Central Committee members confirmed by the Twenty-Sixth Congress in 1981 lost the jobs that gave them this status, in addition to the 10 percent who died in office.

In conformity with past tradition, this housecleaning has been directly reflected in the makeup of the new Central Committee. Of the 319 members installed in 1981, only 171 have been reelected this time to the slightly pared-down body of 307, leaving space for 136 new people who have risen to elite jobs in the last five years. The upheaval contrasts with the 5 to 20 percent turnover rate between congresses that prevailed during the Brezhnev era, pursuant to the now repudiated policy of "stability of cadres." Apart from the purges of the 1930s, the current rate of turn-over has been exceeded only by the 50 percent of replacements in 1961 when the neo-Stalinists were closing ranks against Khrushchev. This time, accelerated change became irresistible, thanks to the aging of so many Stalinist bureaucrats.

What does Gorbachev's reconstructed political foundation mean for the future direction of Soviet policy? Comparisons with the Twentieth Party Congress thirty years ago when Khrushchev launched his de-Stalinization campaign and the peaceful coexistence line are a bit overdone, but there are weighty items on Gorbachev's agenda which needed the imprimatur of a well-orchestrated party congress before he could forge ahead.

Dominating all other issues now is the question of economic reform, to break out of the low-growth doldrums that have beset the country since the last years of Brezhnev. Since taking over as General Secretary Gorbachev has made this not only a priority but a sensational promise: to double the nation's GNP and standard of living by the year 2000. "Acceleration of the socioeconomic development of the country," he repeatedly stressed in his five-hour address to the congress, "is the key to all our problems."

Gorbachev is well aware of the cause of the Soviet Union's economic stagnation. His speeches on the subject sound like the critical writings of American sovietologists. He has called for less central control and more managerial initiative; less unearned guarantees to labor and more monetary incentives; less measurement of performance by quantity of output and more by profitable sales. He speaks of "openness" and "democratization" to get the masses involved in the administrative process, and even uses the Yugoslav expression "self-management."

Agriculture is still the soft underbelly of the Soviet economy. Despite the much-heralded "food program" launched in Brezhnev's last year, with upped investments and prices for the collective farms, Soviet agriculture has been literally flat in terms of per capita production. Gorbachev, himself responsible for this area in years past, has attacked the problem at the top by creating a new "agro-industrial" czar, and at the bottom by proposing small-team and family operations suggestive of recent reforms in China.

Another chronically depressed sector is consumer services. Here Gorbachev has reversed the old strictures on self-employment and moonlighting by plumbers, mechanics, even doctors. At the congress he hinted at allowing the kind of small-scale private enterprise—dressmakers, restaurants, etc.—that Hungarians and Yugoslavs enjoy.

There are precedents in the Communist world for the kind of reforms Gorbachev is promoting, not only in Eastern Europe and China today, but also in the Soviet Union itself under the New Economic Policy of the 1920s. In those years, prior to Stalin's takeover, the Soviets practiced a very effective form of decentralized, market socialism to revive their war-torn economy. Soviet economists have lately been debating how they might apply the experience of the NEP to the massive but sluggish industrial and agricultural system that is still being run on Stalinist lines.

Despite all this obvious need and interest in reform, Gorbachev's plan faces a twofold hazard. It does not, in the eyes of most Western economists, appear sufficiently thoroughgoing to deliver the dramatic upsurge that Gorbachev has promised. On the other hand, it may encounter resistance and sabotage on the part of the bureaucrats who have to carry it out, like the similar-sounding reforms enunciated by Khrushchev and then by Prime Minister Kosygin in the early Brezhnev years. Or in the worst case, the plan may prove so unsettling to the party chieftains as to provoke a top-level political reaction against Gorbachev.

The other main area of attention at the congress, namely foreign policy, is equally fraught with political disappointment or danger. Gorbachev reiterated his endorsement of détente, directing it particularly toward the West Europeans and the Chinese. He spoke of the "complete unacceptability" of nuclear war, assured dissidents in the international Communist movement that Moscow claimed no "monopoly of truth," and dug up the old bogey of revolutionary war only to denounce "the myth of the Soviet or Communist 'threat'." This was, he claimed, a fiction conjured up by "the right wing of the monopoly bourgeoisie of the USA," serving to justify "military appropriations, global ambitions, interference in the affairs of other countries, and an offensive against the interests and rights of the American toilers."

Pursuing his peace offensive, Gorbachev has made some extraordinary offers for a Soviet leader, even though the details may be faulted—a 50 percent cut in strategic missiles, elimination of intermediate missiles from Europe, a complete nuclear testing moratorium with inspection, and eventual banning of nuclear weapons altogether. He sounds almost like Khrushchev in the 1950s. The hazard for Gorbachev, as it proved to be for Khrushchev, may be to get out on a political limb with these gambits, run into rejection or unacceptable conditions from the American side, find his foreign policy exposed as a revelation of Soviet weakness, and open himself in this area, as in economics, to political retribution at home.

Is there any way in which opposition to the Soviet leader, whether principled or opportunistic, could be made effective? The Khrushchev experience demonstrates that this can happen. Soviet power is now more oligarchic than personal, even though the General Secretary has considerable scope to shape policy. Given the relationship of mutual vulnerability between the leader and his immediate subordinates, Gorbachev must have the confidence of the Politburo and the Secretariat in order to keep the bureaucratic political base firmly under his feet. This was the secret of Brezhnev's success, to avoid any serious innovation that would disturb his colleagues.

If Gorbachev signally fails to deliver on his promises in internal or in foreign matters, *apparatchiki* who would like to take advantage of his embarrassment might well try to rally the Central Committee around a harder-line alternative. As a matter of fact a well-positioned candidate for this role is already visible, in the person of Second Secretary Ligachev. Ligachev has already begun to distinguish himself by harping on discipline, chiding the press—including *Pravda*—for publishing "disruptive" criticism, and echoing the patriotic themes of the growing Russian nationalist element in the party. If Gorbachev's political luck should turn against him, he might be remembered as the Khrushchev, or perhaps the Malenkov, of the post-Brezhnev era.

Chapter Eleven

Gorbachev and the Revolution (October 1987)

By the time Gorbachev celebrated the seventieth anniversary of the Russian Revolution in November 1987, it was possible to see a parallel with the eventual return to moderate, constitutional principles in other countries that had gone through the long process of revolutionary fanaticism and postrevolutionary dictatorship. This was the direction of Gorbachev's administrative reforms and his new doctrine of glasnost— "openness"—responding to some of the needs of Soviet society as it modernized. Resistance loomed among the more conservative of Gorbachev's new appointees, led by Second Secretary Ligachev, but in practice this disunity meant more pluralism and less central dictation.

Winding up the seventh decade after the revolution that put his party in exclusive power, Gorbachev has astounded his country by calling for a new revolution. He obviously means it more metaphorically than the chaotic events of 1917, but the expression dramatizes his perception that matters had gone fundamentally wrong somewhere along the line under his predecessors. This did not mean that he rejected the legacy of the original revolution. It did imply rejection of the record that the Russian Revolution had eventually acquired as it unfolded along the trajectory typical of all great revolutions.

The Russian revolutionary heritage can be stated, without serious over-simplification, in three basic principles: the principle of socialism in the economic order; the principle of Communist Party rule in the political order; and the hegemony of Marxism-Leninism in the intellectual order. The complication is that these principles have all meant different things at different times in the Soviet experience.

Socialism exists, in practice as well as in theory, in a variety of models, no one of which can claim exclusivity, though the Soviets under Stalin represented their model of state socialism and the command economy as the sole legitimate version. The French Eurocommunist scholar Jean Elleinstein, recently expelled from the Communist Party, has directed the publication of a remarkable six-volume treatise, "World History of Socialisms"—using the plural to refer to this diversity.[1]

One-party rule in Soviet Russia has gone through major changes. In the 1920s, when Trotsky and his friends were still battling the Stalinists, it might have turned into a multi-faction system within the single-party framework, like Mexico, an analogy that Yugoslav political scientists feel applies to their country today. With Stalin's personal victory at the end of that decade, the course was set instead toward totalitarian rule through the party's bureaucratic apparatus.

As for Marxism-Leninism, it is only one variant in the vast corpus of interpretations of Marx, though it gained preeminent exposure as the version embraced and enforced by the rulers of a great power. Originating as a radical analysis of society with utopian overtones, Marxist theory became obligatory belief for all Soviet citizens at the same time that the leader—Stalin, above all—reserved for himself the power to determine what the doctrine meant at any particular moment. From a revolutionary utopia, Marxism-Leninism turned into a legitimizing ideology, a new form of orthodoxy just as restrictive in the intellectual respect as were the command economy and the totalitarian party in politics.

Two decisive circumstances underlay these selective modifications of the revolutionary legacy under Stalin. One was the natural process of revolution, observed by many historians, moving from the idealistic fanaticism of the early years to the opportunistic authoritarianism that takes hold of the tired postrevolutionary society later on. Like Cromwell in England, Bonaparte in France, and Hitler as the ultimate heir of the German Revolution of 1918, it fell to Stalin to effect in Russia the synthesis characteristic of this stage, between traditionalist nationalism and authoritarianism on the one hand, and revolutionary rhetoric and a new governing elite on the other.

The other force helping redefine the revolution was historic Russian tradition, revived in new guise in the postrevolutionary era under Stalin. As Edward Keenan has recently shown, the old habits of Russian political culture—the often unarticulated reflexes and assumptions about government exhibited by both rulers and ruled—were unusual even among traditional societies in the penchant for central authority, bureaucratic control, conformity of belief, secrecy in all public affairs, and xenophobic distrust of the outside world.[2] It is the irony of ironies that these came to be the governing attitudes in a regime of Marxist revolutionaries, through the advent to power of a new generation of men risen from the peasantry (or from the working class, itself scarcely a generation away from the village), some with Stalin as he climbed to power in the Communist Party in the 1920s, and others to fill the shoes of Stalin's purge victims in the 1930s.

Western sovietologists are still debating the question whether Lenin (or even Marx) was to blame for Stalin, and if so how much. The answer, governed by the very broad forces outlined above, obviously goes beyond the intentions of any individual leader. Revolutions never turn out the way revolutionaries expect; if they could foresee the outcome with certainty, they would usually not be revolutionaries. Having taken the plunge to identify themselves with revolution and to press it by every means, leaders like Lenin cannot escape a measure of responsibility, though their individual forbearance might not necessarily assure a more benign outcome in a country undergoing this sort of historic convulsion. In any case, it is the mix of revolutionary fanaticism, postrevolutionary opportunism, and traditionalist authoritarianism, armed with modern techniques of organization and repression, that creates that distinctive twentieth-century political compound known as totalitarianism.

Does the process end here? Is the totalitarian postrevolutionary regime immutable, as the celebrated thesis of Jeanne Kirkpatrick holds, unless it is overthrown by outside enemies as happened to the major totalitarian-isms of the Right in World War II? The record of certain Communist regimes—Yugoslavia, China, briefly Czechoslovakia—as well as a more distant perspective on revolutions of the past, suggests that this is not an absolute rule. There is reason to believe that the unresolved tensions and pretensions of a postrevolutionary regime will sooner or later make fundamental new changes indispensable if not inevitable.

There are precedents for such an evolution in the history of all the great revolutions, when postrevolutionary authoritarianism was repudi-ated in favor of a return to the early liberating principles of the revolu-tion. In England, France, West Germany, and Spain, early libertarian and constitutionalist aspirations were revived, but without the degree of fa-naticism and devisiveness that originally drove each revolution into dicta-torship of the Left or of the Right.

In Russia such a historic correction has proven difficult, thanks in part to the extraordinary apparatus of coercion and terror that Stalin fash-ioned out of the revolutionary legacy, and in part to the Russian historical experience that made such despotism seem more or less normal. When Khrushchev attempted his reforms after Stalin's death in 1953, he lacked a sufficiently strong following in the politically effective sectors of society. He and his supporters among the intelligentsia were helpless to prevent his overthrow in 1964 and the turn back under Brezhnev, if not to full Stalinism, then at best to neo-Stalinism or Stalinism without the mass terror. The Brezhnev regime, affirming the Stalinist heritage of militarized socialism, monolithic party rule, and blind ideological discipline, repre-sented a historically unique prolongation of the era of postrevolutionary dictatorship.

With the death of Brezhnev, followed in quick succession by his near age-mates Andropov and Chernenko, and the advent to power of a dis-tinctly new, post-Stalin generation, another opportunity has presented itself for the overdue return to early revolutionary principles, in Russia's case the decentralized and democratic soviets of 1917. A practical need for overhaul of Stalin's very Russian model of economic and intellectual control from the center has become more and more obvious in the country's inability to move ahead in the postindustrial age of information and microtechnology. Finally, thanks to the quantitative progress made by the Soviet Union in the 1960s and the early 1970s, there is a much larger and more self-confident educated class ready to back reform. All these elements in combination have presented Gorbachev with both the need and the opportunity for changes that have to be deep and might be lasting.

Immediately after being designated General Secretary of the Communist Party in March 1985, Gorbachev set his sights on the radical reform of the Soviet economy. *Perestroika*—restructuring was the watchword, meaning in practice a partial dismantling of the Stalinist command economy and a revival of some elements of the market socialism practiced under the NEP. Results were less than dramatic, thanks to resistance both in the bureaucracy, which feared the devolution of responsibility, and among the masses, who were afraid they would have to work harder. Gorbachev was hitting Russian political culture head-on.

After a year or so, Gorbachev evidently realized that under Soviet conditions the success of economic reform depended on a change in the political atmosphere. Quite possibly the Chernobyl nuclear disaster in April 1986 and the stupidity of the early cover-up reflexes triggered his change of mind. His response was a series of steps, unprecedented in Soviet experience and even more at odds with Russian political culture, to expose national problems to public discussion and, in effect, unleash the intelligentsia from the dictates of the party apparatus. This is the essential meaning of his slogan of *glasnost*—openness, publicity.

Gorbachev laid bare his concerns at an unusual off-the-record meeting with a group of leading writers in June 1986, in a talk only sketchily reported in the official press but quickly leaked and circulated by the underground network of *samizdat*. "Restructuring is going very badly," he conceded. "We have no opposition. How then can we check up on ourselves?" An extraordinary acknowledgement of the virtues of pluralism. His answer for the Soviet Union was, "Only through criticism and self-criticism. The main thing is—through glasnost. There cannot be a society without glasnost." He went on, revealingly, "Society is ripe for a changeover. If we retreat, society will not agree to a return. We have to make the process irreversible." Echoing a familiar Jewish exhortation that originated with the Rabbi Hillel, Gorbachev declaimed, "If not us, who? If not now, when?"

In his initial phase, Gorbachev set about correcting the basic Stalinist distortion of the revolution in the bureaucratic model of socialism. In his second phase he has undertaken to dismantle the dogmatic control of thought and expression, including the Stalinist suppression of the dark chapters of Soviet history. There remains the rule of the monopoly party and the monopoly position of the bureaucratic hierarchy within that party.

Gorbachev has made some modest gestures in this direction, suggesting contested elections for local party offices. If he really puts an end to the mania for total political unity and opens the door to what the émigré publisher Valery Chalidze calls "one-party democracy,"[3] it would be an epochal development, perhaps truly irreversible—not establishing democracy by Western standards but nevertheless representing a decisive retreat from Stalinism.

The recent emergence of a variety of unofficial environmental and cultural groups, relaxation of the pressure against dissidents such as Andrei Sakharov, and even toleration of the unofficial journal *Glasnost*, shows the direction of the new wind. But democratization is bound to go slowly if only for fear of centrifugal tendencies among the Soviet national minorities and East European satellites. The fervent *Pamyat* (Memory) group has manifested the opposite danger of a conservative Russian nationalist reaction with fascistic overtones.

The forces for and against reform in Russia are often misperceived in the outside world. The revolutionary idea is not an obstacle to reform that is presumably demanded by Russian tradition; it is the tradition that is the obstacle. It is wrong to hold that the totalitarianism of the postrevolutionary regime cannot change; as time goes on, the more anachronistic it becomes, and the more likely is reform in the early spirit of the revolution. The Soviet Union has suffered in every respect because Khrushchev's attempts at reform were too little and too brief. Gorbachev, in a society thirty years more mature, sadder, and wiser, now has the understanding and the opportunity to press reform more fundamentally and more permanently.

Or does he? We still do not know whether Gorbachev can muster enough support within the party apparatus to put an end to its own power—in effect, to invite his own political machine to commit suicide. The further he goes, the more resistance he arouses within the party bureaucracy. Second Secretary Ligachev has openly taken the lead in resisting what he regards as the excesses of reform and glasnost, and the dangers of dwelling on the crimes of Stalin. The two tendencies in the party might be described as the liberals and the Andropovites. The liberals really see the need to revise the principles of the system, whereas Ligachev and the Andropovites—who put Gorbachev in office to begin with—only want to see more discipline and less corruption in the old system.

Gorbachev is still removable by the leaders of the apparatus assembled in the Politburo and the Central Committee, as the fate of Khrushchev reminds us. That could end the push for thoroughgoing reform and arrest the renaissance of Soviet society, though given today's problems and the requirements for survival as a great power, we should not expect a carbon-copy return to Brezhnev's neo-Stalinism.

Failing such an overturn, the Andropovites around Ligachev will remain very much a force of resistance to the liberalizing leadership. Ironically, they will thereby have contributed to a real multifaction political competition, and thus to the very pluralism in government that they have all along set themselves against.

CHAPTER TWELVE

THE NINETEENTH PARTY CONFERENCE AND THE CIRCULAR FLOW OF POWER (JUNE 1988)

By 1988 Gorbachev's attempts at economic reform and glasnost were prompting open opposition within the party apparatus. Under Second Secretary Ligachev the conservatives threatened to use the circular flow of power against Gorbachev himself. He tried to sidestep this challenge by convening an unusual midterm "conference" of the party, and appealing to the rank and file. His success was mixed—limited in the matter of party personnel but significant in the area of constitutional reform.

When Gorbachev called the extraordinary nationwide conference of the Communist Party for 27 June 1988, his intention was to solidify the political foundation for his program of reform—*perestroika, glasnost,* and *demokratizatsiya.* When the conference actually convenes, he may be fighting for his political life.

Frustrated by bureaucratic resistance to his efforts to modernize the Soviet economy, Gorbachev has called into question the foundations of the Soviet political system, not only as Stalin shaped it in the 1930s, but as it took form under Lenin immediately after the revolution and during the Civil War years of 1918 to 1920. In his speeches and in his "theses" prepared for the party conference, Gorbachev proposes to open the Communist Party to competing viewpoints and genuine elections, to decentralize responsibility among the nominal bodies of local government, the soviets, and to curtail the party's direct control and interference in the specialized work of governmental and economic administration. In line with the philosophy of glasnost, he has already gone outside the usual channels of political authority to appeal to the intelligentsia as a social force in support of reform, and has unleashed the press—insofar as individual editors are willing—to expose the failures and abuses of the system that he inherited. All of these moves contradict the structure of political authority as it took form in the Communist Party during Lenin's early years in power, even though Lenin continues to be officially revered and reinterpreted to fit the new line.

To give the party conference the composition that would most vigorously support these reform goals, Gorbachev has attacked the special basis of leadership authority that has operated ever since Stalin's rise to political dominance in the 1920s, the circular flow of power. Created by Stalin, the circular flow of power has to be reaffirmed through the appointment and election process every time the top leader passes from the scene. Khrushchev managed to do this up to a point, though after 1960 the neo-Stalinists in the top leadership broke into the circular flow and turned it against him. The overthrow of Khrushchev in 1964 remains an object lesson—not lost on Gorbachev—in the mutual vulnerability of the top leader and his bureaucratic entourage.

Andropov restarted the circular flow when he succeeded Brezhnev in 1982, and Gorbachev orchestrated it very successfully up to the time of the Twenty-Seventh Party Congress in 1986. This meant removing and replacing the functionaries whose jobs, by tradition, entitled them to Central Committee status; as a result, the Central Committee confirmed by the 1986 Congress included no less that 125 new members out of a total of 307.

This extensive shake-up has proven to be an insufficient political basis for Gorbachev's reforms. Perestroika and glasnost have developed faster than Gorbachev has been able to renovate the leadership. The pace of change has alienated those officials, perhaps even some of Gorbachev's own appointees, who favored the disciplinarian approach to reform in the style of Andropov, now represented by Second Secretary Ligachev. Ironically, it is primarily conservative resistance to fundamental reform that has created the "socialist pluralism" to which Gorbachev now refers with pride.

Gorbachev evidently conceived the forthcoming party conference—the first to be called since Stalin convoked the Eighteenth Conference in 1941—as a mechanism for circumventing the conservative party bureaucracy and appealing to the rank and file party membership and Communist intellectuals to support his program of reform. The success of this ploy depended on his ability to stop the circular flow of power and keep the bureaucracy out of the process of selecting delegates to the conference. Some comments in the press suggest that Gorbachev may have hoped to go so far as to overturn the bureaucratic representational basis of Central Committee membership.

Gorbachev's plan seems to have encountered trouble this spring at the time of the conservative counterattack signalled by the now-famous Andreyeva letter.[1] We know from many complaints in the Soviet press that when the actual selection of conference delegates by local party organizations took place in April and May, the party apparatus simply followed the old practice of the circular flow, and dictated the selection of its own conservative members. Gorbachev's response has been to challenge the whole system of the circular flow even more directly, and to mobilize the rank and file to confront the apparatus and support conference delegates sympathetic to his reforms, particularly from among the leading intellectuals. In this he is going back to the methods and criteria of leadership selection that prevailed before Stalin took it over in 1923. On the popular side, there have even been open street demonstrations to protest the bureaucratic method of delegate selection and to support reformist candidates.

The key test of Gorbachev's attempt to break the dominance of the apparatus was in Moscow, where after considerable turmoil a bevy of the intellectual advocates of reform—the sociologist Tatiana Zaslavskaya, the playwright Mikhail Shatrov, the economist Leonid Abalkin, the historian Gavriil Popov, and the archivist Yuri Afanasiev (an outspoken advocate of the truth about Stalin) were nominated at party meetings. At this writing it appears that all of these except Abalkin and Afanasiev have been screened out by the apparatus. If this is the outcome in Moscow, we can be sure that in the provinces, in most cases, the apparatus will be even more firmly in control. It does not appear that Gorbachev will have a conference that will enthusiastically endorse his reform program and re-staff the party leadership accordingly.

A conference that Gorbachev does not control—as the prospect appears—would not mean that he is destined to be overthrown in the immediate future. By securing Central Committee approval at the brief plenum of 23 May of his far-ranging theses for the conference, he demonstrated that he can still command top-level acquiescence in any broad statement of policy. But if the delegates of the apparatus dominate the conference and the most articulate spokespersons of reform are excluded, the momentum of reform will be lost. A conservative outcome of the conference, expressed perhaps in the watering-down of Gorbachev's theses, would chill the spirits of the reformers and encourage the bureaucratic interest expressed in the Andreyeva letter. On the other hand, if Gorbachev prevails at the conference to the extent of being able to shake up the membership of the Central Committee, it will show not only that he has an open path to extend his reforms in Soviet economic and intellectual life, but that he has succeeded in changing the basic mechanisms of Soviet politics—i.e., apparatus control over the membership and elective bodies of the party—in a truly irreversible way.

CHAPTER THIRTEEN

GORBACHEV'S CULTURAL REVOLUTION (JULY 1988)

By mid-1988, it was evident that Gorbachev was leading a revolution in Soviet governmental thinking, in matters both foreign and domestic. As the Nineteenth Party Conference showed, this aroused such opposition in the party apparatus that Gorbachev had to look for a new, broader political base.

"Politics is the art of the possible. . . ." So spoke Gorbachev at his press conference closing the Moscow Summit in June 1988, explaining why he settled for less than the strategic missile reduction treaty he had hoped for. The phrase may be hackneyed for Americans, but such pragmatic language is unprecedented for a Soviet leader. "And," the General Secretary went on, "we have pushed the possible as far as we can."[1]

Pushing the possible, Gorbachev has presided over some of the most extraordinary changes in both foreign and domestic policy since the founding of the Soviet regime almost seventy-one years ago. While still falling short of Western standards in the extent of his reforms, he has come to the fundamental conclusion that he must live with two old, intractable adversaries, the government of the United States abroad, and the restive but essential intelligentsia at home.

In relations with the United States, Gorbachev seems to have been advised, perhaps by former Ambassador Dobrynin, perhaps by the 1986 Reykjavik experience, that Ronald Reagan has certain fixations, from religion to Star Wars, that one cannot try to meet head-on. They will not interfere in the long run with a pragmatic accommodation. By the end of the Moscow Summit, after enduring with strained patience the homilies on human rights that Mr. Reagan gave at monasteries, universities, or dinner with dissidents, he had the American President retracting his "evil empire" talk and conceding that the Soviet chief was "a serious man seeking serious reform. . . . We must do all that we can to assist it."[2]

Disappointed Reaganites still complain that Gorbachev's concessions in both the foreign and domestic areas are only cosmetic. This overlooks the fact that ideas have always been part of the Soviet system of internal control, and that they are not lightly played with just to pull the wool over foreign eyes. The new statements about history and ideology coming out daily in Moscow mean that fundamental changes are taking place both in the internal basis of power and in the Soviet approach to the outside world. Explaining the radical change in U.S.-Soviet relations since the mid-1980s, the deputy director of the Institute of World Economics and International Relations declared, "In the United States, the alignment of factors that we have talked about has changed. And, of course, in our country what one might call a "post-April" (i.e., 1985, after Gorbachev's first Central Committee plenum) foreign policy has appeared."[3]

Gorbachev announced one of the most drastic revisions ever of Soviet ideology in his book *Perestroika* that appeared last year, when he asserted that certain universal human values—above all the prevention of nuclear war—took precedence over the Marxian values of the class struggle.[4] Since then, one writer after another has attacked the excessively military bias in Soviet foreign policy, to the detriment of successful political and economic competition. Several have spoken of the need to understand Western fears generated by the preponderance of Soviet conventional armaments. One commentator has even called for an alliance with the capitalist powers against the nuclear menace, on the model of the alliance against Hitler in World War II.

Gorbachev acknowledged all this in his opening speech to the Nineteenth Party Conference in June. "It was necessary to achieve strategic parity with the USA and this was accomplished," he said, but "we did not always make use of the political opportunities opened up by the fundamental changes in the world in our efforts to secure the security of our state. . . . As a result, we allowed ourselves to be drawn into an arms race, which could not but affect the country's socioeconomic development and its international standing." He sounded like a Congressional dove berating the influence of the Pentagon.

This unfamiliar language coming from Soviet spokesmen high and low bespeaks not just a change in phrases or even of ideology. It reflects a profound shift in political culture, in the habits and assumptions by which the Soviet leadership has guided itself for decades in dealing both with its own society and with the outside world. Stalinism was distinguished by a reversion to the oldest Muscovite forms of political culture, secretive, conspiratorial, and xenophobic, embodied in the peasantry and in the Stalinist bureaucracy that stemmed from it. Gorbachev advisor (and one-time Khrushchev speech writer) Fyodor Burlatsky has recently invoked this concept to explain the failure of Khrushchev, due, he says, to "the political standards of Khrushchev himself and of the generation of leaders at that time. Those standards were in large part patriarchal, drawn from traditional notions about forms of leadership in the framework of the peasant household. Paternalism, interference in all matters and relations, the infallibility of the patriarch, intolerance of other opinions—all these things made up the typical set of age-old notions about power in Russia."[5]

Gorbachev has clearly recognized the diplomatic, economic, and intellectual impasse into which this old outlook has brought the country. In an extraordinary act of individual leadership, he has shifted to a fundamentally new cultural base for his rule. This is above all the Westernized intelligentsia, with its traditions of openness, creativity, and cosmopolitanism, that the nation must capitalize on if it is to survive competitively in the modern world. One of the resolutions of the Nineteenth Party Conference speaks of "the right to discuss any socially significant matter openly and freely."[6] Nothing could be farther from the Muscovite and Stalinist tradition.

To be sure, the firmness of this trend toward the "new thinking" and the new culture in foreign and domestic policy remains uncertain, dependent as it is on the political balance among the party elite. Opposition to reform is concentrated in the professional apparatus, the hierarchy of appointed officials who heretofore have been the real power in the country and ordinarily the chief instrument of rule in the hands of the leader who controls appointments. When the circular flow of power is fully operating, the General Secretary orchestrates the whole process of elections and congresses that keeps him in power. Although Gorbachev has pursued the circular flow by extensive use of his appointment power ever since he took office in 1985, it appears that the pace of his economic reform and the reality of the new political culture have proved too much for the party bosses, possibly even the new ones. The apparatus is in revolt against him, and he has lost control of the circular flow. This has forced him to look for a new basis of power.

Gorbachev's quest for a new base has involved three distinct strategies. One, now familiar, has been to unleash the press and the intelligentsia and keep the neo-Stalinists of the apparatus off balance with revelations of the criminality, venality, and sheer stupidity that Stalin's system of power permitted. This is the meaning of glasnost. The second approach, capturing most of the headlines about the Nineteenth Conference, is the package of governmental reforms—withdrawing the party apparatus from day-to-day control of administrative and economic matters, revitalizing both the local soviets and the Supreme Soviet, and introducing actual choice in elections. But the most decisive change of all, if it succeeds, remains relatively unsung. This is the relocation of power within the party itself. As the process of selecting delegates to the party conference showed, Gorbachev has undertaken to break the power that the apparatus has exercised over the party membership through the circular flow, and is trying to appeal directly to the rank-and-file against the professional hierarchy.

The ensuing struggle was evident all over the country in contests over the choice of conference delegates. The apparatus tried, in many places successfully, to use its power in the old way and send its own people—enemies of reform or at best lukewarm reformers—to the Moscow gathering. Even in Moscow the apparatus was able to resist Gorbachev's pressure and reject some of his favorite intellectuals as conference delegates. But it could no longer work its will behind the customary veil of secrecy and pre-arranged unanimity: It was met with open protests. The apparatus still has a measure of power, but it is no longer in control in the old way.

The new tone was immediately carried into the conference itself. To be sure, lacking full control over the delegates, Gorbachev was not able to use the gathering as he had hoped he could. He had to back off from his talk of replacing a large fraction of the Central Committee, even though many of the members had by this time become "dead souls" who had lost the bureaucratic positions that originally entitled them to membership according to the old Stalinist custom. But the conference proved to be the scene of the most genuine, unfettered, and often acrimonious debate among Communists since the earliest days of Soviet rule. There has certainly been nothing approaching it since the Twelfth Party Congress in 1923, the last in Lenin's time. Gorbachev welcomed the fracas as evidence of the "pluralism" that he wants to introduce. "This palace of congress has not known such discussions," he commented in his closing speech to the conference, "and I think we will not err from the truth by saying that nothing of the kind has occurred in this country for nearly six decades."[7]

In pursuit of economic success, Gorbachev has undertaken to dig up the deepest foundations of the Communist system as it took shape under Lenin during the Russian Civil War of 1918–1920. These features included the shift of power from the soviets, local and central, to the Communist Party; the shift of power from local institutions, party as well as governmental, to the center; and the shift of power from elected bodies, in both the party and the government, to appointed bureaucrats, above all the newly created party apparatus. The apparatus gained the authority of military command and discipline over the membership, who even lost their right of forming factional groups and presenting alternative platforms at the party congresses. All this was justified for the sake of winning the Civil War against the anti-Communists, but by the time victory was won the power of the apparatus was locked in place.

This was not impossible for most Russians to live with, since in fact it represented a revival of the familiar bureaucratic culture. As the British political scientist Jack Gray has noted, "At each successive crisis there was a choice, and in each case the preferred solution was that which more nearly approximated to tsarist practices."[8] Bureaucratic centralism was a way of political life that proved much more viable under Russian conditions than Lenin's utopian dreams of 1917.

The militarized bureaucratic system that evolved under Lenin was the foundation of Stalin's rise to power and his terroristic despotism. This answers the question of how to explain the "cult of personality," something the Soviets have still not been officially able to do. Gorbachev so far has spoken only of "deformations" in the political system, and the name of Lenin—now invoked, ironically, as the patron saint of perestroika—is still sacred.

The historic dimensions of Gorbachev's reforms make it inevitable that the party apparatus will fight back with every means at its command. It is still not beyond the realm of possibility that the neo-Stalinists, with their base in the Central Committee and their following among the less educated masses, could take advantage of some major domestic or international embarrassment and vote Gorbachev out of office, much as a previous generation of similarly-minded people overthrew Khrushchev in 1964. The initial effect of such an eventuality on the progress of reform would be traumatically depressing and disruptive. Yet the breakup of apparatus control over the party membership and of party control over the general public may have gone so far as to be indeed irreversible. It would be hard to put the Humpty-Dumpty of terrorized conformity and obedience back together again, short of a major purge that would damage most those educated sectors of society essential for the country's progress in the modern world. In a novel sort of materialist dialectic, the forces of economic and technical modernization and the non-military challenge of the industrial democracies have finally made the old Stalinist style of rule obsolete.

Chapter Fourteen

Perestroika at a Turning Point: The September Revolution (October 1988)

Needing a new political base against growing opposition in the party apparatus, Gorbachev struck by surprise at the end of September 1988, to further shake up the party leadership and to implement the constitutional changes approved at the Nineteenth Party Conference.

Waiting in line at a half-empty Moscow restaurant recently and observing newcomers being admitted out of turn by the head waiter, I commented to the Soviet citizen standing next to me that the procedure reminded me of Winston Churchill's description of the Soviet Union, "a riddle wrapped up in a mystery inside an enigma." He laughed knowingly, and answered, "It's a riddle to us, too."

The country remains a riddle as well to the vast school of foreign sovietologists who try to amass clues about the Soviet decision-making process. They draw conclusions all over the political map, often with a degree of certainty that the evidence scarcely warrants. Optimists about Gorbachev's reforms have gone so far as to describe the latest reshuffle as a new revolution. Pessimists have put it down as a veiled victory for the neo-Stalinist conservatives.

No one outside the inner circle in Moscow actually anticipated the sudden shakeup in the Soviet leadership that took place the weekend of 30 September. Nor could they: Top level politics in the Soviet Union are still conducted according to the old Muscovite rules of secrecy within the upper oligarchy. This remains an ingrained habit, even though a KGB official, of all people, published an article just a few weeks earlier berating the "cult of secrecy" and calling for the country's transition to the "information society" that everyone in the West talks about.[1]

On the face of it, Gorbachev scored an important political success when he suddenly convoked special meetings of the Central Committee and the Supreme Soviet to ratify the leadership changes that he had pushed through the Politburo. To be sure, the shakeup was not as broad or dramatic as some observers have hastily suggested. But the General Secretary did shore up his reformist group within the Politburo by adding one new vote, that of the new ideological secretary Vadim Medvedev, to

those of himself, Foreign Minister Eduard Shevardnadze, and party secretary Alexander Yakovlev (who has now been made responsible for international affairs). The presumed middle-of-the-road group lost the
seventy-nine-year-old Gromyko, who had to be retired as Chief of State
to accommodate Gorbachev's plan to combine the party and governmental leadership.

One Politburo conservative was knocked off in the September 30
shakeup, the elderly chairman of the party's disciplinary commission,
Mikhail Solomentsev. The move answered the complaint heard at the
party conference last June that he and Gromyko, though presumably
backers of Gorbachev three years ago, were now dragging their feet on
more substantial reforms.

The most significant steps of all in the reshuffle involved no actual
removals but only a shift in responsibilities. Second Secretary Ligachev,
Gorbachev's obvious conservative rival (however much both parties have
denied it), was shunted to the supervision of agriculture. Though the
area is vital, the move takes away Ligachev's broader responsibilities and
implicitly reduces him to fourth or fifth place in the hierarchy. Secret
police chief Chebrikov was shifted to the party Secretariat and given the
nebulous function of running the new party commission on legal affairs,
where he seems more or less neutralized. Meeting with farmers a few days
ago in Ligachev's absence to announce his commitment to free enterprise
in agriculture, Gorbachev underscored his own dominance in that field.
Ligachev's announced responsibility now seems only pro forma, and may
be just a way station toward his political demise.

Important changes have also been made at the level of the candidate
members of the Politburo. Two Brezhnev holdovers were dropped, and
three new candidate members were designated. One is Alexandra Biryukova, now a deputy prime minister and the first woman to reach this
level in almost thirty years. Another is Anatoly Lukianov, a nuts-and-
bolts administrator from the party Secretariat, who became vice president
under Gorbachev in the Supreme Soviet. The third is Alexander Vlasov,
up to now Minister of Internal Affairs (in charge of the uniformed police), and a close associate of Gorbachev's from the North Caucasus region. His promotion came in anticipation of his designation four days
later to be the new prime minister of the Russian Republic. All direct
police representation in the Politburo has now been eliminated.

Of all the new faces at the top, the most interesting is Vadim Medvedev
(not to be confused with the long-time dissidents, Roy and Zhores
Medvedev). This Medvedev's credentials were not exciting—a party pro-
pagandist under Brezhnev, head of the Central Committee's Academy of
Social Sciences that used to guard the party line, and since 1986 party
secretary in charge of relations with the Soviet satellites. Now, less than a

week after his new promotion, in a speech to a conference of social scientists from the Communist bloc, he made the most advanced statement of the reform philosophy yet heard.[2] He wants to redefine socialism, using "the experience of mankind as a whole, including the non-socialist world," with particular respect for the law of supply and demand and the virtue of individual and cooperative enterprise. Not only peaceful coexistence but world ecology as well take precedence over the Marxist class struggle. Instead of struggling to the death, "capitalism and socialism will inevitably intersect"—an echo of the theory of "convergence" long taboo in the Soviet Union. Medvedev still concedes no place for opposition parties. Free discussion within the Communist Party and measures to represent all the diverse interests in society are supposed to take care of this question, according to the principle of "socialist pluralism." But this is a far cry from the "monolithic unity of the party" and the "iron solidarity" of the party and the masses that was the line through the 1970s.

The mood in Moscow on the eve of the leadership reshuffle was apprehensive. Everyone felt frustrated over the failure of Gorbachev's "restructuring" to improve the performance of the economy. There was concern that the high hopes for glasnost, for speaking the truth about both the present and the past, had reached their limits. And there was widespread fear that the conservative opposition in the Communist Party machine was either forcing Gorbachev to retrench, or preparing to remove him as it had removed Khrushchev back in 1964.

This danger quite possibly explains Gorbachev's haste in convoking the Central Committee and the Supreme Soviet, a move so sudden that Foreign Minister Shevardnadze had to interrupt his negotiations in New York to return for the vote. The shakeup has all the marks of a preemptive strike, launched by the General Secretary without warning so as to catch his conservative opponents off guard and unable to offer effective resistance. Nevertheless his counterattack was rather restrained, taking advantage of the age of individual conservatives and isolating instead of destroying his chief rival.

Another question is the meaning of Gorbachev's taking over the chairmanship of the Supreme Soviet. Surely he did not do it purely out of motives of prestige or protocol, as Brezhnev, Andropov, and Chernenko had. It was a step toward implementing the constitutional reform that he had proposed at the June party conference, to create a strong executive, based on a presidential structure in preference to the existing system of prime minister and cabinet. Another consideration, possibly explaining Gorbachev's haste, was to broaden his institutional power base so that he could rest his authority a little less on the undependable party apparatus and more on the popular interests represented by the soviets. I saw a double-edged political button in Moscow, "All Power to the Soviets." It was the old revolutionary slogan of 1917, but now it implies no confidence in the party.

The perspective now emerging is roughly the following. Gorbachev found his reform program stymied by conservative opposition, especially as it was expressed in the now famous "Andreyeva letter" planted in the paper *Sovetskaya Rossiya* last March to embarrass the reformers' campaign against Stalinism. It began to appear that the party conference set for June would not behave as he hoped, to reaffirm the reform line. Consequently, it seems from the record, Gorbachev made the radical decision to attack his own party apparatus, the traditional power base of Soviet leaders. He would break out of the old and unreliable structure of power by appealing to the intellectuals and writers and to the rank and file membership of the party. The gambit largely failed, and probably stirred up even more opposition. This situation underlay the apprehension felt in Moscow by early fall about Gorbachev's prospects. But this mood underestimated Gorbachev's skill as a politician. He reverted to the old style of secret political maneuver at the top, and directly exerted the force of his personality and the authority of his office to get a Politburo majority behind his surprise blow at the conservatives.

The most immediate effect of Gorbachev's new display of political clout, and especially of Medvedev's new position, will be to encourage the reformers at all levels. By Western standards of intellectual freedom and political pluralism, to be sure, the Soviets still have quite a distance to go. The striking thing, however, is how far they have come from their neo-Stalinist past, and in how short a time. For the observer who has followed the Soviet scene through all the gray years under Brezhnev, the "era of stagnation" as the Soviets now call it, the new atmosphere is extraordinary and exhilarating. Instead of the old dead conformity, the newspapers and literary journals debate with each other, and official organs like *Kommunist* and *Problems of History* have been transformed by their new management. Intellectuals argue publicly with each other from positions all across the political spectrum. American sovietologists are being invited to lecture and contribute articles to Soviet journals. The first Soviet edition of an American monograph, *Stalin in October* by Robert Slusser,[3] is due out this winter.

One historian whom I encountered assured me that there were still more rehabilitations and revelations to come regarding lost figures of the past. I thought I would needle him a little: "Since I have written a lot about Trotsky, I wonder if he will be rehabilitated."

The answer: "I hope so. We can't have any more blank spots and black holes in our history."

As Tocqueville underscored in his work on the French Revolution, attempts to reform a repressive system can unleash radical anger far out-weighing any appreciation they may win for the reformers. Soviet citizens not only complain universally about the economy. They are afflicted with deep cynicism. As far as my small sample suggests, many consider the Communist Party bankrupt, and hope for a fundamental political over-turn, either real democracy or a new dictator like Stalin who can straighten the country out. Some fear a Polish type of crisis; some may even welcome it.[4] "The worse it gets, the better," said one gloomy citizen, convinced that this was the only road to real change. Meanwhile the national minorities are taking advantage of Moscow's new leniency and threatening to tear the country apart at the seams. This pressure has been dramatized by the well-reported demands of the Armenians and the Bal-tic peoples.

From a variety of conversations both with intellectuals and with ordi-nary people I have found that Soviet political attitudes are beginning to crystallize across a broad spectrum from reactionary to ultra-liberal and radical. The reactionary outlook, involving nostalgia, Russian chauvin-ism, anti-Semitism, and a yearning for authoritarian leadership—in short, "traditional values" in the Russian context—is represented in its most extreme form by the Pamyat organization, thought by many Soviets to have great influence ("Some of my best friends . . ."). Other tradition-alists idolize Alexander Solzhenitsyn.

The conservatives, represented by Ligachev, are very strong in the party and among the elderly intellectuals. They want reform, but in the discipli-narian style of the late Yuri Andropov, and they resent the now fashion-able notion that the Soviet system under Stalin and Brezhnev had no positive achievements to its credit. They are typified by Yuri Poliakov, a senior member of the Institute of the History of the USSR, who insists that Stalin, whatever his crimes and errors, sustained the Soviet people's faith in socialism. In other words, don't throw the baby out with the bath water. "I am a Soviet Tory," Poliakov acknowledges candidly.

The liberal position is that of Gorbachev and the party reformers. They believe with Vadim Medvedev that the system really can be reformed and democratized without giving up the Communist Party's political monop-oly. "We now have a normal intellectual life," say scholars at the Institute of Marxism-Leninism, who claim they are giving up that agency's old function of defining ideological conformity.

All this is deeply distrusted by the ultra-liberal or radical camp, repre-sented by the historian Yuri Afanasiev, the weekly papers *Moscow News* and *Ogonyok*, and many eminent writers. They doubt that Gorbachev's political reforms will bring meaningful democratization. People who would have been forced into the dissident underground under Brezhnev, they aim at total honesty about the country's past and present. They complain that the Institute of Marxism-Leninism, guarding the party archives, "still has the right of first night in history." So far, the radicals are mainly critics rather than advocates.

So much for the short-run prospects, where Gorbachev's "new thinking" appears to be rolling ahead. For the long run, things are not so rosy.

Ultimately, everything depends on the performance of the Soviet economy, to validate Gorbachev's premise that his country will respond better to freedom and incentives than to discipline and coercion. His new emphasis on individual farming shows his commitment to such methods. However, apart from small cooperatives, mainly restaurants, the immediate results of this approach have been discouraging, in part for cultural reasons that Gorbachev and his entourage may not fully understand themselves.

Three centuries of serfdom, reinforced by half a century of barracks socialism, have left the Russians a heritage of indifference to work and evasion of responsibility. There is a dearth of middle and lower management capable of coordinating effort and economizing labor time. Unlike the Baltic peoples, for instance, the Russians mostly just wait for orders from above. Instead of changing their own ways, they blame the government, which having claimed all power in the past, now is expected to answer for everything. With the relaxation of the tight grip at the top, the system seems to be performing worse, not better. Many workplaces do not even answer their phones until eleven o'clock in the morning, and then lunch may take a couple of hours. It will take a long time to transform a nation of shirkers into a nation of real workers.

Trying to reverse the old attitudes, Gorbachev mingles with the crowds, a very effective politician, as Soviet television showed him night after night during his Siberian trip in September. He responds to complaints by telling people that the responsibility is theirs for making restructuring work and getting the economy moving again. But despite the latest shakeup, he has only bought time.

CHAPTER FIFTEEN

SOVIET DEMOCRACY AND THE INTELLIGENTSIA (APRIL 1989)

Pursuant to his new constitutional arrangements, Gorbachev initiated his experiment in limited democracy with the election of the Congress of People's Deputies in March 1989. While this innovation was far from perfect, it opened up a degree of free political participation and debate, especially for the intelligentsia, that had not been known since the Bolshevik Revolution.

Not since the voting in November 1917 for the All-Russian Constituent Assembly—when the Bolsheviks came in second and learned not to depend on a popular mandate—has there been any exercise in open political competition in the Soviet Union approaching the election on 23 March 1989 of the new Congress of People's Deputies. The election shows that Gorbachev has rejected not only Stalinism, but also the system of authoritarian rule through the party apparatus under which Russia has been governed ever since the Civil War of 1918–1920.

The obvious limitations and faults in the new Soviet electoral system enacted last year seem to be the result of a political compromise, perhaps even in Gorbachev's own mind. He wants to relieve the country of the burden of bureaucratic authoritarianism without seeing it fall abruptly into a chaos of antithetical philosophies and nationality separatism. Hence the devices of multi-stage elections, institutional apportionment of a third of the deputies, and old-style single-slate candidacies in many jurisdictions. The one hundred congress seats reserved for the party as an institution went almost entirely to the central leadership plus token representatives of the various categories of the population—intellectuals, factory directors, workers, collective farmers, etc.—all without contest. Party bosses in the provinces and the union republics were left to stand for election in their own territorial districts.

The nominating process is the most serious flaw in the new Soviet election procedure. With or without Gorbachev's approval, the apparatus intervened clumsily, with tactics of obstructing meetings and harassing oppositionists more like Third-World or American-style machine politics than the smoothly orchestrated Soviet electoral charades of the past, to assure that local party chiefs would be the only candidate on the ballot.

This behavior illustrates why, if a party organization controls nominations, there can be no democracy without a multi-party system. If there are to be just one or two parties, democracy requires a procedure like the American system of primary elections, where aspirants to office must win the endorsement of a majority of the party's voters in order to become the official candidate of the party in the general election.

Nevertheless, choices have been presented to Soviet voters on a scale undreamed of for decades, and the voters have taken advantage of the opportunity to pronounce a stunning vote of no confidence in the party bureaucracy. Boris Yeltsin's victory in Moscow, the triumph of the Popular Fronts in the Baltic States, and the rejection of leading military figures all show the degree of popular frustration with the status quo, as well as the honesty of the vote-counting in these districts. Most striking has been the repudiation of a number of the local party chiefs who were running unopposed, when voters took advantage of the old theoretical right to cross the name off their ballots, and did so in such numbers that the official candidate was denied the 51 percent of the total vote necessary for election. In a number of places these protests were obviously well organized by informal groups; in Leningrad the defeat of First Secretary Yuri Solovyov (a candidate member of the Politburo) was evidently engineered by the semi-underground Social Democratic Party.

The new congress and the smaller Supreme Soviet elected by it represent a further stage in Gorbachev's efforts to find a political foundation for his reform program and his own leadership. Despairing as early as 1986 of support for perestroika within the party apparatus, Gorbachev turned to the intelligentsia and to the press with his doctrine of glasnost. Then he sought the backing of rank and file party members against the bureaucracy in elections to the party conference of last June. This was at best a limited success, and Gorbachev seems to have decided to shift from the party to the elected government as his principal base of authority. Hence the constitutional changes to create a strong presidency for himself and the new parliamentary process to back it up.

A distinctive feature of this election, furthered by the institutional apportionment of deputies to such entities as the unions of writers and artists, is the prominence of the creative intelligentsia among the candidates. Obviously this reflects the traditional prestige of intellectual accomplishment in Russia. It also reflects the fact that other than intellectuals, few people outside the high bureaucracy have had an opportunity to establish themselves as individual personalities in the public mind, and to achieve that essential advantage that every Western politician appreciates, "name recognition."

The crucial question remaining is how the Congress of People's Deputies will proceed to elect the new Supreme Soviet of 542 members. Even if the congress turns out to have a majority controlled by the party apparatus, it now seems unlikely, in view of the popularity of many opposition candidates, that they would be excluded from a proportionate share of the seats in the higher body. That would discredit the whole electoral process. But proportionality implies the formation of groups within the congress, which Boris Yeltsin and Roy Medvedev have already talked about. This would be a multi-party system in embryo.

There is a possible parallel between the new Supreme Soviet and a previous experiment in representative government. This was the tsarist Duma from 1907 to 1917. Under Prime Minister Peter Stolypin's law, the apportionment of Duma deputies by regions and classes assured a pro-government majority, but debate was nevertheless vigorous, and the radical parties, including the Bolsheviks, had a legal forum for their views. Now, with the many distinctive personalities who appear headed for election to the Supreme Soviet, it could become one of the most interesting parliamentary bodies in the world.

Chapter Sixteen

Dead Souls and Perestroika (May 1989)

As deliberative politics became more meaningful in the Soviet leadership, Gorbachev aimed to remove from the Central Committee those individuals who had lost the jobs entitling them to membership. Unable to accomplish such a purge at the Nineteenth Party Conference, he managed it in the spring of 1989, just after the election of the new Congress of People's Deputies. Reflecting the on-going renovation of the party officialdom, the move for the time being strengthened Gorbachev's hold on power and the progress of his reforms.

With the passage of time, the studies of political science are destined sooner or later to turn into history. Sometimes the course of events can cause this change of perspective to take place within a surprisingly short period. So it was with the precedent-shattering plenum of the Central Committee of the CPSU in April 1989 when seventy-four out of the 300 living members of the Central Committee, together with twenty-four of the 157 candidate members and twelve of the eighty-two members of the Central Auditing Commission, collectively handed in their resignations. The list included no less than four former Politburo members (Aliev, Gromyko, Solomentsev, and Tikhonov) and five former Politburo candidates (P. N. Demichev, V. I. Dolgikh, V. V. Kuznetsov, B. N. Ponomaryov, and Marshal S. L. Sokolov). But, decisive though this event was, it was quickly consigned to the historical dimension by the tumultuous proceedings of the Congress of People's Deputies and the advent at least for the time being of quasi-democratic politics in the Soviet Union.

Nevertheless, the April housecleaning of the Communist Party leadership retains its significance as a benchmark in Gorbachev's step-by-step campaign to consolidate his own leadership, and shift—or at least broaden—the base of his power from the bureaucratic apparatus of the Communist Party to institutions more genuinely founded on the consent of the governed. Between March 1986 and April 1989 the Central Committee elected at the Twenty-Seventh Party Congress had already been thinned out a bit by death and scandal. During the same period, at all three levels of the party's institutionalized elite, there was a rapidly growing number of members who had lost their entitlement to membership, thanks to removal from the bureaucratic positions that conferred elite status on their tenants. The mass resignations announced at the April

Plenum were immediately recognized as a move to get rid of these so-called "dead souls" in the Central Committee.

Use of this Gogolian term—"lame duck" would be the nearest equivalent in American politics—reflects the unwritten law that membership in the Central Committee is based on bureaucratic position and rank in the party apparatus, the civil government, the military, and other national organizations, together with a number of "mass representatives," essentially activists chosen from broad categories of the population such as managers, workers, and collective farmers. For decades the practice has 2been that a bureaucrat at any of the three elite ranks—Central Committee member, candidate member, and member of the Central Auditing Commission—who is removed from his job will automatically be dropped from the slate of Central Committee members and candidates and CAC members that is submitted to the next party congress for unanimous approval. By the same token, with very little variation, the successors to these same bureaucratic positions, be they regional party secretaryships, ministries, or high military commands, will automatically be given the corresponding rank in the Central Committee elite at the next party congress.

In the meantime, the new bureaucrats have attended Central Committee meetings, while their predecessors temporarily retained the right to do so as well.[1] Since voting until recently was prearranged and unanimous, the presence of the dead souls made little difference. But now that the leader's authority is no longer total and automatic, it becomes a serious matter as to who retains the right to vote in a Central Committee decision. It is widely believed that Gorbachev wanted to have the Nineteenth Party Conference get rid of the dead souls and elevate their replacements to the Central Committee. This concern would imply his recognition that the Central Committee was exercising real power and making real decisions where the votes counted. Though he did not succeed in his aim at the conference, the goal obviously remained high among his priorities.

The mass resignations in April were totally without precedent. On occasion, individuals have been expelled from the Central Committee—one member and four candidate members were ousted for corruption in 1988, and Stalin had a large majority of the CC arrested in his purge of 1937–38. Otherwise, membership has not been substantially altered except at party congresses.

It appears that the major reorganization of the Politburo and the Secretariat that Gorbachev pushed through in September 1988 was the key development giving him the strength to proceed with the renovation of the Central Committee. Twenty-four candidate members were promoted to full CC seats by the April plenum. However, there is less to this move than meets the eye. Nine of the promoted candidates came from the category of mass representatives, even though there was only one mass representative type in all the seventy-four resignations. Gorbachev evidently likes the idea of expanding this group, as he had already done at the Twenty-Seventh Congress. Nine promotees were upgraded in their existing posts, including four leaders in the Academy of Sciences. (One, E. M. Primakov, Director of the Institute of World Economics and International Relations, emerged soon afterwards as chairman of the Soviet of the Union in the newly reconstituted Supreme Soviet.) Only six of the promotees represented the usual reason for promotion, namely advancement to a different job already carrying Central Committee rank; they included V. A. Ivashko, the new Second secretary of the Ukraine, a man to watch as the possible successor to Shcherbitsky since he was the only provincial official included in the central party delegation to the Congress of People's Deputies. This bureaucratic parsimony in making promotions results from the party rule that CC vacancies may be filled between congresses only by promoting candidate members. It so happens that relatively few of the replacements for the dead souls in CC-level jobs had been drawn from the ranks of the 1986 candidate members. The majority of the people installed in these positions had not reached candidate status jobs by that time, and so are not eligible for de jure elevation to the CC until the next congress in 1991.

After the April 1989 plenum, thanks to the resignations, deaths, and previous removals, on the one hand, and the promotion of candidate members on the other, the median birth year among the full members of the CC moved from 1924, for the group as it was constituted at the Twenty-Seventh Congress, to 1929. This means that the recent changes have more than compensated for the natural aging process among the CPSU leadership. In the distribution of Central Committee seats among the various functional areas of the Soviet bureaucratic structure, the party apparatus and the military appear to have lost ground, but the real explanation is that the dead souls in those areas were more likely to have been replaced by rapidly advancing younger people who had not yet reached candidate rank in 1986, and hence were not eligible for promotion in 1989.

One bit of data is nevertheless quite revealing. This is the make-up of the Central Committee broken down by the year in which members entered it.[2] In this respect 1986 and 1989 compare as the table shows (with 1981 included as a Brezhnev-era benchmark).

These figures show how thoroughly the Brezhnev era appointees were weeded out between 1986 and 1989—a decisive shift resulting from Gorbachev's efforts to restaff the leadership. Among the victims, as the table indicates, were the last three survivors of Stalin's post-war Central Com-

Entry year of cohort	original number	survivors 1981	survivors 1986	survivors 1989
1952 or before	125	12	3	—
1956	54	7	4	1
1961	108	38	13	6
1966	51	29	10	4
1971	91	67	32	18
1976	86	77	50	32
1981	89	89	60	40
1986	135	—	135	120
1987–89	29	—	—	29
Total		319	307	250

mittee and three of the last four (including Gromyko) who joined the Central Committee in the year of de-Stalinization, 1956, only Kunaev being spared for the time being. Even without filling most of the vacancies left by the April resignations, the General Secretary now has a Central Committee more than half of whose members have joined the body since his accession to the leadership. If the potential additional members already holding Central Committee-rank jobs are counted in, the proportion of new, post-Brezhnev blood approaches two-thirds of the top elite rank. Beyond this, there is bound to be still more turnover of high officeholders by the time of the next party congress in 1991.

This pace of renovation evidently does not guarantee Gorbachev against conservative proclivities, even among the younger apparatchiki, but it does show how far he has gone in restaffing the power structure. As these changes proceed, enlarging the potential for new entrants into the Central Committee in 1991, the possibilities of a successful palace coup by the conservatives become ever more problematical. Moreover, the conservatives would have to reckon with the entire new scene of electoral politics within a more and more autonomous governmental structure. For all its limitations, the April shakeup therefore stands out as another decisive step by a most decisive leader to make his program of perestroika irreversible.

PART FOUR

THE CRISIS AND COLLAPSE OF PERESTROIKA, 1990–1991

CHAPTER SEVENTEEN

"SLAVIC SUPER-SUNDAY"
(MARCH 1990)

The year 1989 was a time of extraordinary developments, as the dominoes of Communist rule in Eastern Europe fell one after another, and the Soviet Union implemented semi-parliamentary government for the first time since 1917. Gorbachev held to his reform course despite rising choruses of opposition both on the "right" (Communist conservatives) and on the "left" (impatient democratizers and non-Russian separatists). He set elections in motion in the spring of 1990, not perfect but freer than the year before, to choose new legislative bodies in all the union republics as well as city and provincial authorities.

An American journalist has termed 4 March 1990 "Slavic Super-Sunday."[1] The analogy is with "Super-Tuesday" in March 1988, when a large number of the American state-by-state presidential primary elections to choose delegates to the Republican and Democratic nominating conventions were scheduled for the same day. In the Soviet Union, "Slavic Super-Sunday" was the day when voters in the three Slavic Republics of the USSR—Russia, the Ukraine, and Belorussia, representing three-quarters of the population of the entire nation—went to the polls to elect new deputies to their local and republic-wide soviets. 4 March was therefore a decisive step on the path toward democratization in Soviet political life.

There is more than a coincidental resemblance between the new Soviet system of representation and voting, and the system in the United States. Deputies to the soviets at all levels are elected from single-member districts, rather than on the basis of party lists in larger districts, as is usual in continental Europe. The Soviet practice of voting in two stages, a first-round election with any number of candidates, followed by a runoff election between the two leading candidates if no one wins an absolute majority in the first round, may be compared with the two-stage American system of primary and general elections.

Technically speaking, the Soviet Union does not yet have multi-party elections, but the two-stage electoral system virtually assures a contest in the runoff stage between the candidate of the Communist Party apparatus and the candidate of all the reform and opposition factions who coalesce against the party bureaucrats. Even the attempts of the local party apparatus, especially in rural areas, to obstruct opposition meetings and publicity work and to falsify the elections themselves, has its American parallel.

The Soviet apparatus can no longer dispose of its opponents by the Stalinist methods of censorship and arrest; it is reduced to tactics of petty fraud and harassment, just like the political machines that used to govern Chicago and many other large American cities.

We will not know accurately the outcome of the current contest between the Soviet reformers and the apparatus until the runoff stage is completed. Nevertheless, it seems probable that the reformers will control the city soviets of Moscow, Leningrad, and other populous centers, and that Boris Yeltsin will be in a good position to win the presidency of the Russian Republic. This will put the reformers in a position to carry out the policies of perestroika with enthusiasm, instead of grudgingly like the old apparatus. To this extent they will aid President Gorbachev in his continuing struggle with the apparatus conservatives, even though he has directed most of his critical rhetoric against the impatience of the reformers. At the same time, the reformers will be responsible for the improvement of economic conditions in the cities under their control.

These March elections in the Soviet Union constitute one further step in the remarkable process of political transformation through which Gorbachev has been leading his country. In all probability, when he began his program of perestroika in 1985, he did not foresee how radical his political reforms would eventually become. But in pursuing the economic recovery and reinvigoration of the Soviet Union, he found it necessary to take one step after another to break down the power of the Stalinist-type apparatus; first, with glasnost and the liberation of public opinion; then by appealing to the party rank and file against the apparatus; then by shifting power from the party hierarchy to the organs of the state; and finally by creating the opportunity for genuinely democratic elections and giving up the principle of the Communist Party's monopoly of power. If not truly a new revolution, the changes Gorbachev has allowed have revived Russia's democratic aims of 1905 and 1917. With each new electoral exercise of the democratic principle, it will become more difficult to deny those long-frustrated hopes.

CHAPTER EIGHTEEN

THE ROCKY ROAD TO PLURALISM
(APRIL 1990)

While Gorbachev pressed ahead in the spring of 1990 with his constitutional revolution—surrender of the Communist Party's political monopoly and confirmation of his own presidential power, as well as the local elections—the old discipline of the party broke down completely, and a split into two or more rival movements loomed.

At its Tenth Congress in March 1921, when the young Soviet regime was struggling to resolve the crisis brought on by revolutionary radicalism and civil war, the Russian Communist Party took its cue from Lenin and resolved, "The unity and solidarity of the ranks of the party . . . are particularly essential at the present juncture. . . . All class-conscious workers must clearly realize the perniciousness and impermissability of factionalism of any kind. . . . The congress . . . orders the immediate dissolution of any groups without exception that have been formed on the basis of one platform or another. . . . Nonobservance of this decision of the congress shall involve absolute and immediate expulsion from the party."

Today, this famous rule has become a dead letter. The democratization of political life that Gorbachev has sponsored, beginning with the election of the Congress of People's Deputies a little more than a year ago, has made possible an extraordinary proliferation of "informal groups" and nascent political parties all over the country. The Communist Party of the Soviet Union has given up its constitutional monopoly, and within the party itself the most diverse and antagonistic currents of opinion are being expressed.

Against the backdrop of unresolved crisis in the economy and in relations with the national minorities, Soviet political life has de facto achieved "more political variety than any other country in the world," in the words of the Soviet social scientist Lilia Shevtsova.[1] As in Eastern Europe, the political culture of pre-Communist times is re-emerging, with all the old philosophical and ethnic cleavages, "politically infantile," as Shevtsova says, in contrast to the political maturation that West European democracy has manifested since 1945.

There are at least five distinct factional positions on the new Soviet political scene. Within the Communist Party Gorbachev's centrist, compromise position is opposed by the impatient reformers, who have organized under the leadership of Yeltsin and Afanasiev as the "Interregional Group" and as the "Democratic Platform." The latter is not to be confused with the "Democratic Union," avowed anti-Communists whose demonstration on the most recent anniversary of the February Revolution of 1917 was broken up by the police.

On the opposite flank, Gorbachev is opposed more quietly but also more dangerously by the apparatus conservatives led by Ligachev. Ironically, in their fight to preserve the old organizational and ideological unity of Leninism against Gorbachev's reform program, these people have done more than anyone else to promote real pluralism within the party.

On the far right a variety of nationalist and traditional movements have taken shape, ranging from the Pamyat group with its openly anti-Semitic sentiments, to a new "Orthodox Monarchist Party," all under the umbrella of the "Bloc of Russian Public-Patriotic Movements." Writers on the left have called this a "bloc of Black Hundred neo-Stalinists and corrupt bureaucrats," and "the first manifestation of fascism."[2]

As Gorbachev's position within the party crumbled, he pressed ahead to establish a new base of power as president in the civil government, despite sharp criticism both from Soviet reformers and from foreign observers. His strongest supporter in the Politburo, Alexander Yakovlev, told the Supreme Soviet in February, "The new approach to the presidency would be yet another barrier against an unconstitutional striving for power. . . . The functions of power are being shifted from the party to constitutional bodies of power."[3]

A clear picture of the relative strength of each tendency was provided by the second round of elections on 18 March 1990 in the Russian Republic, the Ukraine, and Belorussia. The Communist reformers won both in Moscow (under the banner of the "Democratic Russia Bloc") and in Leningrad ("Democratic Elections—90"), while the ultra-Right was badly defeated. The Communist apparatus kept its grip in most rural areas, but its future as a contender in free elections was becoming more and more doubtful. One loyalist, trade-union chief Vladimir Mishin, warned of "the party's falling prestige among the broad masses of people," and added, "We're talking life and death as far as the CPSU is concerned. And maybe even life and death for Soviet society."[4]

Ligachev's answer to the crisis was an apparently deliberate effort to drive the reformers out of the party. At the March 1990 plenum of the Central Committee, he openly called for a party purge, and in an interview early in April he targeted "revisionists, nationalists, and social-democrats."[5] An official statement of the party Secretariat two days later called on the Democratic Platform group to quit the party or be expelled. Meanwhile, a tense confrontation occurred in Leningrad, when the new anti-apparatus majority of the city soviet intervened to suspend censorship in the Leningrad television and oust the local television director.

All sides now agree that a party split is virtually inevitable, probably at the Twenty-Eighth Party Congress scheduled for early July. Departure of the Democratic Platform group would then deprive Gorbachev of the force he needs to balance the conservatives, and would thus compel him to rely more than ever on the electoral process as a power base instead of the apparatus. But if the recent pattern of voting in Eastern Europe is any guide, the disintegrating Communist Party may be supplanted by the conservative nationalists as the dominant political force in Russia.

Alexander Tsipko, the political scientist who achieved notoriety a year ago by blaming Marx for Stalinism, now warns, "There are two distinct processes taking place in Russia: democratization and the reawakening of national self-consciousness. If those two processes are separated, it will be very dangerous."[6] Both, one might add, for democratic reform within the Soviet Union and for ending the Cold War legacy in Europe. As they say in Prague now, there is no chance of another Soviet intervention in Eastern Europe—unless a coup should bring the chauvinists and militarists to power in Moscow. Ligachev himself has called the democratization of Eastern Europe "just a passing setback for socialism; Communist ideas will prevail in the end."[7]

CHAPTER NINETEEN

THE LAST PARTY CONGRESS? (JULY 1990)

The Twenty-Eighth Party Congress in July 1990 was the high-water mark of Gorbachev's reformism, as the party lost power to the civil government and dissolved into a chaos of warring factions. Yeltsin took his cause of radical opposition out of the party altogether, with a demonstrative walkout from the congress.

The Twenty-Eighth Congress of the Communist Party of the Soviet Union reflects the transformation that five years of *perestroika, glasnost,* and "new thinking" have brought to the USSR. Compared with party congresses of the past, even with the Twenty-Seventh (held when Gorbachev had already been party leader for a year), it is an event of a different order. In all probability this will be the last congress of the CPSU as we have known it.

The most obvious change is the demise of the old mores of official unity and unanimity. Both the reformist and conservative wings of the party are already behaving not just as separate factions but as independent parties, subjecting Gorbachev's leadership to criticism just as sharp as that voiced by the opposition in any Western parliament. The Italian journalist Giulietto Chiesa has identified seven distinct factional positions that could be the nuclei of new parties—"radicals" (e.g., Afanasiev, Andrei Sakharov); "left independents"; "mediators" such as Roy Medvedev; "centrists" around Gorbachev; *apparatchiki;* "right independents," that is, Russian nationalists and Slavophiles; and the "pre-perestroika" types, "the swamp," who vote as they are told.[1]

It appears that in the Twenty-Eighth Congress, as in the Nineteenth Party Conference in 1988, the conservatives of the party apparatus have been able to achieve solid majorities by their old methods of manipulating the delegate selection process, in defiance of the surge of democratization and political pluralism in the country at large. This makes Gorbachev's attainment of firm authority as president in the civil government appear all the more significant as a base of power independent of the party.

Gorbachev approached this congress in his characteristic style—broad verbal attacks on both dissident wings, appeals for unity, and heavy-handed exercise of the position of chairman to steer unruly assemblies toward a compromise position. This time, however, he has been less successful. Though he managed to stop attacks on individual Politburo members, the conservatives made scathing criticisms of the leadership's "capitulation to capitalism," betrayal of socialist values, and "losing Eastern Europe." Meanwhile, with Yeltsin as their catalyst, the reformers left little doubt about their intention to leave the party altogether and set themselves up as a social-democratic movement.

Under this pressure, Gorbachev and his centrist supporters have blamed the country's difficulties more and more on their predecessors of the Brezhnev era, to the point of exaggeration. "It was an extremely grim legacy that we inherited," Gorbachev asserted in his opening report to the congress. He cited the crisis in agriculture, the waste of natural resources, and the innumerable environmental disasters. Foreign Minister Shevardnadze scored the "militarization" of the Soviet economy under the Stalinist command system that had channeled one-fourth of the country's economic resources to the armed forces (confirming estimates of the most alarmist Western analysts).

These arguments have done little to help Gorbachev's declining popularity among the Soviet population as well as on both wings of the party. All hold him accountable for the failure to improve economic conditions, and many fault him for always trying to reach compromises. One congress delegate complained, "What people can't understand is Gorbachev, who maneuvers between the two poles. They do not understand this centrist vacillation." He applauded both the conservative Ligachev and the liberal Yakovlev—"At least these are both clear, distinctive personalities."

Paradoxically, Gorbachev's prestige has continued to rise abroad while falling at home. In particular, the Reagan-Bush leadership in Washington, after first holding that Gorbachev's reforms were merely cosmetic, and then warning that he could not possibly succeed, now acknowledge that he is the only leader who can hold the Soviet Union to a stable role in international relations. The only issue, as the Western powers consider aid for Moscow, is whether it will really help or will only allow the Soviets to perpetuate their bad economic habits. But aid is also an issue among the potential recipients, a basis for suspicion among Soviet conservatives that it may be the entering wedge of capitalism.

As the body that ratifies national policy and the national leadership, the Soviet party congress is already an anachronism. The elected governmental bodies—the Congress of People's Deputies and the Supreme Soviet—already deal more authoritatively with national issues and represent more accurately the spectrum of public opinion. The Politburo has already yielded to the Presidential Council as the body that deliberates on executive decisions. The expansion of the Politburo ordered by the congress dilutes its authority even more. The shift in real power was underscored by Yakovlev's decision to leave the Politburo in order to concentrate on work in the Presidential Council. Similarly, a number of provincial party secretaries (who are automatic Central Committee members) have resigned their party positions in order to chair committees of the Supreme Soviet. The prospects are for party institutions at all levels to be pushed to the side and left only with responsibility for the party's internal organization.

Will the party organization accept such a marginal role as it attempts to compete with the far more popular political forces that are leaving its ranks or organizing entirely outside the old monolithic framework? There is no longer any alternative, except resort to force. That could only be attempted by a coalition of the armed forces, the KGB, the Russian nationalists, and workers who fear reform, all with an anti-Western and anti-Semitic flavor. They would revive Stalin without Marx, so to speak, and they would still control the Soviet Union's nuclear arsenal. That would be the destabilizing event that Western governments now fear much more than a revival of Soviet power through Gorbachev-style reform.

CHAPTER TWENTY

GORBACHEV AT A DEAD END
(NOVEMBER 1990)

As Gorbachev continued to maneuver between the reformist and conservative elements on the Soviet political scene, the nation's problems in the economy and in relations among nationalities reached a critical point. Growing disorder prompted incessant rumors of some kind of impending coup.

Mikhail Gorbachev has achieved two epochal successes, and has suffered two painful failures. The successes, virtually unprecedented in the history of any country, were to dismantle the Stalinist dictatorship internally, and to withdraw from superpower competition externally, in both instances without the use of force. The failures stemmed from these successes—the near-paralysis of the Soviet economic system, and the virtual dissolution of the Soviet Union into its constituent nationality elements.

Ironically, Gorbachev is now being destroyed politically by the very forces that his democratic reforms unleashed. The stagnation of the Soviet economy was the first target in his reform agenda of 1985, but within a year of his accession to power he found himself compelled to shift his emphasis to the political system. He had to attack the power of the Communist Party's bureaucratic apparatus to obstruct reform and potentially to overthrow the chief reformer himself. Gorbachev has always proceeded with the lesson of the downfall of Nikita Khrushchev foremost in his mind.

From the middle of 1986 until the Twenty-Eighth Party Congress in July 1990 Gorbachev's primary attention was continuously preempted by the resistance of the conservative party bureaucracy. As he broadened his political base from the party to the entire Soviet electorate in free elections, he provoked more anxiety and resistance within the party machinery, in an escalating dialectic of political confrontation. By the time he prevailed at the Twenty-Eighth Congress, he had decapitated the party by restaffing the Politburo and excluding it from government policymaking. He deprived the party of its political monopoly and pushed it to the margin of the Soviet political arena, while he built for himself a new power base as president in the constitutional government.

Gorbachev showed himself to be a master of political maneuver to reach this goal without provoking a dangerous counteraction by the conservatives. He would allow other reformers to prepare public opinion for an innovation and even to criticize him for moving too slowly. Thus he let the conservatives believe that he was their best hope. Then he would advance into the reform position himself and strike another in a series of organizational blows against rule by the party apparatus. Examples range from the 1988 constitutional reform to the repeal of Article 6 in the constitution (the Communist Party's privileged role).

While these tactics were successful in pulling the teeth of the party apparatus, Gorbachev's focus on political reform and foreign policy allowed the country to drift as regards the economy and relations among the nationalities, where democratization and *glasnost* permitted the troubles bottled up under the pre-Gorbachev regime to erupt into the open. The two problem areas are related, for the demands of the national republics for autonomy and "sovereignty" create great uncertainty for the future of any economic reform. The principle difference between the "five hundred days" proposal of Stanislav Shatalin and Grigori Yavlinsky, and the government position of Prime Minister Ryzhkov, was whether ultimate responsibility for marketizing the economy should lie with the Union government or with the several republics.

A very important commentary on the relation between the nationality problem and the economy was published by the historian and People's Deputy Andranik Migranyan.[1] Noting "a two-fold collapse of the center," between the reformers and the conservatives, Migranyan argued that the hope to improve the economy first and thereby dissuade the minorities from seceding was no longer viable. "The shift of power from the center to the republics . . . has become a hindrance to the changeover to a market and the continuation of democratization." Therefore it was necessary to recognize the responsibility of the republics for carrying through the economic reform, leaving union concerns to a "coordinating committee"—an anticipation of the "Federation Council" that Gorbachev has just proposed to bring the leaders of the republics into the central decision-making process.

The alternative, according to Migranyan, might be "great-power Russian nationalism—orientation toward a special path, isolationism, nonacceptance of Western institutions and values." Here was a hint of the often-rumored military coup supported by party conservatives and nationalist intellectuals. Meanwhile, the Union government and the governments of the republics are trying to nullify each other's legislative acts, without any conception of a constitutional demarcation of the spheres of action of the Union and of its constituent republics such as has been the basis of the American federal union. Moscow as the Union and Moscow as the Russian Republic now fight for control even of such functions as the central television.

The demand of the Russians and the Russian Federation for "sover-

eignty" means above all to endorse this status for all fifteen union republics. Under Yeltsin's leadership, the Russian Republic has started to
conclude treaties and trade agreements with the other republics, just as if
they were independent countries. But for the huge Russian Republic, with
over half the population of the Union and three-fourths of its land area,
this redistribution of power does not necessarily mean decentralization;
it is only a shift of power from one set of offices and officials in Moscow
to another one. Yeltsin and the Russian government in Moscow have
their own problems with the dozens of smaller national minorities within
the Russian Federation who are claiming sovereignty for themselves and
control over natural resources in their respective territories.

The real issue between the two foci of central power in Moscow is
generational: The government of the Russian Federation, formed a year
later than the present Union regime, through more fully democratic elections, is committed much more unambiguously to the decentralization
and marketization of the economy, as well as to the right of the other
republics to leave the Union. Then there is the personal factor: Yeltsin
seems never to have forgiven Gorbachev for ousting him from the Communist Party leadership in 1987, and now as president of the Russian
Federation he uses every opportunity to attack Gorbachev for delaying
reform—even though it was Gorbachev's reform of the political structure
that enabled Yeltsin to survive politically and regain high office. Gorbachev's plan for the Federation Council, in which each republic would
have an equal voice, might be construed as a maneuver to hem in the
Russian Republic; in any case, Yeltsin sharply attacked the plan. Another
ironic note is the fact that the new, separate Communist Party organization for the Russian Republic is dominated by the conservatives led by
Ivan Polozkov, who had made a name for himself in Krasnodar Province
by suppressing newly-formed cooperative enterprises.

Both in private and in public, Soviet citizens are expressing more and
more often their fear of chaos, civil war, or a military coup, if the crisis
in the economy and among the nationalities cannot be resolved legally
and democratically. Migranyan speaks of "the abyss toward which we are
rushing at full steam."[2] To be sure, there is no Soviet precedent for the
seizure of power by the military and/or the secret police. Up to now the
party's political controls have kept them loyal to the leadership. Now,
however, removal of the party's role in the armed forces is on the reform
agenda. Add to this the grievances of the officer corps over reduced bud-
gets, withdrawal from Eastern Europe, a general diminution of their prestige, and the prospect of being cast loose in the Soviet economy, and
intervention in the present political crisis acquires a motive as well as an
opportunity. Correspondents Rick Atkinson and Gary Lee write, "The
armed forces will be the first and worst victims of an inexorable effort to
demilitarize one of the world's most martial societies."[3]

The Soviet-backed coup of General Jaruzelski in Poland in 1981 is an example of what the military might do in the USSR, though there is no prospect of their being able to turn the clock back any more permanently than Jaruzelski could. In their current state of demoralization, deprived of their main raison d'être and torn within their ranks by open hostility among the troops of different nationalities, the Soviet armed forces do not seem to have any clear idea of an alternative to the present course.

The fate that threatens democratization under Gorbachev is, rather, to be the victim of its own success, as the Russian democracy of 1917 was. Once relieved from the reflexes of obedience under a repressive autocracy, citizens of the Empire then and now have responded with a veritable orgy of democratic behavior, defying the minimum requirements of social discipline on the job, in governmental administration, and in military service. Now democratic decentralization has gone to the point where one Moscow borough is disputing with the city soviet the question of jurisdiction over the Bolshoi Theater. Citizens of the union republics are encouraged by their own leaders to defy calls for Union military service outside their own territories.

At the moment it is as difficult for Soviet commentators to predict the outcome of the crisis as it is for foreign observers. Gorbachev has progressively lost the public support necessary to lead the social forces he has liberated. A coalition of reformers might keep some if not all of the national minorities within the Union. Yet Gorbachev would still be necessary to the reformers and the national minorities to ward off a Russian nationalist reaction. The latter could conceivably bring together the military, the party conservatives, the rightist intellectuals, and the Orthodox Church, with strong support by the working class in Russia proper. In any case, the Soviet Union stands at an epochal crossroads where its future, peaceful or bloody, may hang on the unpredictable action of people who have lost both their fear and their patience.

CHAPTER TWENTY-ONE

GORBACHEV'S "THERMIDOR"
(JANUARY 1991)

Towards the end of 1990, Gorbachev apparently decided to resolve his political di-
lemma by turning back in the conservative direction, in effect executing a "Thermi-
dorean reaction" in his own revolution. Recoiling from the challenges of free-market
economic reform and autonomy for the nationalities, he provoked a veritable fire-
storm of controversy at the Congress of People's Deputies in December 1990.

If Gorbachev's reforms since 1985 constitute a revolution, as he has said himself, then the Fourth Congress of People's Deputies, held in December 1990 in Moscow, marked the Thermidorean reaction.

Warning of the immaturity of "Russian political culture," Gorbachev sounded the retreat in his opening speech to the congress: "What is most necessary now to overcome the crisis is to restore order in the country. . . . If we do not accomplish this, greater discord, a rampage of dark forces, and the disintegration of the state are inevitable." He faced the body of more than two thousand deputies riven by the passions of national separatism; two republics, Lithuania and Armenia, had refused to send their delegations, and the deputies from Estonia and Moldavia were at the point of walking out. Support crumbled on both of the president's flanks. A conservative deputy actually called for a vote of no confidence, accusing him of indecisiveness. Foreign Minister Shevardnadze, one of Gorbachev's closest allies in *perestroika*, shocked the congress—and the president—by announcing his resignation to protest the danger to reform: "A dictatorship is coming." On the left, Yeltsin alleged that such warnings were simply contrived to justify Gorbachev's desire for greater presidential powers. KGB chief Vladimir Kriuchkov, on the right, delivered an old-style Cold War speech, blaming the West for all the Soviet Union's troubles and calling for "decisive actions" against the separatists, even if "we will have to agree knowingly to the prospect that blood will be shed."

Caught in this crossfire, with his popularity dropping, Gorbachev opted for the conservative side. He nominated as his vice president under the new constitutional arrangements Gennadi Yanaev, a long-time but inconspicuous party and trade-union functionary who had been given the post of chief of the Communist Party's International Department in the reorganization of July 1990. Nevertheless, it took two days and two ballots for Gorbachev to secure approval of Yanaev by the congress.

The congress left the reformers in disarray, while the conservatives, coalescing as the *Soyuz* ("union") group of deputies, saw their chances brighten. Military hard-liners ostentatiously threw their support to this position. Yeltsin warned, "The proposed scope of the president's powers has no equal in Soviet history. Neither Stalin nor Brezhnev had so much legislatively established power."

How does all this add up to a Thermidorean reaction? The pattern of events in any revolution is to swing from an initial phase of moderate reform to radical reconstruction, and then to undergo a retrenchment. Normally this does not mean a counterrevolution against all the ideas of the revolution, but only a retreat from its most radical aims, and sooner or later a reconsolidation of authority. To be sure, in the framework of Soviet politics in the 1980s there was no literal revolution in the sense of the violent overthrow of the system of power, but there was at least what we might call a quasi-revolution, initially orchestrated by the regime itself, that evidenced the same dynamics in a more modest way. Gorbachev's government, sponsoring gradual reform, was being overtaken by the impatient popular forces that reform had set free, particularly among the nationalities. Losing his deft political touch, Gorbachev awarded himself wide presidential power to rule by decree, and turned back to rely on the military and the police to replace his shrinking popularity among the public.

The high-water mark of perestroika, so it seems in retrospect, was reached in July 1990 at the Twenty-Eighth Party Congress. Although conservatives were in the majority among the delegates, the party congress acceded to Gorbachev's will by surrendering the infamous Article 6 of the constitution that had conferred a political monopoly on the Communist Party, and by ending the policy-making function of the Politburo (which was expanded and restaffed to make it a weak and undistinguished body).

Then the country's two great challenges—the difficult problem of the economy and the insoluble problem of the national minorities—closed in on Gorbachev. His popularity, first seriously damaged last spring when he had the Supreme Soviet elect him president instead of standing for direct election by the people, fell precipitously. Under all this pressure Gorbachev seems to have lost his fine political touch, and perhaps even panicked. Instead of taking steps that might restore his real authority with the public, he turned to the Supreme Soviet for measures to enhance his formal powers as president.

From September 1990 on, Gorbachev took the conservative road in dealing with the economy and with the national minorities. He warned the parliamentarians in November, "Political forces of an openly brown color," i.e., fascists, were undertaking "a shameless manipulation of public opinion."[1] He still spoke of moving to the free market economy, but

he flinched when he was confronted with the "five hundred days" program of his reformist advisor Shatalin. He campaigned for a new treaty
of union among the republics of the USSR, but insisted at the same time
that the Union must be preserved at all cost. "If we have strong government, strict discipline and control over the implementation of decisions,"
he told the Congress of People's Deputies, "then we will be able to nor-
malize the food supply, restrain crime, and put a stop to nationality discord." Even before the session of the congress, he began to implement
this approach: in the economy by decreeing the formation of "workers'
committees," i.e. auxiliary police, to supervise the allocation of food supplies; towards the minorities, by authorizing the Soviet army to use force
to defend itself and its supply lines against separatist obstruction.

Gorbachev underscored his turn to the right by changes in his governmental entourage. The first such sign was the replacement in November
of the liberal minister of internal affairs, Vadim Bakatin, by the conservative Boris Pugo (a former KGB chief in Latvia, and an affront to the
minorities). He abolished his Presidential Council, which had represented
both the liberal and conservative wings of opinion, and left Yakovlev, the
chief architect of perestroika, with no government post at all.

The new Council of the Federation was no substitute. It represented
not only the union republics (that is, all those who chose to participate)
but also the "autonomous republics" within the Russian Federation. But
it had no definite power other than to advise the President on nationality
interests.

Then Gorbachev had the congress create a new inner cabinet in lieu of
the eighty-member Council of Ministers, eliminating the post of prime
minister (held by Nikolai Ryzhkov, a target of the reformers, who meanwhile fell critically ill). But this did not eliminate the dozens of actual
ministries administering the economy; it only enhanced the president's
direct control over them. The change brought the Soviets' formal consti
tutional structure close to the American model, with the executive power
of the president at least co-equal to the powers of the parliamentary bodies. In the minds of the reformists, Shevardnadze's resignation was only
the final, dramatic signal that a coup d'état by stages was underway, or
what the economist Yuri Levada called "a creeping paramilitary coup."[2]

The nationality problem has always been the most challenging aspect
of democratization. Gorbachev secured approval by the congress of the
text of a new treaty of union among the republics, but he made it clear
that he would not tolerate any republic's refusal to join. The prominent
reformist deputy Galina Starovoitova, comparing the USSR to France and
Algeria, warned that "the process of decolonization could be upset by the
millions of Russians living in the minority republics, and by the imperial
mentality of a large part of the population."[3]

If the December congress really has marked the Thermidor of the Gorbachev revolution, what are the prospects? Most obviously, a trend toward authoritarian and forceful measures—presidential decrees and military and police action—in dealing with the crisis in the Soviet economy and the crisis in nationality relations. An end to glasnost and democratic elections? Perhaps not directly, but efforts by the government to limit the effectiveness of these basic steps in the Gorbachev revolution. A return to Marxist-Leninist doctrine? This Humpty-Dumpty has been too thoroughly smashed; the ideology of Thermidor is more likely to be Russian nationalism in Soviet dress. A renewal of the Cold War? The Soviet government can in no way afford this, even if its retreat from reform cools Western eagerness to send aid. In the long run? In the long run it seems impossible for the Soviets to avoid the imperative of reform as Gorbachev tried for five years to pursue it.

Chapter Twenty-Two

WHITHER GORBACHEV?
(JANUARY 1991)

Gorbachev's retreat from reform at the end of 1990 was a good occasion for taking stock about the accomplishments and shortcomings of his reforms over the preceding five years, an assessment that left the Soviet future highly uncertain.

Revolutions do not go on forever. Sooner or later, Gorbachev's revolution in the Soviet Union, as he has styled it himself, had to fall back. The main uncertainty was whether the chief reformer would retreat with the receding tide, or be left high and dry by it.

The reason for natural limits in any process of radical change is simple. Reform (or revolution) opens up the political playing field to forces that seem at first to serve the cause of the chief reformer, but which really have their own agendas. Some militants strain to go beyond the movement's original goals, while other, less ambitious supporters of reform are turned off by the excesses of the zealots. Friedrich Engel's words of 1885 about the revolution he saw impending in Russia could well describe Gorbachev: "People who boasted that they had *made* a revolution have always seen the next day that they had no idea what they were doing, that the revolution *made* did not in the least resemble the one they would have liked to make."[1]

By last year, Gorbachev had traversed an incredible distance to marginalize the party and democratize the country. He swept the old neo-Stalinists out of the leadership, called for real contested elections within the party, got the party to agree to a democratic constitutional reform, held national elections that were at least partially democratic, shifted basic decision-making from the party to the government after making himself president, presided over a new and genuine (if not fault-free) parliamentary process, and finally (and most amazingly) got the party to surrender its constitutional monopoly of power and give up the Politburo as a serious policy-making body. With this record, one certainly cannot say, as is heard nowadays, that Gorbachev's reforms were just a manipulative trick. All the evidence is that he believed in what he was doing—up to a point.

What, then, went wrong, to turn Gorbachev against the people and the policies that he had fought so successfully to promote? Why, after his series of triumphs in democratizing the country, has he turned back to the people and the methods that stand for dictatorship? The answer lies in his two great failures, with the economy and with the national minorities.

Gorbachev was convinced from the start—from before the start, actually, in discussions with his liberal friends who had worked for Khrushchev—that the Stalinist "command-administrative system" in the economy had to be broken up. His model for reform was the NEP, with individual farming and private enterprise in trade and services, while large-scale business (banking, heavy industry, energy, transportation, the "commanding heights") was kept under state ownership, but were put on a profit-and-loss, supply-and-demand basis that Trotsky dubbed "market socialism."

To implement this vision Gorbachev extracted one law after another from the Supreme Soviet, a law on enterprise responsibility, a law facilitating individual and cooperative business, laws on joint enterprises and direct foreign dealings by Soviet firms, a law on leasing land for individual farms. If the results were less than spectacular, the blame can be placed on local party bureaucrats who, with the progress of democratization at the center, ironically found themselves less under Moscow's thumb and more able to obstruct policies with which they were out of sympathy. As many Soviets now describe it, Gorbachev broke up the old economic system, but did not put anything in its place.

The trouble with the economic reform seems to have been a philosophical one. Gorbachev remained wedded to something called "socialism," loose as that term may be. When his economic advisers such as Shatalin and Nikolai Petrakov began to advocate a crash program to revive the economy through marketization and privatization, Gorbachev balked and tried to compromise over their "five hundred days" plan. This was his first critical step in the retreat from reform. He got the Supreme Soviet to vote him emergency power to rule by decree, ostensibly to speed up reform. Instead he issued four panicky, retrogressive orders: One set up auxiliary police units of workers to assure distribution of goods; another gave the police unlimited power to raid enterprises (including joint enterprises with foreigners) to verify the legality of their earnings; the third called on army troops to accompany local police in their regular patrols (above all to curb sympathy with the minorities); the fourth and most astounding called large rouble bills out of circulation and effectively expropriated every grandmother who kept the family savings in a mattress. These are totalitarian measures, 180 degrees opposed to the "law-governed state" that Gorbachev claims to advocate. They suggest that despite his reformist convictions he has fallen back to the time-honored Russian methods of the decree and the whip, now that the going has gotten tough.

Even so, in recent months the economy has not been Gorbachev's most serious problem. Despite the pictures of long queues and empty shelves, there are ample reports that consumers manage, through their enterprises, in the black market, or by exchanging goods they have hoarded. The critical issue now is the national minorities and the future of the Soviet Union as a state.

It has been clear from the start of the Gorbachev era that the nationality problem was the Achilles Heel of democratization in the Soviet Union. If democracy were introduced, the first thing the minorities (particularly the more developed and Western-oriented) would want to do with it would be to leave the Union, and the one thing that many Russians and certainly the conservative bureaucracy would insist on more than democracy would be to keep the minorities forcibly within the Union and thus within the base for Russia's international power. The only surprise is that Gorbachev has managed to stave off the crisis until now.

One paradoxical fact is that the government of the Russian Republic, headed by Yeltsin and administering over half the Soviet population and two-thirds of its area, supports free choice for the nationalities and declares its own sovereignty. Russian autonomy in the Soviet framework is an oxymoron, a contradiction in terms. Russia *is* the center. It cannot be autonomous from itself. For Russia to be anti-centralist means that it is willing to forego Russian domination over the peripheral nationalities. The struggle between the Union government and the Russian government is a struggle between two authorities in Moscow, one in the Kremlin and the other on Krasnopresnenskaya Embankment, over the question of a looser or tighter relationship between the Russian center and the minorities. The Russian government is more pro-autonomy than the Union government for two reasons: (1) it was elected more recently and more democratically, and thus is more prepared to abandon the centralist heritage of the past; and (2) the Russian leader Yeltsin has carried his enmity toward the Union leader Gorbachev to the point of opposing everything the latter stands for. If Gorbachev rejects full independence for the minorities, Yeltsin will endorse it.

The turning point for Gorbachev seems to have come sometime last fall. The government's power to command obedience had dissolved, almost as it had in 1917, and rumors of a possible military coup flew about. In the Soviet press and from individual Soviet citizens one constantly encounters variations on the theme of chaos: they sense catastrophe, they see the "abyss," they fear civil war. The liberal paper *Literaturnaya Gazeta* wrote just a few days ago, "Today our fate is being decided. Today it is being decided whether we will begin to live honorably, boldly, according to our consciences, or whether we will remain mute slaves, blindly obeying whoever tries with a devilish smirk to rule in our name."[2]

Unfortunately, every step Gorbachev has taken since last fall to address the crisis has been in the conservative, Stalinist direction. Ligachev, squeezed out of the power structure last summer, has taken open satisfaction at the turn of events.[3] Naturally, speculation has arisen as to whether Gorbachev's moves against reform, and above all his condoning of military action in the Baltic states, means that he has become a prisoner of the conservatives. This seems unlikely, considering the political strength he displayed up to last summer in chipping away at the institutions of conservative power. More plausible is what Gorbachev has stressed himself—his own ultimate commitments. Economic reform must not go so far as to eliminate everything he could call socialism, and relations with the national minorities must not allow the complete breakup of the Union. He is willing to decentralize the economy and encourage individual initiative, but he balks at legally private ownership, particularly in land. He offers the minorities a new Union Treaty guaranteeing wide autonomy but stopping short of complete independence; if a republic will not sign, it will be stuck with its status under the bogus treaty of 1922.

The limits to reform in the USSR are the limits in the mind of its leader. Seeing the surge of reform threatening to get out of control both in the economy and in nationality relations, and fearing the anarchy that these developments portended, Gorbachev has turned back to the traditional forces of order, Russian-style. By all appearances this is not one of the tactical retreats that he habitually executed between leaps of reform to keep the conservatives off balance; this is a basic strategic reversal of direction.

How far back can Gorbachev take the Soviet peoples, after having brought them so far ahead? No doubt he can stall reform for a while, but it is inconceivable that he can hold the clock back indefinitely. Soviet society is now far too modern, sophisticated, and complex to be run in the old monolithic way.

CHAPTER TWENTY-THREE

THE END OF THE REVOLUTION?
(DECEMBER 1991)

The long-expected coup attempt by Communist conservatives in August 1991 served only to delegitimize the entire Soviet system, reformed or unreformed. It triggered the rapid disintegration of the USSR, as well as a host of attempts to explain the collapse of Communism.

Rarely in history has a brief event so arrested the world's attention as the abortive Communist coup in Moscow on 19–21 August 1991. Like any riveting occurrence, the coup immediately set off an avalanche of journalistic accounts and I-was-there memoirs. Unlike anything previous in the Soviet realm the coup was the occasion for public commentaries and confidences by the highest leaders involved.

Gorbachev's own version of the August crisis made news when HarperCollins paid him a reported $500,000 advance for it.[1] Actually *The August Coup* is only a slightly reworked compilation of its author's statements during and immediately after the events, plus the hitherto unpublished article that he had been working on at the time he was sequestered in his Crimean *dacha* by the plotters, pleading, as he had so many times before, for peace, democracy, the Union, and "the socialist perspective."[2] Nevertheless, the book is a useful compendium with its dramatic moments, above all Gorbachev's account of his house arrest and the secret videotape he made to preserve his case for history. The Crimean article and similar post-coup comments gain poignancy in the light of the more recent collapse of the Union government. At the emergency session of the Supreme Soviet immediately after the coup Gorbachev affirmed "the idea of socialism . . . , an idea which embraces values developed in the course of a search for a juster society and a better world." As to the Stalinist past, "It was the model of socialism that we had in our country which proved a failure, and not the socialist idea itself."[3]

Gorbachev puts great stress on the September session of the Congress of People's Deputies, when he persuaded it to surrender its powers to a new government dominated by the individual republics. Ironically, that step cut out from under him the political base from which he might have contended more successfully with Yeltsin and the movement to break up the Union. Gorbachev comes across as a very sincere man who accomplished monumental changes, but ultimately could not rise above his own limitations—truly a tragic figure.

Michel Tatu, the famed Moscow correspondent of *Le Monde*, described Gorbachev as the leader of *perestroika* "who helped the Soviet Union to get back on course, who made socialism more human," indeed "a sort of Dubček à la soviétique."[4] The estimate that he wrote shortly before the coup sounds like a news dispatch of 19 August: "Let us hazard a guess. Some time in 1991 or even later, the situation has become so chaotic that a delegation of high-ranking officers and top conservative officials meets the President to beg him to restore order. They have prepared a decree to declare a state of emergency. . . . How will President Gorbachev react when he is told that the decree is the only way to stop the army from acting independently, as well as keeping his power, especially if he is reminded that his prestige abroad can ensure that the West will prove understanding and allow a return to naked power, since he is the only person capable of explaining to Bush, Mitterand, and Major that the putsch is not illegal and that it is only a regrettable parenthesis on the way to perestroika?"[5]

Another Old Moscow Hand, Giulietto Chiesa, enjoys a unique background of high-level access: He was for many years Moscow correspondent for the Rome Communist daily *L'Unità*. He recounts the dramatic emergency meeting of the Presidium of the Russian Supreme Soviet in the "White House" on Monday the 19th, where Speaker Ruslan Khasbulatov rushed in to read Yeltsin's appeal to the people while everyone wondered if the Russian president, who had not yet appeared, would escape arrest by the surrounding troops. Chiesa, his wife Fiammetta Cucurnia of *La Repubblica*, and Pilar Bonet of the Madrid *El País*, were the only foreigners present. Dashing around Moscow, Chiesa was one of the first to sense the hesitancy of the plotters: "The putschists appear uncertain, they do not seem to have a plan, they do not have any prospects without letting flow a river of blood, without repeating a Tienanmen of monstrous proportions. . . . Tomorrow a power without consent and without any future will have to decide whether to turn to armed struggle."[6]

At the coup leaders' televised press conference Monday afternoon when they alleged Gorbachev's illness, Chiesa put the first question: "Mr. Yanaev, can you tell me what is the state of your own health?" He went on, "Your action is anticonstitutional. Does your program at least include convening the Supreme Soviet?"[7] At Gorbachev's press conference after the collapse of the coup Chiesa boldly asked the Soviet president why he had appointed the conservatives who then turned against him. Gorbachev evaded the question.

Gorbachev, Chiesa suggests, was "the Louis XVI of the second Soviet revolution." Though the Soviet president tried to hang on, he inadvertently sealed his own doom when he forced the Congress of People's Deputies to "commit suicide" in September. "The Soviet Union is finished," Chiesa concluded, well before Yeltsin proclaimed the fact this December.[8] He hesitated to predict what would follow, not foreseeing the apparent resurrection of the Union according to Yeltsin's "commonwealth" model.

The real winner coming out of the coup was, of course, Gorbachev's rival on the reformist side, namely Yeltsin. Yeltsin's image remains something of an enigma: Is he a savior or a menace? The history of perestroika can practically be written as the contest between the gradualist Gorbachev and the radical Yeltsin, a duel enlivened by personal rivalry and bitterness as well as a widening philosophical gulf. At bottom, according to Yeltsin's biographer John Morrison, is "the Russian question," Russia's "dual history, as both empire and nation-state."[9] Morrison finds it paradoxical that the two protagonists should line up as Gorbachev the imperialist and Yeltsin the Russian nationalist, but in fact this is what the politics of their rivalry dictated: Yeltsin, winning the leadership of the Russian Republic, could prevail only by allowing all the republics to become sovereign as against the Union, and Gorbachev conversely had to try to maintain the Union in order to keep his job.

In his peasant background and his career progress through the party Yeltsin was remarkably like his age-mate Gorbachev, though he only reached the top a decade later. Gorbachev and Ligachev, working together in the initial, Andropovite phase of disciplinarian perestroika, brought Yeltsin to Moscow in April 1985 and turned him loose to attack the corruption and privileges of the Moscow bureaucracy. He overreached, and Ligachev started to conspire against him, just when Gorbachev was trying to mollify conservatives resisting the reforms. Fatefully—an episode Morrison misses—when promotions were being made from candidate member to full member of the Politburo in June 1987, Yeltsin was conspicuously passed over, and this blow to his pride seems to have governed his relations with Gorbachev ever since.

Of all the players in the Kremlin game, Morrison observes, Yeltsin had the best sense of the logic of history. The August Coup, like the Chernobyl nuclear disaster, was "an explosion that was both inevitable and avoidable," though Gorbachev ignored the warnings of what lay in store.[10] Yeltsin was at his best in rallying resistance to the plotters and working through his military contacts to shake the will of the armed forces. In the aftermath, he adroitly identified himself with the winning issues of democracy and independence for the republics, together with much free-market rhetoric and a touch of religion thrown in for good measure.

Morrison makes no bones about Yeltsin's limitations, "his authoritarian and abrasive personality," his "impulsiveness and a prickly sensitivity to real or imagined insults."[11] Most intellectuals distrust him as he distrusts them, though he is a quick study. Morrison quotes the writer Vladi-

mir Bukovsky on his first glimpse of Yeltsin on television: "A typical
Bolshevik, a Bolshevik straight out of central casting. Stubborn, overbear-
ing, self-assured, honest, irresistible, a human engine without brakes."[12]

Yeltsin's record since the coup supports these concerns—a penchant
for rule by decree, reliance on his old Communist cronies from Sverdlovsk, centralization of power through his own agents in the provinces,
and surprises like the Russian-Ukrainian-Belorussian "commonwealth."
Orthodox Communists truly fear him. On the other hand, the man's
courage, tactical adroitness, and popularity, particularly among "middle-
aged Russian women," are not to be denied.[13] Perhaps the Communist
Party could not have been eradicated except by a charismatic ex-Communist using Communist methods. But where will this lead Russia? "Opposition to totalitarianism must confront the danger of new totalitarian
structures replacing the old," Anatoly Sobchak warns.[14]

In Western minds Yeltsin has come to personify almost exclusively the
democratic opposition to Gorbachev and to any form of the old Communist regime, however sanitized. But there are a host of other impressive
figures who won prominence at the same time that Yeltsin made his
comeback, in the election of the Congress of People's Deputies in 1989.
One among these has stood out in Russian minds as a natural leader for
the future—Sobchak, the former Leningrad law professor, now Mayor of
St. Petersburg. Sobchak's political philosophy is like Yeltsin's, but more
reflective and more convincing—democracy, rule of law, private property. "Only in the last two years," he confesses, "have I fully realized the
value of private life and personal freedom."[15] The old ideas are nothing
but dead weight: "We live in a country where the ideological framework
remains long after ideological content has vanished."[16]

Sobchak's real hero is Sakharov, and the qualities that come through
most impressively in his book are his reasonableness and moderation,
quite un-Russian traits, but they seem to explain his popularity, along
with his negotiating skills and his contribution to the mechanics of the
new parliamentary system. He is equally the man of action: In his account
of the August Coup, Sobchak becomes his own hero, as he stiffens Yeltsin
in Moscow and then hurries back to Leningrad to shame the local military
into distancing themselves from the coup. His writing almost reminds
one of Leon Trotsky on himself in 1917.

The story of the decline and fall of Soviet Communism turns above all
on the mysterious problem of power. How could the Communist dictatorship, still embodied in the institutions commanded by the coup leaders, have collapsed so totally and abruptly just because those individuals
decided to tighten up a bit and present Gorbachev with the demands that
Tatu foresaw? "The coup d'état," writes Chiesa, "advertised for months;
organized by the most potent of armies, by the best organized and experi-

enced of political police forces; born in the innards of the Communist Party, the beacon and guide for decades of an international movement of colossal proportions; backed by forces that had struck fear into the entire West—was defeated in the course of three days, almost without fighting. The whole repressive machine collapsed upon itself, revealing fearful splits in its apparent solidity. Its sponsors lay down their arms and fled in panic when they realized that the country would not follow them."[17]

As the collapse of the coup revealed, political power does not inhere in vast organizations or simply come out of the mouth of a gun, contrary to Mao Tse-tung. Power is a psychological substance, not a material one, resting on a delicate interplay of perceptions between ruler and ruled: Like beauty, it exists mostly in the eye of the beholder. Sobchak recognized this truth when he wrote that the coup might easily have succeeded, "if the people had remained silent." Even more, "I want to make a special point of praising . . . those who hesitated . . . , those thousands and thousands of waverers—the militia and KGB personnel, soldiers and officers—who sent the coup to its downfall."[18] If the people will not obey and the troops will not shoot, power, like the Emperor's New Clothes, vanishes. So it was on the morning of Wednesday, 21 August: The KGB had not attacked the White House, the curfew had not been enforced, and the populace ranged the streets at will. Once this point had been reached, nothing could save the old structures of power, the Communist Party and the Union of Soviet Socialist Republics.

CHAPTER TWENTY-FOUR

OVERTHROWING UTOPIA
(FEBRUARY 1994)

Following the failed coup of August 1991 and the collapse of the Soviet system, Alexander Yakovlev, the theoretician of perestroika, published an impassioned condemnation of Marxism. Opting for democracy and moderation, he raised more questions than he answered about both the Old Regime and its successors.

Was Marxism invalidated by the collapse of Communism in the Soviet Union, as the conventional wisdom holds? It was not, for the simple reason that it had already been invalidated or proven irrelevant within the first few years of the Soviet experience.

As Alfred G. Meyer pointed out more than three decades ago,[1] Marxism contains two contradictory elements. One Marxism is the "scientific" vision of the inevitable course of history towards "socialism" and then "communism"; the other is a call for revolutionary struggle to make the inevitable come true. Marxism was never intended to be a blueprint for the future society; hence the lack of practical guidance for legislating a socialist society into existence. The laws of history would take care of things.

But what would happen if—as events turned out—Marxism as scientific prognosis turned out to be wrong? If Marxists continued their revolutionary efforts to make their utopian vision come true, this could then lead to an altogether unexpected, and even unwanted, outcome. In fact, Marxism in the scientific sense did prove to be wrong in many vital respects. It was wrong in predicting proletarian revolution in the capitalist West, and it was equally wrong in failing to anticipate Marxist-inspired revolution in countries thought to be too backward for socialism, such as Russia and China (unless one takes the position, as some Social Democrats have, that the Russian Revolution was not at all the kind that Marx predicted). Marxism was wrong in playing down the political force of religions and of ethnic and national differences. It was highly simplistic about the division of modern society into classes, and it was fundamentally wrong about the proletariat as the successor to the entrepreneurial class or "bourgeoisie"; if there has been any definable trend in this century either through democratic evolution or through revolutionary dictatorship, it is the movement toward what Milovan Djilas labelled as rule by the "New Class," or what James Burnham described as the "managerial revolution."[2]

As a genuine experiment in Russia, Marxism lasted no more than six months. The whole subsequent history of Soviet Russia was a struggle for survival in a hostile world, and for personal and oligarchic power over a beaten-down country. After Lenin seized power during a revolution that he did not start and that his Marxist theory failed to map out correctly, his Bolsheviks imagined for a time that they would make the Marxist vision come true by force and despite Russia's unpromising circumstances. By 1921 Lenin realized that this would never succeed, and proclaimed in the New Economic Policy a course of gradual evolution toward socialism. In turn, Stalin rejected this direction (while deifying his predecessor), and built a system of militarized industrialism ruled by terror that had nothing in common with the Marxist utopia.

What actually became of Marxism under the revolutionary rule of the Russian Communists? In Alexander Yakovlev's words, Marxist doctrine was converted by "coercive manipulation" into "a pseudo-neo-religion" to legitimize—fraudently—"the interests and caprices" of a "monopolistic, absolutist power," a new bureaucracy fitting into the Russian tradition of absolutism and fashioning a new society of total militarization.[3] Marxism thus became a new form of "false consciousness," in the phrase coined by Friedrich Engels.

Yakovlev's thoughts are important because he was the chief architect of *perestroika* under Gorbachev. He had already become a highly placed figure in the Communist *nomenklatura*: chief of propaganda, and then ambassador to Canada, where his doubts, perhaps seeded as an exchange student at Columbia University, may have matured. Gorbachev elevated him rapidly to chief of propaganda again in 1985, member of the party Secretariat in 1986, and in 1987 member of the Politburo, where he became the strongest voice for *glasnost* and reform. *The Fate of Marxism in Russia* is the record of his efforts to define the philosophical defects of Communist doctrine and the responsibility he believes it bore both for the horrors of Stalinism and for the failure of Gorbachev's efforts to reform the Communist system from within.

Like most people steeped all their lives in the mendacious dogma of Stalinism, Yakovlev is not entirely consistent about the relation that Marxist theory has to Soviet reality—whether utopian drive or false consciousness. He shares the assumption common among both Communists and anti-Marxists that Marxism led to Leninism and Leninism led to Stalinism in an inexorable progression. By this reasoning, any anti-Lenin Marxist was a weak Marxist and any anti-Stalin Leninist was a false Leninist. Thus, it is the embrace of a dangerous doctrine that is held accountable for dangerous behavior, like a religious heresy, though Yakovlev concedes that fanatical and authoritarian features of the Russian tradition supported the choice of an extremist creed.

Along with the Polish philosopher Leszek Kolakowski, among others, Yakovlev maintains that Marxist doctrine, with its fusion of determinism and messianism, serves uniquely to exclude ethics from politics and to justify the employment of the most inhuman means to serve a noble as well as inevitable goal. This commitment to ruthless struggle to achieve what is going to happen anyway is illogical, but it is true psychologically for the Bolshevik type of fanatical and authoritarian personality. The analogy with early Calvinism and the doctrine of predestination has often been cited. Logically, people who embrace a determinist doctrine should be completely passive. Otherwise they have to contradict themselves as the Communists do. For the latter, Marxist determinism was only an excuse for furious action, and the logical contradiction had to be concealed at the cost of suppressing all independent thought about the doctrine.

The philosophical dangers that Yakovlev now sees in Marxism include the materialist denigration of individual creativity and moral values, and "reductionism" of human affairs to abstract "essences," along with the failed predictions that everyone is now aware of. He aims, he says, not to establish the "responsibility" or "guilt" of Marxism, but rather at "understanding ourselves . . . , how and why our country followed this particular social messianism and what become of it."[4]

The consequences for Russia of this Marxist choice, Yakovlev contends, were catastrophic, as Marx's Bolshevik disciples attempted to bring his utopia to life at the cost of terrible oppression and degradation and the militarization of society. "The Marxist program of eliminating the market and market relations proved in fact to be a program to destroy the pillars of human civilization."[5] Conceding that barracks socialism found receptive soil in the Russian statist tradition, he holds that the socialist idea is now exhausted and that capitalism is the only alternative in order to continue human progress.

Reflecting on the unfolding of reform under Gorbachev and the stumbling blocks left in its path by the authoritarian Marxist heritage, Yakovlev takes note of the internal weaknesses of the old regime—its loss of "spiritual monopoly," general awareness of "ideological fraud, a coerced world view," the difficulty of controlling the proliferating interests of regions and specialists, and the temptations of corruption. In fact, "Perestroika was many years too late" for a new idealism to take charge.[6] Under Gorbachev it went too slowly. Under his successor it went too fast, and Russia never ceased to suffer.

Yakovlev had largely completed *The Fate of Marxism in Russia* before the August Coup of 1991; in fact, he acknowledged the project at a caucus of reformist delegates to the Twenty-Eighth Party Congress in July 1990, and opined, "If I publish those pages *now*, I'll be hanged from the nearest tree."[7] He finished the book early in 1992, lamenting the breakup of the Soviet Union, though he says nothing directly about the new Yeltsin government of Russia. (Yeltsin is not even in his index.) In a contemporaneous speech Yakovlev continued his assault on the collectivist utopia, with more explicit recognition of the input from the Russian tradition of authoritarian violence. However, he also warned of the counterutopia of pure capitalist individualism untamed by humanistic ethics.[8] His hope for Russia and the world is a rational, pluralistic, and ethical balance of the individual and the collective.

Yakovlev constantly polemicizes against utopianism and any attempts to impose utopia forcibly and dogmatically, which he holds to be the essence of Communist rule in Russia from Lenin to Andropov and Chernenko. He takes it for granted that Stalinism was only a more frenetic form of Leninism, both being driven by the commitment to compel an ideology to come true, regardless of the circumstances and no matter at what cost. Much of this thinking Yakovlev outlined earlier, on the two-hundredth anniversary of the French Revolution, when he compared the Bolsheviks with the Jacobins in deciding "to use the means of terror not only to put an end to counterrevolutionary activities, but also to stimulate the processes involved in building a new society. A cruel price had to be paid for these mistakes, for the immorality of pseudorevolutionary behavior."[9]

Along with this lament there is a strong second theme in Yakovlev, namely the exercise of ethics and common sense to work out a civilized future, avoiding the dogmatic extremes of capitalist individualism and communist collectivism. Without saying so directly, he had become a social democrat and an adherent of the mixed economy, as well as an enemy of all forms of authoritarianism and monopolies of thought.

Yakovlev recounts how painful it is to break with the past, and, for him, particularly from the Marxist past, because it embodied the inspiring socialist idea. However, he does not quite clarify the distinction between socialism in general, in its wide variety, and the particular creed of Marxism. Orthodox Marxism captured the European socialist movement as a whole only very briefly at the turn of the century, before revisionism began to water it down in the West and Bolshevism built on its most extreme implications in the East. Yakovlev would no doubt agree that by identifying socialism with the horrors of revolutionary dictatorship in a cruel and authoritarian country, the Russian Revolution was the worst thing that could have happened to that ideal.

Chapter Twenty-Five

The Limits of Federalism and the Collapse of the USSR (April 1992)

The Soviet Union was liquidated in favor of a "Commonwealth of Independent States" on 8 December 1991 by an agreement among the presidents of Russia (Yeltsin), Ukraine (Leonid Kravchuk), and Belarus (Stanislav Shushkevich), meeting secretly at the governmental retreat of Belovezhsk near Minsk in Belarus. This decision was the outcome of many factors—the multinational character of the Russian Empire and the urge for self-determination among its minorities, the pseudo-federalism of the Soviet system, the new democratization, and the rivalry between Yeltsin and Gorbachev. The path of federalism having failed, the Soviet successor states faced an uncertain future.

The collapse of the Communist Party of the Soviet Union and the liquidation of the Union itself in 1991 are generally regarded both in the former Soviet republics and in the West as triumphs of democracy and national self-determination. These views are at best oversimplifications.

Whatever other judgments one may make about it, the breakup of the Soviet Union was a failure of federalism. The conception and experience of federalism in the Soviet Union were inadequate, and in any case the circumstances challenging the federalist experiment of the era of *perestroika* might have overwhelmed even the best-conceived institutions of federalism.

The great impediment to successful federalism in the Soviet Union was the diverse ethnic makeup of the country, the very reason for the nominally federal structure of the Communist regime. Whenever the Russian center was weakened by revolutionary events or democratic reforms—in 1905, in 1917, and again under perestroika—the automatic response of the minorities was to strive for independence. To them, democracy has meant above all the opportunity to escape from Russian rule, while this prospect in turn has raised doubts about democracy among the Russians if the result were to dismantle the Empire and topple Russia from the ranks of the major world powers.

In contrast to the avowed centralism of the tsarist state, the Soviet regime attempted in its early years to come to terms with the multinational character of the country by adopting on paper a federal system of government. This was formalized in the establishment of the Union of

Soviet Socialist Republics in 1924, though all of its entities, Russian and minority alike, were governed by the totally centralized dictatorship of the Communist Party, whose members running the union republics and other jurisdictions were appointed by and worked under the discipline of the party leadership in Moscow. Thus the federal structure of the USSR was an utter sham. Nevertheless, with the reforms of perestroika, the dummy federalism of the USSR came to life, and the union republics and the lesser nationality units became the political framework within which the forces of minority separatism were expressed.

Though the Communist leadership cultivated the myth of the Soviet Union as a genuine multinational state, distinct from its Russian component, in fact the center has always been a Russian center, under the Empire, under the Soviet system, and today. In this context we cannot really speak of the "collapse" of the USSR. The Russian center is still intact. What has happened in the last couple of years has not been a "collapse" but rather a struggle for power at the center, and a weakening of the center's control over the non-Russian periphery.

Nowhere in the Russian experience, unfortunately, has there been any awareness of the fundamental principle of federalism: the distribution of different powers among the various levels of government (not to be confused with the separation of powers among the legislative, executive, and judicial authorities at any level). Whenever a lower jurisdiction could assert its independence against the higher, as in 1917 and again after 1989, it would try to assert unlimited "sovereignty," lay claim to all public property within its boundaries, and defy all outside authority. Among the union republics after 1989 this attitude led to the so-called "war of laws," as republics acted to suspend the application to their territory of Union legislation that was not to their taste. The dispute recalled the nullification controversy in the USA before the Civil War, when several Southern states defied federal legislation infringing on their interests concerning slavery, the tariff, and "states' rights" in general.

As the American example illustrates, the question of demarcating the powers of the federal and local authorities is not an easy one to answer. Yet a clear resolution is vital to the effective functioning of a federal system. And it was just such a clear resolution that was so conspicuously lacking in the Soviet experiment in federalism under perestroika. Neither the Union government nor the republics had any sense of the limits on their own authority imposed by the sharing of jurisdiction with the other level. Some of the trouble went back to the pre-perestroika regime and its failure to observe even the forms of federalism in certain key areas, notably taxation and the judiciary. Executive functions were complicated by the distinction among all-union ministries (heavy industry, transport, etc.); republic ministries (health, education, local industry); and "union-republican" ministries (finance, agriculture, the police, social services, and foreign affairs—Stalin's idea in 1945 to get more UN seats), where the ministry at the republic level functioned as a branch of the Union ministry—something like Social Welfare and Employment Security in American practice.

Other weaknesses of Soviet federalism were rooted in the attempt to accommodate the national minorities without compromising the power of the Russian center. The basis of the primary units, the union republics, was not a division into roughly equivalent territorial entities, as in American or German federalism, but ethnicity (as marked by language). This left the Russian Republic as one entity overwhelming all the others. Any system of representation in a central government would either give the Russians domination (if by population) or diminish them absurdly (if by republic), though until Gorbachev's reforms this quandary was not felt because the Supreme Soviet in Moscow was representative (one house by population, the other by nationality) only pro forma. Matters would have been quite different if there were no parallel government of the Russian Republic in Moscow, and the Russian part of the USSR had been divided into regions—ten or twelve can readily be suggested, as some Russian constitutional theorists have proposed—roughly equivalent in power and importance to the non-Russian republics. Then there could have been no question of dissolving the Union government, even if certain non-Russian republics ultimately decided to secede.

The surge of minority nationalism after the electoral reforms of 1989 quickly altered the federalism issue and made it rather one of confederation at best. The demands posed by the non-Russian republics—separate currencies, separate military forces, independence from the legislative competence of the Union parliament—pushed the terms of the argument to the confederal extreme even before the August Coup.

This direction was clear in the "Union Treaty" finally drawn up in March 1991 and accepted in principle in the "Novo-Ogarevo Agreement" of the "nine plus one" in April 1991. The treaty—the document that was scheduled to be formally signed the day after the August Coup was launched—was intended to replace the coercive treaty of 1922 that created the USSR, and to provide the basis for a new Union constitution. Its language leaned heavily to the rights of the republics, "sovereign states" that "possess full state power" and "retain the right to the independent resolution of all questions of their development."[1] But in the assignment of powers to the Union and the republics the Union Treaty was so vague and confusing that it would be a nightmare for an American constitutional lawyer. The draft specified the logical Union responsibilities— defense, state security, foreign policy, communications, the space program—but promised the republics a share in formulating policy for all these areas, while putting the bulk of governmental responsibilities for the economy and social policy in the hands of "the USSR . . . in conjunction with the republics." Then, as though to compensate, it declared, "Republic laws have supremacy on all questions, with the exception of those falling within the Union's jurisdiction." The new Constitutional Court was supposed to sort all this out if disputes arose.

The stakes in the struggle over federation or confederation were raised by the socialized character of the Soviet economy, where all industry and natural resources were state-owned. If the republics were to gain preeminent powers, this would include ownership of the economic assets within their borders. There was no clear formula to determine what properties, if any, should remain the domain of the Union government. Yet the Soviet economy was actually highly integrated and centralized, a system which would be—and in fact was—grievously disrupted by the independence of the republics. Generally speaking, within any economic entity, planned or market, that operates as an undivided whole, it is unrealistic to speak of significant economic powers for lower levels of government. This is equally true for the American federal system, where, states' rights ideology to the contrary notwithstanding, states cannot exert economic power against nationwide business organizations or even tax them as they might wish. If, as the Soviet republics demanded, lower entities were to get real control over their respective economies, this would—and did—doom the functioning of the overall Soviet economy as a single unit.

Perhaps a distinctive line between federation and confederation is the right of a constituent entity to secede. To be sure, union republics had the right to secede under the Stalin Constitution, but anyone who took it seriously was purged. The issue was forced by the new anti-Communist Baltic governments that were elected democratically in 1990, and Gorbachev refused to face it squarely. He referred to a complex process of secession, subject to a Union-wide referendum, and made it clear that he would do anything within the terms of his democratized system—or even outside those terms—to prevent a republic from seceding. This attitude led him to order or condone military and economic action against separatists in Georgia in 1989 and in Lithuania in 1990 and again in early 1991. He responded to calls for "sovereignty" by alleging "fascistic tendencies," "superfragmentation and chaos," and "furious attempts to discredit the institutions of state power which embody the idea of a federal union state."[2] Alarm about the separatism that his own reforms had unleashed was undoubtedly the major factor in Gorbachev's shift toward the party conservatives in the winter of 1990–91.

At Novo-Ogarevo, in the course of his zig-zag back towards reform, Gorbachev accepted language affirming the right of republics to secede, or to become independent if they declined to sign the treaty. Interestingly,

the nine signatories at Novo-Ogarevo were the Slavic and Moslem republics where Communists and ex-Communists remained in command even
after the August Coup; the six non-signers were the non-Slavic-speaking
European republics led (except for Moldova) by former anti-Communist
dissidents. In any case, the prospect of the actual or virtual dissolution
of the Union pursuant to the treaty was anathema to the Communist
conservatives, and appeared as a major item on the agenda of the August
plotters against Gorbachev: "The confrontation between nationalities and
the chaos and anarchy that are threatening the lives and security of the
citizens of the Soviet Union and the sovereignty, territorial integrity, freedom and independence of our fatherland. . . . A mortal danger threatens
our homeland . . . , the breakup of the state."[3] But even at the end,
Gorbachev himself was unreconciled to the breakup of the Union. "I
suppport the preservation of the union state and the integrity of this
country," he said in his resignation statement on 25 December 1991.
"Developments took a different course. The policy prevailed of dismem-
bering this country and disuniting the state, which is something I cannot
subscribe to."[4]

The survival of the Union, dubious enough between the pressures of
minority separatism and the weakness of any conception of federalism,
was further threatened by the emergence of purely political considerations. These involved two elements, one institutional, the other personal.
The institutional element was the existence of the huge Russian Republic,
the main body of the Union with its capital in Moscow like the capital of
the Union as a whole. As long as the governments of the union republics,
Russia included, were mere appendages of the Russian-dominated Communist Party, this division created no problem. But once Gorbachev
began democratization in 1989, the possibility arose for what Lenin called
"dual power" in Moscow, and an automatic struggle for power between
the Union and Russian governments.

The potential institutional conflict quickly became a personal political
contest, as the former Moscow party secretary Boris Yeltsin returned from
the political wilderness to challenge his former leader Gorbachev. Gorbachev's failure to promote Yeltsin to full member of the Politburo in June
1987 accounts for the latter's futile defiance in the fall of that year. Yeltsin
has repeatedly referred back to 1987 as the point when Gorbachev "began
to go wrong" and "began . . . deceiving the people."[5] The record since
that time suggests a firm determination on Yeltsin's part to settle scores.

Yet in the spirit of his new democratization program Gorbachev had
to leave Yeltsin free to speak out and to run in March 1989 for a seat in
the Congress of People's Deputies, which he won triumphantly as a voice
for accelerated reform. A year later, after the series of more fully democratic elections in the union republics, the radical reformers advanced

Yeltsin as a candidate for the chairmanship of the newly democratized Supreme Soviet of the Russian Republic. Gorbachev campaigned vehemently against him, but took no steps contrary to his own new constitution to stop his rival.

Once in command of the Russian Republic, Yeltsin worked consistently to undermine Gorbachev's power as president of the Union. His approach was simple—to support the calls for "sovereignty" on the part of all the union republics, including his own, thereby curbing the authority of the Union government and enhancing the authority of his own alternative regime in Moscow. It did not matter that for Russia to be "sovereign" against a Russian-dominated Union was to be sovereign against itself, a patent absurdity. Russian "sovereignty" within the old structure of the Union could only mean Russian non-sovereignty over the other republics. The real question was which Russian government, under which Russian leader, would prevail. To win, Yeltsin was willing to pay the price, for the time being, of dissolving the authority of the Russian center exercised by Gorbachev's Union government. This process was underway well before the August Coup, and directly underlay the final collapse of Union authority that followed the coup attempt.

After the August Coup, Yeltsin moved relentlessly to liquidate the Union government, while Gorbachev tried to sustain its ebbing life by reviving his project of the Union Treaty. The decisive undoing of this hope was the matter of taxation. Revenues had been transferred to the republics, who were then supposed to share Union expenses, including the armed forces. Literally bankrupt, Gorbachev was helpless to resist Yeltsin's physical takeover of Union government ministries and assets, even the Kremlin itself. Finally came the Belovezhsk Agreement of 8 December between Russia, Ukraine, and Belarus to declare the Soviet Union dissolved. This was a coup d'état no less real than the Communist coup of October 1917, technically preempting the rights of the nine other remaining members of the Union, though in fact none of them objected.

There is a curious parallel between the events of 1917 that brought the Communist regime into being, and the events of 1991 that put an end to it. Kerensky's Provisional Government faced the Bolshevik-controlled Petrograd Soviet in a situation of dual power, just as Gorbachev's Union government faced Yeltsin's Russian government and the radical reformers. Before the Bolsheviks ever acted, Kerensky lost virtually all popular confidence as support drained away to the left and to the right—just as Gorbachev's support had drained away. There is even a parallel between the August Coup, crippling Gorbachev politically, and the abortive right-wing coup led by the chief of staff, General Lavr Kornilov, in August 1917, which was equally damaging to Kerensky. After the 1991 coup attempt, it was as easy for Yeltsin to step in as it had been for Lenin, when, as the latter said, he found power lying in the streets, and picked it up.

Ironically, once Yeltsin had disposed of Gorbachev and the Union, he found himself face to face with the same urges and problems. Under the umbrella of the "Commonwealth of Independent States" he hoped to maintain some semblance of Russian influence over the former Union, with emphasis on the minimal features of a confederation, namely the military, the currency, and foreign relations. He took it as a matter of course that the Russian government should inherit the position of the Soviet Union in international matters, including the embassies abroad, treaty obligations, and the UN Security Council seat. Yet he had gone so far in advancing the sovereignty of the republics against Gorbachev that there was no restraining them now, certainly not Ukraine with its assertion of complete economic independence and its claim on an independent share of the Commonwealth's armed forces. At the same time, Yeltsin was confronted within the Russian Federation with a series of separatist movements among the smaller minorities—notably the Tatars and the Chechen-Ingush—analogous to those that had challenged Gorbachev in the Union at large. Toward these movements within the Russian Federation Yeltsin has proved so far to be an even more adamant centralist than Gorbachev (though not enough to satisfy the Russian nationalists in his entourage, led by Vice President Alexander Rutskoi). His "Federation Treaty" between the Russian government and its subordinate minority units, the autonomous republics, has run into all the problems that Gorbachev's Union Treaty encountered.

Yeltsin's position after the breakup of the Union lends some credence to the notion that his embrace of sovereignty for the union republics was as much a matter of expediency as of principle. Nor has he consistently observed the principles of federalism in dealing with the Russian provinces under his rule, though in many cases they had also asserted powers of local self-government well before the August Coup. He responded immediately to the coup by dispatching his personal representatives to the Russian provinces to impose his authority over the local Communists who, ironically, hoped to use their "states' rights" to survive politically. Unfortunately, Yeltsin's methods remind the historian of the manner in which Stalin built his apparatus of personal power in the 1920s.

The circumstances of the Soviet Union in 1991 cried for a federal solution. Genuine federalism, made possible by the dismantling of the Communist Party dictatorship, would have given the minorities full scope for cultural self-expression. At the same time it could have avoided the divisive concept of citizenship based on ethnicity rather than territory, a principle that implied second-class citizenship for the sub-minorities present in every ethnic subdivision because of the historic mixing of nationalities. Federalism could have maintained the union-wide economy and avoided barriers among highly interdependent regions. It would have allowed institutions of democratic local administration to be fashioned more gradually and more constructively. It would have avoided the unnerving problems of dividing the Soviet armed forces while trying to maintain some form of responsible control over the nuclear weapons stockpile, and it would have preserved the Soviet Union, despite all its problems, as a more influential and less troublesome power on the international scene.

Yet the obstacles to successful federalism were daunting, given the urges of long-suppressed nationalism colliding with the old habits of centralism, as well as the defects in the federal structure that the reformers inherited. More statesmanship in all quarters might have made a difference. If Gorbachev had been more flexible toward the nationalities at an earlier point in perestroika, if Yeltsin had not chosen to use the Russian Republic as a weapon against Gorbachev, if some of the ex-Communist leaders in the other republics had not yielded to the political pressure to outdo former dissident nationalists, the federal—or confederal—union might have been preserved, at least with its essential powers in defense, money matters, and foreign relations. In the absence of these might-have-beens, the democratized Union was a lost cause, and the individual Soviet republics were left to cope with each other and with the outside world under very unpromising circumstances.

CHAPTER TWENTY-SIX

IS SOVIETOLOGY DEAD TOO?
(SEPTEMBER 1991)

The August Coup and the overthrow of Communist Party rule in the Soviet republics immediately made it plain that the West would have to reconsider its assumptions about the whole region. This was a moment for rethinking the propositions of sovietology and developing new approaches to the understanding of the former Soviet realm, even as Russia plunged into a new utopian experiment.

The spectacular collapse of Communist governments from the Elbe to Vladivostok is going to have an equally earthshaking effect in those Western and particularly American academic circles devoted to the sometimes occult discipline known as sovietology. Sovietology may be defined as the scholarly study, in political science and closely related fields, of the Soviet system of power and of other Communist regimes planted by Moscow or copied from it. For decades it has been a flourishing academic industry. Now its reason for being has been wiped out.

Sovietology has become the victim not only of events but of its own rigorous conclusions. It targeted an odious but presumably immutable adversary of the Western way of life, and explained that hostile system by constructing a rigid, schematic model of its characteristics and behavior. The Soviet system was totalitarian, like the right-wing dictatorships of Hitler and Mussolini, only more so; it was driven by a relentless ideology of utopian transformation; it was managed by a centralized bureaucracy in which power-hungry individuals battled for primacy behind the façade of official unanimity; it was locked in an unyielding contest with the West—the Cold War—for world supremacy. Now all this is gone, and going with it is the whole school of sovietological analysis, bereft of anything more to do.

Or rather, the subject-matter of sovietology, ceasing to be a present reality, will be consigned to history, where it can live on like any other ghoulish curiosity in the museum of the past. But this transference to history will require a rethinking of all the sovietological models, to recast them from seeming permanence into the time dimension, a mode of thinking not particularly congenial to American social science. In other words, we now have to understand totalitarianism, ideology, bureaucratic behavior, international confrontation, as political patterns rooted in particular historical situations, that rise, flourish, and then—under new circumstances—decline and collapse. We have to recognize the connection between totalitarianism and revolution, for instance; the roots of revolution when a country's social and economic development outruns its government; the changing meaning and function of Marxist ideology over the long history of "communism"; and the multifarious factors in international conflict that antedate and survive the Soviet Union.

❖   ❖   ❖

To say that Communist totalitarianism is now history (apart from some of its Asian and Third-World variants) does not mean that it has become exclusively a subject of academic contemplation. The totalitarian past has bequeathed a unique and complex legacy to the formerly Communist societies. Their problems and potential cannot be properly understood, either by themselves or by outsiders, without ongoing reference to this background. Nor will it be very enlightening merely to invoke this background to blame it for every sort of pain and difficulty that post-Communist societies may experience.

The challenge to rethink the propositions of sovietology in historical terms is compounded by the emotional need expressed by more and more people in Eastern Europe and the Soviet republics to purge themselves of the entire experience of Communism since 1917. To give one example, the new "classical" high school just now opening in Leningrad/St. Petersburg will not teach the history of the Soviet period *at all!* Understandably, the former subjects of Communism would like to regard that epoch as one long dark night that suddenly fell and just as suddenly lifted, and not concern themselves about the circumstances that contributed to the Soviet model in its creation, its development, and its decline. Many Easterners, steeped all their lives in the ideological pretenses of Soviet-style regimes, now look back on that period just as many sovietologists have, as the undiluted reign of a perverse ideology. They thus risk creating a mammoth new "blank spot" in their nations' historical consciousness, possibly equalling the blank spots and black holes that marked the Communists' own version of the past.

A major example of the new historical blindness is the abandonment of any distinction between Lenin's revolution and Stalin's, between the Bolsheviks' original utopian drive, however fanatic and misguided it may have been, and the reactionary militarized despotism that Stalin later created in the name of that utopia. The Russian Revolution, animated by socialism, ultimately generated a disgusted rejection of anything going by that name. This has left the new societies of the East with no model to guide their quest for human betterment, other than narrow nationalism and the tender mercies of the free market, a utopia of another kind.

Sovietologists for years charged themselves with the responsibility of keeping alive the true historical record of the Communist countries. Now, potentially, a new but analogous task may be presenting itself to Western scholars. This is to preserve an objective understanding of the Communist past and its relevance to the post-Communist present, if a new anti-Communist orthodoxy in Eastern Europe and the Soviet republics should lead to its own distortions and oversimplifications. To accomplish this mission, Western scholars may themselves have to restrain the urge to exult over the demise of the Old Regime and embrace its successors uncritically. The challenge is to sustain critical thought under all circumstances, not just in the direction of what was perceived to have been a Communist revolutionary threat.

It was among the Mensheviks and other Social Democrats, in the United States and in Europe, that the earliest realistic and time-tested appraisal of the phenomenon of Communism emerged. This was no accident: Sharing some of the philosophical background of Bolshevism, the moderate Left could see clearly how personal fanaticism plus the inhospitable circumstances of Russian backwardness led step by step to the total departure of the Soviet dictatorship from its initial revolutionary inspiration, saving the latter only as a cynically imposed false consciousness. Social Democrats have never had any trouble distinguishing between Communist propaganda and Communist reality (so often confused on the left) or between the Soviet model and the real issues of social reform in Western societies (so often obfuscated on the right).

The demise of the system that sovietology thought it would be analyzing and critiquing indefinitely does not, of course, eliminate the need for Western study and understanding of the nations of the former Communist realm, as regards their present problems and future prospects as well as their pasts. The matters that will most challenge our skill and our intuition are obvious. We will need to track the evolving forms of the new political and economic systems in the ex-Communist lands, appraising how well they adapt to Western notions of democracy and market economics, and unfortunately, how they may lapse into authoritarianism and autarchy. We will have to follow with great care the newly released passions of ethnicity and nationalism, with their potential for regression to the worst of pre-Communist times that we can observe already in Yugoslavia and in Transcaucasia. It has long been clear that suppressed ethnic aspirations were the Achilles Heel of democratization in the Soviet Union and in the bloc, threatening to exploit any loosening of the Kremlin's rule and thereby provoke the Russians to abandon reform and crack down. At least this turned out to be true for the older generation of Communist leaders in their desperate coup of August.

The urge to assert old national identities is not unique to Eastern Europe by any means. We can see in American society and all over the world that ethnic distinctiveness has taken the place of the class struggle as the current wellspring of political radicalism. But in the old Communist realm, ethnic conflicts have a special history which only outsiders, in all probability, can save from the morass of inter-ethnic recrimination and apologetics.

The mood in the West today is understandably one of self-congratulation on the seeming triumph of its values over Communism. The tradition of sovietology, by contrast, has been to probe the basic differences between East and West and try to explain them in terms of institutions, cultures, and ideologies. This more skeptical approach, leavened with a strong measure of history, will stand us in good stead if and when democratic experiments in the East begin to go awry.

Democracy is still at risk all over the East bloc. Students of Russian history have often noted the pattern of Russian political culture, among a people who break out in ungovernable fits of anarchy whenever the hand of the authoritarian center is lightened, while passively submitting betweentimes. On a small scale the defiant outburst, the *bunt*, was the endemic history of prerevolutionary peasant revolts and urban riots; on the grand scale it was the "Time of Troubles" of 1604–1613 and the revolutions of 1905 and 1917. Now we may be seeing the same phenomenon again, in the radical decentralization and defiance of authority set off by the failed conservative coup. How far this anti-authoritarian reflex may go and what it will do to the former Soviet republics we cannot yet say, but a sovietological and historical perspective can at least alert us to the problem.

To take another example of the hazards of reform, the competitive market economy in the productive sense (excluding bazaar trading and sheer speculation) has little cultural foundation in Russia, where the state has always been the engine of economic development. Neither Soviet reformers nor their Western cheerleaders have taken this background properly into account. Reform, too much and too fast, has unfortunately contributed to one of the most abrupt economic setbacks that any country has ever experienced short of invasion and physical devastation. This is a point where the complaints of the Communist conservatives have some merit. It is not that Russians and their neighbors do not want freedom, economic as well as political—they do, desperately, so desperately that they risk turning its advent into their own undoing.

Perhaps the greatest fault that can retrospectively be attributed to sovietology was to overestimate grossly the strength of the Soviet bloc, in its physical and economic capabilities as well as in its political cohesion and its psychological stamina. Much of this error resides in the unhistorical totalitarian model and its ideological corollaries. Totalitarianism was supposed to mean the maximum mobilization of a nation's resources to crush opposition, sustain the regime, and support its international adventures. But the theory distorted the appraisal of Soviet reality. The totalitarian model as popularized by Hannah Arendt drew more from the Nazi experience than from the Soviet.[1] German culture was in fact far more adapted to efficient performance under strict control than was Russian, and we know from post-World War II studies how inefficient even the Nazi administration was. Without denying the horrors of purges, camps, and genocide, scholars as diverse as Moshe Lewin and J. Arch Getty have demonstrated how clumsily, erratically, and inefficiently totalitarian controls functioned at the everyday level of Soviet life.[2]

Sovietology erred further by not taking sufficient account of the changes wrought in Soviet society under the totalitarian regime, including industrial growth, urbanization, and mass education. The resulting revolution of rising expectations was met with corrupt indifference and immobilism on the part of an aging Stalinist and neo-Stalinist leadership. Tensions grew everywhere between the expanding professional and intellectual class and the bullheaded controllers of the party *nomenklatura*. Here was the old recipe for revolution, as the Soviet system sowed the seeds of its own destruction. Sovietology took seriously the "New Soviet Man," whom we now know to have been a total fiction of Communist propaganda; the only "new" types were the grafters, sycophants, and bribe-takers in the nomenklatura. By the end of the Brezhnev era, the vast majority of people at all levels and among all nationalities were utterly fatigued with the old system and consumed by disbelief, while discipline sagged everywhere from the factory floor to the demands of "socialist realism" in the arts. Post-Stalinist Communism was a stultifying shell, waiting to be pushed off its wall. "We can breath now," was the universal response once Gorbachev had set democratization in motion and shattered the old restraints.

Our problems with the countries of the old East bloc are not over, even if they will reside at a far lower level of concern than the nuclear standoff with what we used to think of as the Soviet superpower. These nations will not easily resolve the political, economic, and ethnic problems that confront them as they emerge from the pressure cooker of neo-Stalinist Communism. Sovietologists, in their altered identity as practitioners of Russian and East European studies, will have a new role as interpreters to bridge the gap between West and East. As educated citizens of the West who also enjoy expertise on the East, they are the only people who can really explain Western values and institutions to the Easterners. They can translate Western advice into the Eastern context, and explain the inevitable limitations and perversities of the East to the sometimes hesitant aid-givers in the West. Thanks to their experience in critiquing ideologies, sovietologists are also in a position to filter out the utopian aspects of Western free-market ideology accompanying aid programs. To date, unfortunately, they have not been used as much as they might in the important and sensitive job of communicating Western solutions to the ex-Communist world.

Sovietology is not yet dead and it must not die. But it has to change and recognize that many of its most cherished propositions are time-bound and have been shunted from the foreground into the background. This is not to diminish the role of Russian and East European studies; we need the background of historical and cultural insight in order to under-stand the former bloc and the transformation it is going through. Soviet-ologists are the people trained to do this, and their special lore, with new content, will continue to be indispensable as we strive to communicate with a part of the world that has won our sympathy and admiration but may yet try our patience, our compassion, and our generosity.

PART FIVE

RUSSIA SEEKS SALVATION, 1992–1995

CHAPTER TWENTY-SEVEN

IN SEARCH OF A USABLE TRADITION (JULY 1992)

As Russia entered its post-Communist future in 1992 it faced a void in its philosophical sources of national identity. Westernism of the radical persuasion was ruled out by the reaction against Communism, and native traditionalism was ruled out by the realities of modernization. Apart from a strange alliance among the nostalgics who still clung to one or the other of these old positions, Russia's leaders saw no alternative to the free-market utopia of Western classical liberalism. Carried to an abstract (and thus very Russian) extreme, this became the guiding philosophy of the Yeltsin regime.

For three hundred years Russian thought has been impaled on the horns of a dilemma—tradition or modernity, faith or reason, the Russian way or the foreign way.

No person and no nation, of course, can exist without some measure of tradition. A country needs a sense of meaningful context, some faith in itself, even if it is trying to map out a new path for its future. But Russian tradition and Russian faith have been continuously assaulted, from within as well as from without, by those who find it wanting in the face of the challenges and opportunities posed by modern life. This predicament is by no means unique to Russia. Pulled backwards and forwards at the same time, between the nativists and the modernizers, Russia is a paradigm for that great part of the world that has found itself prodded into change by the alien models of the West.

What is, however, more nearly unique to Russia is the powerful form taken by the rejection of tradition and the embrace of Western norms. From the late eighteenth century on, this reaction became embodied in the Russian intelligentsia, understood broadly as the consumers as well as producers of books and ideas. Initially the more educated and critically-minded segment of the privileged aristocracy, the intelligentsia broadened its compass in the course of the nineteenth century to include the so-called *raznochintsy*, the "people from all ranks." Still, it sustained and even intensified its attachment to Western political and philosophical ideas and its sense of a mission to apply those ideas to Russia. It leaned steadily to the most advanced and radical ideas coming from the West— philosophical materialism, revolution, and socialism, culminating in Marxism.

Thus, the westernist reaction against native tradition before long gave

Russia a second philosophical tradition, based on the Enlightenment, rationalism, science, the Rights of Man, and revolution. This outlook was not, however, a representative mirroring of Western thought; it selected the most advanced, radical, and antitraditional elements in Western thought, and it embraced them in a distinctly un-Western, absolutist fashion. It developed an antireligious stance more extreme than Western anticlericalism, and an anticommercial socialism more uncompromising than most Western varieties—all this before Marx. Said N. V. Butashevich-Petrashevsky, organizer of the famous Petrashevsky Circle that included the young Dostoevsky when the police of Nicholas I put them behind bars, "The social science of the West has said the final word, has given us the forms in which the final development of mankind must be molded."[1] By the second half of the nineteenth century the intelligentsia had become the seedbed of a small but self-conscious and violent revolutionary movement.

To be sure, the intelligentsia was neither unanimous in its opinions nor monolithic in its actions. All along there was a countercurrent of nativism, initially represented by the so-called Slavophiles of the mid-nineteenth century, with their romantic attachment to a pre-Petrine vision of the peasants and the Church. Around the turn of the century there arose a distinctly new trend of thought, neither nativist nor conforming to the fashions of Western-style radicalism and materialism. It was expressed in the so-called Silver Age of Russian literature and had many affinities with the new schools of modernism in thought and culture in the West. Exemplified by the Symbolists in literature, and in political thought and philosophy by the *Vekhi* ("Signposts") group of one-time Marxists (Peter Struve, Mikhail Bulgakov, Nikolai Berdiaev, etc.),[2] the new school of thought stemmed mainly from westernizers among the intelligentsia who had second thoughts about revolution and science. Thus they expressed a traditionalism that was more ecumenical than native. While it hardly had time to become established as a new tradition in itself, this body of early twentieth-century thought has become a popular source of inspiration today for those who reject Communism, avoid nativism, and nevertheless look askance at the rationalist mainstream in the West.

❖   ❖   ❖

Russian philosophizing has rarely been as abstracted from the issues of human life in society as the metaphysical classics of Western thought have usually been. Russian philosophy could never avoid the primal question of salvation for Russia, whether this goal was to be achieved through religion, for the traditionalists, or through politics, for the modernizers. Westerners who think of philosophy in more ethereal terms must make a constant effort to keep this Russian preoccupation in mind. On the other hand, Russian thinking directed toward the worldly issues of society ran heavily toward the abstract and the theoretical in its approach, always seeking a grand scheme or magic formula that would resolve the destiny of Russia. Once these recurring features of Russian thought are understood, they help explain the succession of impassioned cleavages and ideological battles that have marked Russian intellectual life in the past and will inevitably do so in the future.

Ardent though the westernizing urge was, it was always vulnerable to surreptitious nativistic deviations, starting with the habit of turning selected Western ideas into abstract absolutes. Nativism welled up even in the patron saint of westernism, Alexander Herzen, who suffered exile by Nicholas I for his views, but then found the European object of his idealism to be wanting in the moral qualities that a Russian sought. Revolutionary socialism, initially inspired by Western theories, split in Russia between those—the Marxists—who were convinced that the country had to follow the Western stages of development through capitalism to proletarian revolution, and those—the *narodniki* or "Populists" and the Party of Socialist Revolutionaries—who believed that Russia could and should proceed in its own way to its own form of socialism based on the legendary collectivism of the peasant village. Then the Marxists split, between those—the Mensheviks—who adhered dogmatically to the Western Social-Democratic orthodoxy of achieving a bourgeois democratic revolution before attempting socialism, and those—the Bolsheviks—who embraced methods of conspiracy and terror out of the Russian revolutionary tradition in order to achieve socialism overnight. Repeatedly, a spirit of Russian messianism cropped up on the nativist side of each of these splits, among radicals convinced that Russia should export the true revolutionary spirit to the West. Eventually the Bolsheviks themselves split, or rather were shaved way, faction by faction, as Stalin liquidated all the genuine Marxists and internationalists, and fashioned his imperial despotism under the double-headed banner of Karl Marx and Peter the Great.

When we examine the Communist phenomenon objectively, without concessions to Stalin's ideological obfuscation, we must recognize that it was a complex synthesis of traditional and revolutionary elements. Furthermore, the Bolshevik Revolution was not an alien violation of all Russian tradition, as Alexander Solzhenitsyn, for example, would argue. Rather, it was the violent imposition of one particular Russian tradition, that of the modernizers, or more exactly the imposition of one variant of the modernizing tradition. This was a variant, as Nikolai Berdiaev pointed out long ago, that incorporated much of the nativist tradition in an unacknowledged way.[3] Under Stalin's aegis, again if we discount the labels, the nativism became paramount.

Looking back on the Communist experience in the context of alternative Russian traditions, we find a peculiar amalgam. Once it was remolded and stabilized by Stalin, Communism supplied its own tradition. In verbal form it rested on the Bolshevik, nativized version of the westernist-modernizing tradition, requiring all public discourse and all philosophical speculation to be conducted in the language of Marxism-Leninism. But in functioning as a substitute state religion with emphasis on liturgical correctness, Marxism-Leninism as codified and enforced by Stalin took a giant step back towards the nativist tradition of authority, faith, and national exclusivity—in other words, back to "autocracy, Orthodoxy, nationality." This was the tradition embraced by the Communist "conservatives" who resisted *perestroika* and backed the August Putsch. The notorious Andreyeva letter inspired by the conservatives to attack Gorbachev in 1988 defended Stalinist socialism with attacks on "militant cosmopolitanism," "pacifist erosion of defense and patriotic consciousness," and "nihilistic views" extending to "ideological omnivorousness."[4] In August 1991 the State Committee on the Emergency Situation promised to fight "chaos and anarchy" and to salvage "the sovereignty, territorial integrity, freedom and independence of our fatherland," without ever mentioning socialism or communism.[5] The parallel between these views and the nativist tradition that finally was able to express itself openly under perestroika helps explain the odd political affinity between Communist conservatives and old-fashioned conservatives that has marked the Russian political scene since the coup and the demise of the Communist Party.

❖   ❖   ❖

In Russia's response to the collapse of Communism there is a great paradox. Most of the country's leaders have understandably rejected the tradition that had been created by the Communists, and with it much of the older westernist-rationalist tradition that the Communists had appropriated, particularly as expressed in any concept of socialism and social engineering. On the other hand, the new leadership (mostly ex-Communist themselves) are much too modern in their outlook to return to the nativist tradition. In politics this has been left to the far-right fringe, including monarchists, anti-Semites, and Vladimir Zhirnovsky's so-called "Liberal-Democratic Party." Apart from these people, the new Russian democracy has dispensed with Russian tradition altogether, and has sought salvation in a new—actually very old—Western orthodoxy, namely classical liberalism and free-market economics. This is yet another example of Russians embracing a Western utopia, in this case more ancient than the socialist doctrines that the Russian intelligentsia found so attractive after the middle of the nineteenth century. Otherwise the only element of tradition that manifests a wide hold at the present time is nationalism, in the meanest sense of struggling to hold on to Russian hegemony against the aspirations for self-determination on the part both of the former union republics and of the remaining minorities within what is now called, pursuant to an impossible compromise, "The Russian Federation. Russia."

The rejection of the Communist past and the unacceptability or unreachability of the prerevolutionary past leave the leaders of the new Russian republic with no past at all to which it can orient itself. This void is neither inevitable nor incurable, but only a momentary consequence of the politics of dismantling Communism. Nevertheless Russia finds itself—or has chosen to place itself—in a position where it has no tradition of its own and no faith in itself by which to be guided, but only the borrowed terms of a Western doctrine which has been highly debatable for many decades in the West, and is to say the least anachronistic. To correct this deficiency, Russia needs to take a more discriminating look at many phases of its own experience. Only in so doing can it find the elements of tradition and faith, whether from the purely nativist pool of thought or from the successive varieties of westernism that have held intellectual sway in the country, that will give it the guideposts it needs to chart its future.

One example of such selective mining of the traditions of the past is the rediscovery of Stolypin, prime minister in the semiconstitutional government under Nicholas II from 1907 until his assassination in 1911. Stolypin is regarded by his admirers as the prototype of a capitalist path modernizer, albeit by authoritarian means. His example encourages those who talk of the need of a "Russian Pinochet" to manage the transition from socialism to capitalism (hopefully then yielding to a new democratic political process).[6] But this is just a new instance of a westernist idea being infiltrated by old Russian assumptions about the necessity of centralized authoritarian power to accomplish desirable social goals.

Another example of the search for usable tradition was the rediscovery of the New Economic Policy by the Gorbachevian reformers. They took the market socialism and the cultural laissez-faire policies of the pre-Stalin Communist government of the 1920s as their model for perestroika and *glasnost*, while still preserving the so-called "socialist choice" of the October Revolution. But Gorbachev's liberated Communism proved to be a contradiction in terms. It violated the substance of nativist tradition incorporated in the Stalinist form of Communism, and it was eventually crushed between the forces of Communist conservatism and anti-Communist outrage.

Identification of the whole Communist experience with Stalinist terror has not only left Russians disinclined to seek any usable tradition in the history of the Communist era, but threatens to turn the entire seventy-four years of Soviet rule into a historical black hole. This could leave Russians with no historical basis for comprehending their own modern society, vastly transformed for better or worse from what the Communists took over in 1917. These changes make much native Russian tradition—the village mystique, for instance—largely irrelevant as a practical matter, while anti-Communist sentiment rules out the quest for postrevolutionary sources of tradition. Hence the only place to turn is to the West, and to that version of Western thought which seems most opposed to the Communist tradition, i. e., the free-market ideology.

❖   ❖   ❖

The historical traditions outlined here offer at least five distinct sources of philosophical inspiration in addressing the problems that have always stood in the foreground of Russian thought. First is the truly nativist position of the Slavophiles. Second comes the classical Westernizer position of rationalism and revolution. Thirdly there is the neo-traditionalism of the immediate prerevolutionary years. Fourthly, not to be discounted, is the Communist (i.e. Stalinist) synthesis of westernizing ideas and language with nativist sentiments and dogmatic style. Finally there is the new fashion, hardly traditional at all in the Russian context, that we might call neo-westernism, harking back to the terms of classical liberalism that had failed to make much of a dent in the Russian psyche when they were originally proclaimed in the West.

It is interesting that even the latest ideas of neo-westernism have been colored by traditional Russian habits of mind, for example the abstract extremism of free-market doctrine under conditions of distress equivalent to wartime, when the West has always suspended its free-market convictions. An authoritarian style in advancing any political or philosophical position seems to be eternally popular. Then there are the doubts about current official programs, deeply rooted in old attitudes such as resistance to speculative commerce and private land ownership (i.e., as a salable commodity, in distinction to family use), and reactions against Western mass culture as corruption of superior Russian ethical values.

Russia confronts great problems in adjusting any and all of its traditional sources of thought to the realities of modern life, realities made much more pervasive by the social and economic changes—industrialization, urbanization, mass education, etc.—wrought under the Communists. It is impossible simply to go back to prerevolutionary traditions, no matter which one, for the political or philosophical answers to the problems posed by these realities. The religious revival may seem comforting, but it is accompanied by some of the most archaic and irrational cultural elements—astrology, faith healing, "drunken nationalism," and anti-Semitism, to mention a few—encouraged by the discrediting of Communism's artificial modernism. Nor is neo-westernism enough, rooted as it is in Western premises that have long since been outdated by the evolution of modern society. Somehow the rationalist tradition of consciously addressing social problems and mobilizing society's powers to deal with them must be cleansed of the Communist encrustations that have dragged it down. At the same time Russian abstractness and extremism must be tempered by a new appreciation of Western pragmatism. Hopefully this will not be too large an order in overcoming the burdens of the remote past and the scars of recent times.

CHAPTER TWENTY-EIGHT

BORIS YELTSIN AND THE NEW WORLD ORDER (JUNE 1992)

As president of the Russian Federation, after the liquidation of the USSR Yeltsin was chief executive of an independent country, a role he vigorously pursued in international affairs, in relations with the other former Soviet republics, and in free-market economic reforms. As opposition arose, however, he came into confrontation with the legislative branch of government and began to show authoritarian tendencies.

Boris Yeltsin came to life on the North American television screen when he visited Washington, Kansas, and Canada in mid-June 1992, and proved himself one of the world's most dynamic leaders. Still the hero of the August Coup and his country's post-Communist transformation, he demonstrated all the political skills that put him at the head of Russia's new revolution.

In Washington, there was the bold stroke—nuclear cuts beyond everything agreed on. There was the sensational spur-of-the-moment allusion to American prisoners in Russian camps and the promise to do all he could to find them—an offer that made his honesty seem so different from his predecessors, even though the archivists had already said they could not document the issue. And in Montreal, there was the folksy politician telling his audience of entrepreneurs, "Business people are the flower of all nations, who guard prosperity and transform dreams into reality, who see to the welfare of the people."[1]

With a little imagination one can make out a certain resemblance between Yeltsin and H. Ross Perot. Both are self-made men from the provinces who have risen high within the system, Communist or capitalist as the case may be. Both have scored tremendous popularity as outsiders preaching against the system. Both have a knack for the dramatic surprise, along with prickly personalities and authoritarian reflexes. Both find their respective countries in serious trouble, while each is short on specifics apart from scoring the errors of previous administrations.

Views of Yeltsin among Russians back up this comparison. He is widely considered to be rash and mercurial. *Moscow News* calls him "nervous, unpredictable, and difficult to understand even for his closest aides," and a man of "revolutionary temperament."[2] Yeltsin's background closely parallels that of his archrival Mikhail Gorbachev, though the ambitions and styles of the two clashed irreconcilably. Born in the same year as Gorbachev, 1931, Yeltsin also had village roots in a remote province (Sverdlovsk, in the Urals). Like Gorbachev, he entered the professional service of the Communist Party, though much later and, it seems, more casually. Nonetheless, he scored with the leadership in Moscow, and in 1976 the Brezhnev Politburo appointed him First Secretary of the party for Sverdlovsk Province, in effect proconsul on his home ground. In 1985 he replaced the corrupt Brezhnevite Viktor Grishin as party boss of the city of Moscow.

In Moscow Yeltsin swept hard with a new broom, and generated all kinds of anecdotes about his impetuousness, such as waking up school principals at two a.m. on a winter's night to go out and superintend snow removal. His zeal roused the ire of the Communist conservatives with whom Gorbachev still had to deal, and when the logical moment came in June 1987 for Yeltsin's promotion from candidate member of the Politburo to full member, he was snubbed.

This setback, overlooked in practically every account of Yeltsin's background, seems to have deeply wounded him and set him bitterly against Gorbachev. The upshot was the well-publicized events of the fall of 1987, when Yeltsin lashed out publicly at Gorbachev for lagging in reform, and in return was removed from his Moscow post. Consigned to the position of deputy chairman of the State Committee for Construction, his old field, Yeltsin bided his time while Gorbachev took the offensive against the conservatives once again and prepared the elections of March 1989.

At this point, with Gorbachev's grudging tolerance, Yeltsin shattered all Soviet precedent by staging a political comeback. He ran for one of the Moscow City seats in the new Congress of People's Deputies, rallied a coalition of reformers, and scored an overwhelming personal victory. The conservatives tried to exclude him from the smaller, more potent Supreme Soviet that was elected by the congress out of its own membership, but a Siberian deputy resigned his seat so that Yeltsin could move up. He was now the undisputed leader of the reformist opposition to Gorbachev.

Gorbachev nevertheless pressed on, and in the spring of 1990 launched a new wave of democratization by holding elections in the fifteen union republics. In the Russian Federation, backed by the reformist coalition "Democratic Russia," Yeltsin won a seat in the People's Congress and in the Supreme Soviet of the republic. Then, against Gorbachev's bitter opposition, he narrowly won the post of Chairman of the Russian Supreme Soviet.

As the head of what amounted to a second government in Moscow after 1990, Yeltsin identified himself with all the forces and issues that put Gorbachev on the defensive. He endorsed the demands for "sovereignty" being asserted by the Baltic republics and others, and backed proposals for radical economic reform, notably the "five hundred days" plan to speed up decentralization and the free market. He firmed up his position further by changing the constitution of the Russian Federation to parallel Gorbachev's new structure in the Union, moving away from the parliamentary principle in favor of the separation of powers and a president directly chosen by the voters. To this position he was overwhelmingly elected, against the liberal Communist interior minister Vadim Bakatin, the conservative Communist prime minister Ryzhkov, and the ultra-nationalist Zhirinovsky. Gorbachev himself had not dared to take such a plunge, and had relied on the Union Congress of People's Deputies to elect him president, a mortal political weakness when his rivalry with Yeltsin was finally played out after the August Coup.

Just hours after he returned to Moscow from house arrest in the Crimea, Gorbachev joined Yeltsin at the Russian Supreme Soviet only to be humiliated before the world's television cameras. From that moment on, the Russian president had the upper hand. The real coup came with ridiculous ease on 8 December 1991, when Yeltsin met with the presidents of Ukraine and Belarus and proclaimed the Union of Soviet Socialist Republics dissolved. Compelled to resign, Gorbachev said plaintively at his farewell reception, "I just could not go on. Everything I did in the last few months, Yeltsin was always opposing it. There was just no way. No way."[3]

Up to now, Yeltsin has identified himself with four basic policies—international cooperation, free-market economic reform, liquidation of the union of the fifteen Soviet republics, and eradication of the Communist Party. Internationally, he has only picked up where Gorbachev left off. The failure of the August Coup took care of the Communist Party. Where Yeltsin has pushed hardest is in decolonizing the Soviet republics and radicalizing the economic reform, both issues that he used tellingly against Gorbachev.

Each of these last two commitments—the breakup of the Union and the drive to marketize—has so far created more problems than it has solved. The two issues are a focus for the growing opposition to Yeltsin that has appeared in the People's Congress and the Supreme Soviet of the Russian Federation. Yeltsin has by and large stayed the course, but he has given more and more signs in recent weeks of backing off a bit—delaying the free energy prices and budget-balancing demanded by the International Monetary Fund, for instance, and articulating nationalist worries about the twenty-five million Russians stranded as minorities in the other former Soviet republics.

In the run-up to the Washington summit with President Bush, Yeltsin made it clear that he had no intention of abandoning the great-power role of his country. Defying what he called the "diktat" of the International Monetary Fund, he asserted, "We have a Russia that the IMF does not know, and a Russian people that the IMF does not know."[4] The IMF has become a bête noire for the Russians; Yeltsin advisors have been publicly quoted to the effect that the IMF's cold-shower tight-money requirements would be worse for Russia than the failure to get its aid.

Yeltsin showed uncanny political skill when the Congress of People's Deputies of the Russian Federation met in April. The congress battered him in one vote after another against his economic course and his softness on the other ex-Soviet republics, and nearly passed a motion of no confidence. Yet by standing aloof like General Charles de Gaulle (he never appeared at the congress until its last day); by letting his economics chief Yegor Gaidar take the slings and arrows of the opposition; and by daring his critics to find another leader and another program, he carried the day.

Yeltsin's troubles with the congress have generally been attributed to a strong bloc of old Communists, but unlike the old Union congress of 1989, the Russian congress was elected in 1990 without special privileges for the Communist Party. It chose the Supreme Soviet that made Yeltsin its leader. Now it is highly fragmented; the Democratic Russia movement that boosted Yeltsin to the leadership broke up after the Communist collapse, much like Solidarity in Poland and the Civic Forum in Czechoslovakia. Even the surviving Communists in Russia are splintered, and they count only by allying themselves with Yeltsin's ultra-nationalist critics on the right.

Neither the Russian congress nor the Russian Supreme Soviet manifests the coherent parliamentary and party politics of government versus opposition that had developed in the Union congress and Supreme Soviet under Gorbachev, when Yeltsin and his sympathizers formed a clear-cut opposition. Ideological positions have dissolved into followings of individual leaders. Most of the strong figures who stood with Yeltsin against Gorbachev—Vice President Rutskoi, Supreme Soviet Chairman Khasbulatov, St. Petersburg mayor Sobchak, even the noted economic reformer Grigory Yavlinsky—have turned against the Russian president, over the economy, over the ethnic situation, and over their fears of Yeltsin's authoritarian proclivities. They are repelled by the "Sverdlovsk Mafia" of old Communist associates whom Yeltsin has brought into his inner circle, particularly Gennady Burbulis, the "state secretary" and former professor of "scientific communism" who is promoting a new cult of personality around his boss. Russian polls show Yeltsin's popularity turning down (from 57 percent in April to 32 percent in May), as the citizenry loses confidence in all its brawling leaders and in government in general.[5]

Ever since the first of the year there has been a running controversy in Russia over the country's ultimate constitutional setup, whether a parliamentary or a presidential republic. Since last fall the President has enjoyed temporary powers to rule by decree. If the Supreme Soviet blocks one of his proposals, as it recently did, for instance, on privatization, Yeltsin puts it through anyway by decree. The opposition naturally prefers stronger legislative control, a position of some merit in the light of Third-World experiences with presidential dictatorship. They want a constituent assembly to draft a new constitution to this effect. Yeltsin periodically threatens to dissolve the congress and the Supreme Soviet and submit his own version of a constitution to a popular referendum—including the future prerogative of the president to call a referendum at any time on any issue. Ross Perot again! Or shades of Napoleon Bonaparte's "plebiscitary democracy"?

Sensing instinctively what his country will and will not tolerate, Yeltsin may be persisting in his reformist commitment only in the hope of gaining Western aid under acceptable conditions. Failing that, he could well maneuver to rescue his failing popularity and disarm his opposition by backing away from the free market, ruble convertibility, and the rest of the IMF dream, and then turning back to the statist self-sufficiency of his predecessors, doubtless still in the name of reform. We often hear the fear that Yeltsin might be replaced by a Russian Pinochet if his policies falter. Yeltsin is not the type to stand back and allow this. More likely, if need be, he would become his own Pinochet.

CHAPTER TWENTY-NINE

INTERDEPENDENCE, OR A
RUSSIAN PINOCHET?
(OCTOBER 1992)

By the fall of 1992 Yeltsin's authoritarianism and his persistence in the free-market reform line he had adopted against Gorbachev led to a running battle with the Russian Supreme Soviet and Congress of People's Deputies that had originally elected him their leader. This confrontation called into question the prospects for democracy in Russia.

The changes in Russia since 1991 manifest a rash and catastrophic renunciation of the principle of interdependence. Both in the political and economic respects Gorbachev's program for the old Soviet Union has truly failed. In ethnic relations the principle of interdependence among nationalities and regions expressed in federalism has failed. In the economic reforms the principle of interdependence among individuals expressed in socialism, or at least in the mixed economy, has failed. In the political sphere the principle of interdependence between the individual and the state expressed in parliamentary democracy has nearly failed.

At the beginning of the period of *perestroika* the Soviet Union had reached a critical point of historical indeterminacy. The revolution was played out, or rather was lost in a postrevolutionary dictatorship, which in turn was played out. With Gorbachev, the country arrived at the historic stage of the moderate revolutionary revival, i.e., a return to the democratic hopes of 1917, after the fall of the tsar and before the Bolshevik coup. But the exact character of this new phase of democratic revival was historically indeterminate. Practically everything depended on the character of the country's leadership, on its level of statesmanship.

It is easy to point out limitations and errors in the Soviet leadership in the period of perestroika. From the start, Gorbachev had the opportunity for profound reform, thanks to the exhaustion of the Stalinist and neo-Stalinist regime, and to the advent of a new generation of leaders in the Communist Party. But it seems that Gorbachev was slow to see the depth of the problems and the possibilities of reform. Moreover, he was afraid of the party apparatus. At his private meeting with the writers in 1986 he declared, "Our enemies [i.e., Western sovietologists] write about the apparatus, that it broke Khrushchev's neck and will now break the neck of our new leadership." From time to time Gorbachev compromised with the apparatus conservatives, and this tactic made possible the conservative attempt against him in the August Coup. In the economy, Gorbachev erred from the start, trying to decentralize state enterprises too fast and allowing a fatal rise in the deficit in the state budget. The Gorbachevian reformers did not sufficiently analyze the defects of the "command-administrative" system. I maintain that its main defect was not in the concept of central planning, but rather in the practical conduct of planning carried out by stupid people, in secret, and with mainly military priorities.

Even more serious, Gorbachev underestimated the force of nationalism among the Soviet minorities released by democratization. He did not understand that genuine federalism depends on a clear division of powers between the center and the regions. However, up to 1990–91, despite these deficiencies, Gorbachev led the country a long way toward the universal human values of which he had constantly spoken, both domestically and internationally.

In the course of these efforts Gorbachev was challenged by contradictory forces: the Right, i.e. the Communist conservatives; and the Left, i.e., the radical reformers, separatists, and anti-Communists. Here the factor of personal politics comes in.

It is well known that in 1989 the former Communist secretary Boris Yeltsin enjoyed an unprecedented political comeback, after his fall in 1987. Then Yeltsin commenced a campaign against Gorbachev that could only be described as a vendetta. The history of Yeltsin's personal vendetta against Gorbachev is important because it explains the political choices that he made in the course of his return to power. To undermine Gorbachev, Yeltsin steered the policy of the Russian Republic toward collaboration with the forces of ethnic separatism and toward radical economic reform, i.e., in the anti-socialist sense of the free market. By the time of the August Coup, he had become committed to pursue these lines as ends in themselves. Thus he supported the dissolution of the Union and the steps to create an economy of the unfettered market, with destructive rigor, to justify the positions that he had taken against Gorbachev. All this involved a great cost as regards the principle of human interdependence on the territory of the former Soviet Union.

With regard to the Russian economy, we now see a catastrophic rupture in all the connections of social responsibility, in the name of the free market. In today's Russia the free market is an anachronistic utopia. Normal life today depends above all on centralized organizations, social complexity, and the interdependence of individuals, groups, regions, countries. The challenge today is how to guide such interdependence democratically.

On the ethnic plane, we now see in Russia and in the republics of the ex-USSR a possibly hopeless situation of nationalistic conflicts. With the abandonment of the goal of federalism in the USSR, and the apotheosis of the principle of territorial self-determination, the concept of the rights and equality of the human individual apart from the ethnic group has been placed in great danger. Moreover, the ethnic fragmentation of the country has fractured the economy even more, and aggravated the danger of nuclear proliferation.

Parliamentary democracy represents the ultimate political expression of human interdependence, as a coordinated system in which all the currents and interests of a society can have their voice in the common governance. Such a parliamentarism had begun to develop in the USSR with the constitutional reforms of 1988–89 and with the formation of an opposition bloc under the labels "Interregional Group" or "Democratic Platform" or "Democratic Russia." But the irony of fate, since the August Coup, is that the Russian Supreme Soviet no longer functions at the level that the Union Supreme Soviet had reached under Gorbachev. We now see in Russia a growing personalism, with the tendency to govern by presidential decree. On the parliamentary side there is disorder and irresponsibility, and a clear structure of government and opposition is lacking. More recently we have seen a return to the tactic of the political trial, but in this case a trial without any defendant, directed only against the ghost of the Communist Party. (As regards individuals, Yeltsin had been just as much a Communist as Gorbachev, Ligachev, Yanayev, and almost all the other political figures in contemporary Russia.) The trial of the Communist Party is nothing but a trial of history and a form of exorcism.

In this context, what can we see in Russia's future? Unfortunately it is not possible to be very optimistic. Under the label of the market, the economy is becoming weaker and weaker. Ethnic antagonisms are becoming more and more violent, and there remains the question of the future of the 25 million Russians in the other republics. In politics, people write in Russia about the possibility of a Russian Pinochet, i.e., of a dictatorship on the model of Chile. I am afraid of the possibility that Yeltsin could become a Pinochet himself. We must remember that Yeltsin adopted his lines of reform and democracy out of political motives more than motives of principle, above all to destroy Gorbachev. Having accomplished this objective, he will doubtless be capable of responding to economic and ethnic crises with rejection of these lines and a return to dictatorship. Stalin without Marx, one might say. But this vision is only the anticipation of a danger. Let us hope that it does not come true.

Chapter Thirty

Who Is Our Man In Moscow?
(March 1993)

In the early months of 1993 open confrontation broke out between the Russian president and the parliament. Western commentators tried to identify the latter with the Communist regime, despite Yeltsin's clear challenge to parliamentary democracy.

George Bush ultimately conceded his mistake in relying too long and too heavily on Mikhail Gorbachev as the man to preserve peace and stability in Russia. Bill Clinton is making the same mistake with Boris Yeltsin, but apparently he does not realize it yet.

Part of the trouble is our tendency to make convenient assumptions that are then recycled by the media until they sound like absolute fact. Yeltsin the "passionate democrat" versus the "hard-line," "pro-Communist," even "Brezhnevite" congress operating under an "old-style constitution." Free-market reform versus a return to Communist dictatorship. With "our horse," to quote ex-Ambassador Robert Strauss, or against all our values and interests.

To begin with, the Russian Congress of People's Deputies is no anti-democratic monolith, as it is so commonly represented. It spreads all along the spectrum and more or less represents the country, with a Yeltsinite reformist wing, a wing of Communist and nationalist conservatives, and a center counting perhaps 40 percent of the deputies. Headed by Yeltsin's erstwhile protégés, Speaker Khasbulatov and Vice President Rutskoi, as well as the industrial leader Arkady Volsky, the center is the unsung element in Russian politics as far as most American observers are concerned. Yet Gorbachev's former press aide, Georgi Shakhnazarov, recently called the centrists "the key to the solution of Russia's complicated problems" and the only alternative to authoritarian rule.[1]

In starkly contrasting Yeltsin and the congress, we seem to forget that the President is just as much a former Communist as any of the parliamentarians: The question is who has changed his spots and under what terms. The Russian congress is not a "Communist holdover" any more than President Yeltsin; it was elected in the spring of 1990 in the heyday of Gorbachev's reforms, shortly after he persuaded the Communist Party to give up its legally privileged position, and is not to be confused with the Union congress elected a year previously with a protected majority of Communist officials. The Russian Supreme Soviet chosen by this congress is the same one that voted to make Yeltsin its chairman, before he had the Russian constitution amended to create the present popularly-elected executive president.

Nor can the old constitution be blamed for Yeltsin's troubles. The problem with the Communist constitution was not its form, which was more or less a European-style parliamentary republic like West Germany, but the practice, which was always a charade until Gorbachev started to breath life into the document in 1989. Today's constitutional struggles mainly stem from the amendments Gorbachev introduced in the Union constitution, tracked by Yeltsin's amendments to the constitution of the Russian Republic. One was the curious innovation of the Congress of People's Deputies, elected by the voters with the power to amend the constitution and to chose the smaller working legislature or Supreme Soviet from among its own membership. Secondly came the addition of an executive presidency, creating a French-style system with all its ambiguities in the distribution of powers between the president, the prime minister and his cabinet, and the parliament. The constitutional stand-off of the past year has been over which way to push this awkward animal—towards an American-style presidency with full control of the executive branch, as Yeltsin wants, or toward parliamentary supremacy over the executive, which Speaker Khasbulatov almost managed to affirm at the March session of the congress.

None of the contenders in Russia really understands the separation of powers. This is not as serious for the parliamentarians, who have the West European model in mind, as it is for the president, who could be speaking General de Gaulle's words today: "The indivisible authority of the State is wholly conferred on the president by the people."[2] At the same time Yeltsin aspires to remain above partisan strife, which is appropriate only for a figurehead president on the German model. He has lost his chance to build an effective government party.

Similarly the Russians fail to understand federalism, which they still confuse with ethnicity. Ethnic minorities within the Russian Federation, resenting Russian hegemony, are trying to claim "sovereignty" just as the union republics did before the dissolution of the USSR, while the Russian majority fears federalism as an invitation to anarchy. There is no clear demarcation of state and federal powers or even of taxing and judicial authority. Yeltsin still tries to control local politics by appointing provincial governors and then sending out presidential representatives to watch the governors.

Yeltsin's influence reached its peak in the fall of 1991, when the Russian Supreme Soviet voted him power to reform the economy by presidential decree. Then two unexpected events intervened: Yeltsin's meeting with the presidents of Ukraine and Belarus in December 1991 to proclaim the end of the Soviet Union; and the decision to decontrol most prices in January 1992 (letting galloping inflation loose). These surprises were accompanied by growing personality conflicts, fed by the budding ambitions of Yeltsin's former lieutenants and resentment of his personal entourage. On top of all this, fears spread of Yeltsin's authoritarian proclivities. Last summer, for example, *Moscow News* protested Yeltsin's "quiet coup" giving his new Security Council "unconstitutional powers": "From now on, a very narrow circle of officials will make decisions related to Russia's security (which essentially means all decisions)."[3]

The liquidation of the USSR in December 1991 started reverberations of instability that will long be felt. The centrists now accuse Yeltsin's entourage of beginning to plot the end of the Union right after the August Coup, in order to eradicate the rival Gorbachev government. Though decolonization of the Russian Empire was long overdue, it left millions of Russians stranded beyond their borders, and unleashed a rash of irreconcilable conflicts among the smaller ethnic groups. By breaking up old trading relationships it compounded the economic crisis. The breakup certainly went further than Yeltsin intended, thanks to the Ukraine's uncooperativeness, but no Russian government can indefinitely abandon the idea of great-power hegemony in the former Soviet realm.

Yeltsin's embrace of the economic reforms urged by the West is riddled with ironies. American commentaries have made the free market the litmus test of democracy, even more than constitutional processes. Yeltsin equates criticism of the reforms with treason to the state, even though a host of observers as diverse as Khrushchev's son Sergei and Alexander Solzhenitsyn have faulted the dogmatic extremes of the privatization program. In the short run, Russia's policies run opposite to the state controls that all Western governments have turned to at comparable moments of crisis in wartime or depression. In the long run, they defy the realities of the modern economy marked by corporate concentration, government intervention, and managed markets in everything from agriculture to health care.

Yeltsin is a fearless politician, capable of bold strokes as when he ran for president, defied the coup plotters, dissolved the Soviet Union, and plunged into free-market reform. But he is stubborn and mercurial, and hardly the type to work in tandem with a parliamentary body. He comes down to the wire with imprecations and threats. This time, he charged, the congress was plotting to restore Communism, but he would take resolute steps—unspecified—to prevent his reforms being derailed. Then at the last minute he yields, as when he sacrificed Prime Minister Gaidar in December 1992, and disappears from view to sulk, or—as many in Moscow believe—to drink.

Rebuffed by the latest session of the congress, Yeltsin still talks of a referendum on whether the people prefer him or the congress to carry on the reforms. Such a question cuts away all constitutional moorings in the separation of powers. It is as if Bill Clinton, without any authority of law, decided to call a national referendum on his economic program, to ask the voters whether they wanted him or Congress to carry it out. Yeltsin could well win, but this would not be the first time in history that a country voted democratically to liquidate democracy.

Are the alternatives to Yeltsin only chaos or dictatorship? This is naturally the way Yeltsin's supporters and the Russian Embassy want us to see the choices. But the argument can be made that Yeltsin's intransigence only plays into the hands of the Communists and nationalists by weakening the center. Democratic practice might be better served if the executive submitted to parliamentary control and a coalition government that could, in Shaknazarov's words, overcome "personal ambition and considerations of prestige" and do something to ameliorate the lot of the people.[4] A Polish-type evolution in the distribution of political power between president and parliament might be something to hope for.

Yeltsin's fate is now inextricably entwined with the question of American aid to Russia. The conventional wisdom, pitting Yeltsin against the forces of darkness, calls for an all-out, unconditional effort, though some of its advocates blanch a bit at the prospect of Yeltsin imposing a presidential dictatorship in the name of democracy. And there are practical considerations. In the present disorganized and demoralized state of the Russian economy, aid that is not carefully targeted is all too likely to end up subsidizing corruption, profiteering, and capital export. In any case, Russian democracy, if left to the Russians themselves, has more potential than is suggested by calls for emergency aid to one particular leader.

CHAPTER THIRTY-ONE

DESTROYING DEMOCRACY IN ORDER TO SAVE IT (MARCH–APRIL 1993)

Russia was plunged into a constitutional crisis on 20 March 1993 when Yeltsin threatened to dissolve the parliament. Eventually both sides agreed to submit to a popular referendum. The West, identifying Yeltsin with anti-Communism, strongly supported him.

I

Boris Yeltsin's proclamation of emergency presidential power on 20 March 1993 came as a shock to most leaders and experts in the West who had seen him as a pillar of democracy. Yet his move could have been expected. What is more surprising is the insensitivity of so many Western leaders and experts who rushed to justify Yeltsin in disregard of the constitutional principles involved, and then rushed to forget what Yeltsin did after he backed down and sought a compromise. Yeltsin himself has begun the rewriting of this history by claiming that all he did on 20 March was to call for a referendum to let "the people" decide.

Something obviously happened between 20 March and the issuance of Yeltsin's watered-down decree on 24 March. Warnings by the Russian military? Back-channel cautioning by Western governments? A clever ruse to frighten the constitutional court and his parliamentary opponents to go out on a limb where he could cut them off? We do not know.

The universal excuse for Yeltsin is that he is "the duly elected president of Russia," to quote President Clinton[1] (even though the similarly elected vice president, Rutskoi, denounced Yeltsin's action). Does election, however, give Yeltsin the right, any more than President Clinton himself, to rule by decree and ignore the elected parliament? And is this the way to nurture Russia's budding democratic experiment? Alberto Fujimori was the elected president of Peru when he put democratic government out of business there in 1992.

Escaping an impeachment verdict which he had vowed not to respect in any case, Yeltsin turned to the crowds to claim the victory that eluded him after his 20 March proclamation. This was clever political stagecraft with totalitarian implications: "Yeltsin and the People are One," read one placard, a conscious or unconscious transposition of the old Communist slogan, "The Party and the People are One." Russian television, the bête noire of the congress, cooperated by putting a transparently pro-Yeltsin spin on events. The congress adjourned 29 March after deciding on its own version of a referendum in competition with Yeltsin's.

II

As the April 25 date for the Russian referendum approaches, it is becoming less and less clear what the ballot will decide. This is not to say that there is anything wrong in principle with holding referenda to let the people decide public issues. In most American states referenda are held to do anything from amending the constitution to approving town taxes. But as part of a constitutional process, a referendum must proceed within a clear legal framework, to decide a definite question that must be formulated by constituted authority for the voters to answer.

In the Russian case referenda are provided for in one of the many democratizing amendments to the much-abused constitution. Gorbachev held one early in 1991 and eked out a victory for the principle of keeping the USSR together, which of course soon proved to be meaningless. Ever since the August Coup a referendum has been talked about to legitimize a new Russian constitution, though so far no such document has been readied for the voters. Instead, the referendum idea has been turned to the service of political as distinct from constitutional legitimation.

Last December, as part of a deal with the Russian Congress of People's Deputies, Yeltsin won agreement to a referendum of confidence in his own leadership, or a "plebiscite," as he sometimes called it. The agreement briefly foundered in March and then was reaffirmed by the congress with further conditions, adding the questions of confidence in the economic reforms and "early" elections (in Russian, *dosrochny*, "before the end of the term") both for president and for the congress.

Only the latter—the early elections—could qualify as a fit subject for a referendum to decide something, and even then the dates are not specified. The questions of confidence in the president or in the economic reforms have no more constitutional force than a public opinion poll. They have been put forth—one by Yeltsin, the other by the congress— purely for the purpose of strengthening their respective political positions in the ongoing battle for supremacy between these two branches of government.

Each side is now trying to define "victory" on these questions according to their own terms—a majority of all eligible voters, as the congress has resolved, or only a majority of those voting, as Yeltsin maintains. In all probability, Yeltsin will win a majority of those voting for confidence in his presidency but not a majority of all voters, due to low turnout. Probably he will lose on confidence in the economy. But no matter what the outcome, nothing will be legally decided: It is pure political posturing on both sides. Policy differences have been intensified by the emerging personal factor, including the rising ambition of Speaker Khasbulatov, and resentment against Yeltsin's inner circle of brash young academics and former Sverdlovsk *apparatchiki.* Yeltsin himself is the kind of politician who seems compelled to justify himself and humiliate his opponents, from Gorbachev in 1991 to Rutskoi today.

Now, thrust up by these tensions, the fundamental question of power dominates the fight between the executive and legislative branches of government. Despite the legal vacuity of the referendum, both Yeltsin and the legislators are taking it very seriously as a decisive test of strength. Campaigning American style with a British public relations firm and all kinds of populist promises, Yeltsin has staked his career on a favorable outcome by threatening to resign if he does not prevail.

The G-7 governments, for their part, have staked their own future relations with Russia on the same outcome, and promise vast amounts of aid to bolster Yeltsin, taking their chances on any Russian nationalist backlash. If this reaction materializes, as many Russians fear, Yeltsin may find himself, as Gorbachev was, more popular abroad than at home.

By pitting the executive and legislative powers against each other, the referendum is disrupting the tenuous separation of powers in Russia. So far Yeltsin has not shown the essential ability to work with a legislative body, or to tolerate the conditions of gridlock that are bound to arise sometimes under a system of checks and balances. What Yeltsin may do about his congressional adversaries in the likely event that he wins the referendum according to his definition but not according to theirs is anybody's guess. If he tries to return to the emergency presidential rule that he threatened on 20 March and has threatened again, his Western supporters will find it far more difficult than they did in March to sustain their faith in his democratic intentions. Let us not forget that it was Napoleon Bonaparte who made "plebiscite" a household word.

CHAPTER THIRTY-TWO

THE RIDDLE OF RUSSIAN REFORM (JUNE 1993)

Having prevailed in the referenda of April 1993, Yeltsin forged ahead with plans for a new presidentialist constitution. Bent on discrediting Gorbachev's "socialist choice," he persevered in his free-market program, despite the country's economic collapse and the impasse in his relations with the parliament.

Communist Russia, though tragically oppressive and secretive, was an open book compared to the murky contradictions and competing ideological illusions that mark the new Russia. The country is far freer than its old incarnation, but it makes less sense. To be sure, some of the difficulty for outsiders in coming to an accurate understanding of post-Communist life is self-imposed. Westerners' misguided assumptions about Russia, and the self-deceptions they project upon it, make the country seem more of a riddle than it really is.

In particular, far too much nonsense has been disseminated in recent months about the background of the Yeltsin government's reforms and the alternatives to it. Reform in Russia after the 1991 putsch was a politically motivated lurch toward extreme positions in politics, in nationality relations, and in economics, based on democratization, decolonization, and desocialization. This phase is now being followed by a little-acknowledged retreat from reform in each of these areas.

❖   ❖   ❖

In economics, as in politics and the national question, Yeltsin was bent on total destruction of the old system, where Gorbachev was trying to clean it up. While Gorbachev clung to the end to the "socialist choice," despite his rejection of the old "command-administrative system," Yeltsin repudiated any and all policies even verbally associated with the socialism practiced by the old regime. He surrounded himself with a cadre of youthful academic economists who had become entranced by the Britzlish and American free-market economic theory that *glasnost* had permitted them to study. Thus he embraced a model of reform based not on the realities of capitalism as practiced in the West, let alone any objective analysis of Russia's real needs, but on an eighteenth-century utopian vision of the market economy. Together with his new deputy prime minister, Gaidar, Yeltsin plumped for a program of instant marketizing, privatization, deregulation, and monetary shock therapy, under circumstances of crisis when Western governments usually resort to more controls and planning, not less. Such was "the catastrophic policy conducted by 'Gaidar's Team,'" in the words of the chairman of the centrist Civic Union.[1]

There is something here of the classic Russian tendency to borrow radical foreign ideas and carry them to a thrilling extreme—a sort of Bolshevism in reverse. Indeed, the analogy can be pursued further: the youthful and impassioned Bolsheviks, rallying around their charismatic leader and their bible of doctrine (in this case Adam Smith and his apostles), intoxicated by power and self-righteousness, and condemning the older and more cautious Menshevik-centrists as tools of the reactionaries (a role now played by the "Red-Brown coalition" of diehard Communists and ultranationalists).

Naturally the Yeltsinites echo the Western notion that free enterprise is the basis of democracy—despite the evidence that large enterprise is inherently undemocratic unless it is constrained from outside, and the frequency in this century of authoritarian regimes presiding over capitalistic economies. In fact, among capitalist countries there is a good correlation between the degree of social-democratic economics and the political performance of democracy. Socialism has never led a democracy to dictatorship, though dictatorships have often instituted socialism of one sort or another.

A deeper motive, occasionally expressed by Gaidar, was the promotion of a new sort of class struggle. Determined to extirpate what they regarded as the social fundaments of the old regime in the *nomenklatura* bureaucracy, Gaidar and his team aimed to make reform "irreversible" by replacing the bureaucracy with a new entrepreneurial class, even before they put in place the elementary financial and legal foundations for a market economy. They welcomed economic collapse as a scourge of their enemies, much as the Bolsheviks rationalized the economic collapse of the Civil War years to eradicate the former bourgeoisie. They thought of privatization of enterprise as a way to create a new middle class that would support the fledgling Russian democracy, while they overlooked the huge existing middle class of professionals, technicians, and white-collar workers. They targeted the nomenklatura of Communist-appointed bureaucrats, but confused the productive nomenklatura of managers—indispensable in any modern society—with the controller nomenklatura of the party apparatus, an incubus on the back of society. Instead, what reform has mostly generated is a parasitical new robber-baron class of speculators and mafiosi.

In their zeal, the radical Russian reformers were encouraged by Western advisors who seemed to be trying to validate at Russian expense their own ideological false consciousness about the free-market economy. Yeltsin's people were led to overlook all the limitations and problems of the free market that have been the subject of a hundred years of debate and struggle in the West—the problem of externalities such as the environmental impact of business that the market cannot govern; public services ranging from transportation to culture that cannot be sustained on a market basis; the trend to corporate concentration and monopoly if it is not curbed by the state; the vulnerability of the agricultural sector if it is not subsidized and protected; the role of the labor movement and social-democratic legislation in achieving advanced living standards, the welfare state, trade-union rights, regulation of business in the public interest, and the fiscal and monetary balance wheel that has compensated for the worst of the business cycle. Instead, the Russian leadership and their Western advisors undertook to extirpate everything in the revolutionary and socialist heritage, Russian or Western, that had arisen to address the problems created by capitalism. The unfettered market was supposed to take care of the very ills that it caused.

The market, of course, has its place in any economic scheme that is not hopelessly utopian. But the reformers under Yeltsin rejected the distinction that the Gorbachevians tried to make between the market and private ownership. They did not realize that there is a vast difference between permitting private enterprise to be initiated again, and artificially recasting state-created enterprise on capitalist lines, with the added disruption this effort entails. As plenty of West European experience shows, the market is not incompatible either with public ownership of enterprise, or with planning.

Indirect planning through state intervention in the market was actually the direction taken by Soviet economic planners in the 1920s, before Stalin destroyed scientific planning during the First Five-Year Plan and replaced it with his irrational and wasteful practices of military-style output commands and material allocations. Thanks to this experience, planning became a bad word, and Gorbachev's government denied itself the use of the planning tool to effect a more sensible deployment of the country's resources. Yeltsin simply went on to make a virtue out of the abandonment of any rational supervision of the economy, and turned Gorbachev's economic muddle into a self-inflicted disaster. Tragically, the old barracks regime has yielded not to a higher sense of social responsibility, but to a pervasive atmosphere of crime, corruption, and greed.

❖   ❖   ❖

As I have observed already, Yeltsin adopted the extreme positions in reform, namely anti-Communism, self-determination, and free-market economics, not as ends in themselves but primarily to advance his personal political objectives. Recent events show how far he is capable of modifying his stands as circumstances alter the agenda, and lead him to back away from those original extreme positions. His changes are most serious in the political realm, less so regarding the federal principle, and up to now ambiguous as regards the economy.

Yeltsin has never been entirely comfortable with the chaos that he helped to bring about when he dissolved the Soviet Union to get at Gorbachev. Probably he did not anticipate how totally the Union would collapse, or the severe economic consequences of its breakup. Nevertheless, he has dealt with the former union republics with relative restraint, despite the explosive problem of the large Russian minorities outside Russia and the political time-bomb of Russia's imperial humiliation in the events of 1989-1991. He appears to be having some success in bringing most of the republics of the Commonwealth of Independent States back into some form of practical cooperation, which he is quite prepared to favor in the absence of any union government headed by his rival.

By contrast, Yeltsin has taken an increasingly firm line toward the nationalities of the autonomous republics within the Russian Federation, and toward the Russian provinces as well, where the issue is his own authority. Without any legal basis, he began immediately after the August Putsch to appoint provincial governors, and then designated personal representatives to watch over the governors—all reminiscent of central control by the Communist regime over both local government chiefs and the local party secretaries who kept the government people in line. In his recent constitutional proposals Yeltsin made it clear that threats to the unity of the Russian state would not be tolerated.

Like most Russians, Yeltsin does not understand federalism, and confuses it with ethnicity. He counterposes the Russian center to the minority autonomies instead of extending general and equal federal rights to the Russian provinces as well. Apart from one unexplicated reference to the "right of peoples to self-determination," his draft constitution essentially left the republics and provinces as administrative subdivisions of the central power.

❖   ❖   ❖

In the economic realm, in the early months of radical reform, it was easy to forget that for Yeltsin his program was not an end in itself, but primarily a way of defining himself and discrediting his enemies. Once this was accomplished, he seemed to lose interest or vigor in matters economic, while the political confrontation with the parliament absorbed his attention. By mid-1992 he was ready to back away pragmatically from purist economic reform. He stopped short of total price decontrol on food and energy, and after the fall of Gaidar in December 1992 he reached out to the industrial lobby for his new prime minister, Viktor Cherno-myrdin, and other cabinet appointments, all the while asserting the true cause of reform. He talked of a social safety net, and he indexed minimum wages and pensions to the rate of inflation, though in practice the main safety-net program was the inflationary credits accorded to industry by the Central Bank to avert unemployment. In the campaign to pass his referendum in April 1993 Yeltsin outdid his rivals in populist promises of economic benefits, despite their implications of even worse inflation.

Not surprisingly, privatization proceeded most successfully in the sector of small-scale trade and services where it had been most irrational to nationalize in the first place. Privatization of larger enterprise through a complicated voucher system took unexpected forms—buy-outs by workers' collectives; "nomenklatura privatization" by the old managers; and retention of a major share of state ownership in most new joint-stock companies. Reformists began to take the Chernomyrdin cabinet to task for attempting to revive the State Planning Commission and undertake industrial policy. Yeltsin himself came down firmly on both sides of the economic question, calling in a speech just after the April referendum, for example, for "the formation of a socially oriented market economy," and simultaneously denouncing "irresponsible, inflationary financing of social production programs."[2] Nonetheless, he may find himself as a practical matter presiding over the formation of a mixed economy based on strong governmental direction and welfare-state promises. Not long ago I commented to a Russian historian that Russia had russified Communism more than Communism communized Russia. He agreed, but added, "The same thing will happen with capitalism."

❖   ❖   ❖

In March 1993 Yeltsin had provoked yet another special session of the Congress of People's Deputies, which rejected all compromise and came within seventy-two votes of the two thirds constitutionally required to impeach the president. Demonstrating again his instinctive understanding of power, Yeltsin staged a mass rally to turn this narrow escape into a psychological victory, and went on to win the referendum, thereby achieving his strongest political position since the heady days just after the August Putsch. In the name of democracy he forged ahead to write a new constitution legitimating presidential dominance, if not dictatorship.

Yeltsin's authoritarian instincts were visibly written into his proposed constitutional draft. This document was an amalgam of the US and French systems, but with a special twist, to resolve all of Yeltsin's recent disagreements with Russia's representative bodies in favor of the president. The French-style prime minister in the previous set-up was kept, but he was to be designated by the president, and the parliament could be dissolved if it did not accept him, while presidential appointments of individual ministers, ambassadors, and military commanders were not subject to parliamentary confirmation at all. There appeared to be no limits on how often the president could dissolve uncooperative parliaments. All legislative initiative respecting taxes and expenditures was reserved to the president and the cabinet, while the two houses of the parliament could only "confirm" the budget. Not surprisingly, the draft spelled out the president's power to call a popular referendum, without specifying the purposes, and it allowed the president to proclaim emergency rule or martial law by merely informing the parliament. He could suspend any act of the parliament or of local government and refer it to the courts. On the other hand, he could be impeached on the motion of the lower house only if this were confirmed by the "higher judicial presence"—which he would appoint.

There is actually a third constitutional model behind these arrangements favoring the executive power. A clue is the name the constitution drafters gave the lower house of the parliament— the "State Duma," just how the representative body under Tsar Nicholas II was styled between 1905 and 1917. Thus Yeltsin endeavored to carry reform back to the earliest and most tentative era of Russia's revolutionary experience under a semi-constitutional monarchy, with a subservient parliament and an executive aspiring to embody the national will.

Russian centrists responded to Yeltsin's plan with dire warnings. Oleg Rumiantsev, leader of the Social-Democratic Party and chair of the constitutional committee of the Supreme Soviet, called Yeltsin's plan "undemocratic and unrepublican."[3] Georgi Shakhnazarov said it was "for a country just having broken out of the clamps of totalitarianism, a straitjacket of a new cut."[4] The actual danger of a Russian Pinochet has now been manifested in the March crisis and highlighted in the draft constitution—that it might materialize in the person of Yeltsin himself.

❖   ❖   ❖

Yeltsin is an enigmatic figure, who has done more than his share to becloud the realities of post-Communist Russia. There is no denying his charismatic impact and his boldness in tight situations. He relishes confrontation and simplifies politics into a death struggle between his democratic loyalists and the totalitarian conspirators. In his campaign for personal vindication he has seized upon the formulas of democracy, market economy, and national self-determination that attract admiration from Westerners. Yet his record makes one wonder how much he really understands these categories, and how much his own turbulent psyche and the deeper authoritarian habits of Russian culture actually shape his leadership beneath the labels of classical liberalism.

Yeltsin does not appreciate the function of political parties in a democracy. He has failed to weld his own supporters into an effective party, just as he has failed to accept the principle of a loyal opposition or the pragmatic virtue of coalition politics. The centrist elements as a distinct political force, who reject nostalgia for the Communist past but criticize the current reforms and the new authoritarian climate, do not exist for him.

Lacking the temperament to work with any parliamentary body on an equal footing, Yeltsin has pursued the popular referendum to legitimize executive supremacy in the style of Charles de Gaulle or even Napoleon Bonaparte. This, unfortunately, is a direction toward democracy in name only, a condition that Russians are familiar with. Let us hope that this is not the only way that the new Russia can be ruled.

CHAPTER THIRTY-THREE

THE EIGHTEENTH BRUMAIRE OF BORIS YELTSIN (OCTOBER 1993)

The impasse between President Yeltsin and the Russian parliament was broken on 21 September 1993 when Yeltsin proclaimed the dissolution of the parliament. The upshot was the violent confrontation of 3–4 October, when rioters attempted to defend the parliament, and the president called in the military to shell the parliament building and disband the legislative branch by force.

President Yeltsin's forceful move of 3 and 4 October to suppress the Russian parliament and its defenders has overshadowed awareness of the steps that led to this tragedy. It is frequently being argued that Yeltsin had no other choice in the face of revolutionary actions by right and left extremists, who undoubtedly predominated among the proparliament crowd at the Russian White House during those bloody days. But the short-lived uprising was a direct consequence of Yeltsin's illegal and unconstitutional decision of 21 September to dissolve the parliament and impose presidential rule. Ironically, the anti-democratic extremists became the most determined defenders of constitutional government.

Yeltsin's dissolution of the Russian parliament (i.e., the Congress of People's Deputies and the smaller Supreme Soviet) came as a great surprise, considering his narrow escape from impeachment last March when he attempted the same action, as well as the effort he made this summer to have a new constitution drafted. What is even more surprising, however, is the insensitivity of so many Western leaders and experts who have rushed to justify Yeltsin's actions in disregard of the constitutional principles involved.

Particularly shocking is the unconditional support for Yeltsin and his actions expressed by the Clinton Administration in the United States ever since the March crisis. One wonders how President Clinton could be so grossly misinformed as to be able to hail Yeltsin's suppression of representative government as a triumph of democracy. Or whether *raison d'état*—hopes for a cooperative Russian foreign policy or stable investment opportunity—has prevailed over respect for the factual record. In any case, in March President Clinton and his Western allies effectively gave Yeltsin *carte blanche* to impose personal rule in the name of democ-

racy and free-market reform, and helped clear the way for Yeltsin's aboli
tion of the Russian parliament.

Yeltsin's defenders claim that the now banned Russian parliament was
a Communist holdover based on a Communist constitution. Nonsense.
No Soviet parliament had any power prior to Gorbachev's reforms. All
the essentials of the Russian government up to 21 September were based
on constitutional amendments enacted since 1989.

The Russian parliament that we have just seen crushed was elected in
1990 without any legal privileges or set-aside of seats for the Communist
Party, unlike Gorbachev's Union parliament elected the year before. Most
of its members had been Communist Party members, to be sure, but so
had Yeltsin—at the highest level of the party apparatus—though not
many of them had believed the Communist doctrine. When Gorbachev
lifted party discipline, the parliamentarians spread all across the political
spectrum, with perhaps 10 percent clinging to Communist ideology and
another 10 percent embracing extreme nationalist and fascist views; the
remainder endorsed democracy and, up to a point, economic reform.

At first the Russian parliament gave Yeltsin everything he wanted: It
elected him its chairman in 1990; it agreed to amend the Russian constitution so that he could get himself elected president in June 1991; it
backed him against the hardline coup attempt in August 1991; and it
voted him temporary decree powers to reform the economy in the fall of
1991. Its chairman, Khasbulatov, was Yeltsin's hand-picked successor in
that post and his right-hand man when they defied the August Coup
together. Yeltsin had no complaints about the parliament as long as it
followed his lead.

Why, then, is the Russian constitutional experiment in such deep jeop-
ardy today? The answer lies both in policy and in personalities. The parliamentarians were chagrined over Yeltsin's peremptory dissolution of the
Soviet Union in December 1991 and his embrace of economic shock
therapy in January 1992. As the economy plummeted and corruption
mounted under Yeltsin's free-market reforms, they tried to put on the
brakes and steer a more pragmatic course toward a mixed economy and
a welfare state, a position perhaps vindicated by the recent election results
in Poland. Conflict between the Russian executive power and the legislative branch of government then escalated for a year and a half.

Under an American-style constitution with its checks and balances,
such as Russia had adopted, the executive has to share policy decisions
with the legislative branch and work within the law, despite the risk of a
political impasse. But Yeltsin has repeatedly shown that he cannot tolerate
legislative opposition, and that he does not really understand the separation of powers. He consistently failed to seek a coalition with the large
centrist contingent in the parliament, and like Lenin in times past, pre-

ferred to rely only on a minority of undeviating followers. Thus, instead of building a consensus, Yeltsin polarized Russian politics. Sadly, he demonstrates how attempts to copy the American presidential system are likely to end up in dictatorship, as they have so often in Latin America.

Yeltsin has justified his actions by the April referendum that backed his leadership, but it was of course for the same purpose that Bonaparte made "plebiscite" a familiar term. Yeltsin's September coup was almost an exact re-play of the coup by Bonaparte the nephew, Louis Napoleon, the elected president of France who liquidated the Second Republic in 1851 and made himself emperor.

The transcendent issue now in Russia is not who is the best leader or what is the best economic policy. It is much more fundamental. The issue is whether young institutions of limited government and the rule of law will be allowed to grow and blossom, or whether a new personalistic authoritarianism will be imposed on the country. More and more, Russians have expressed fear of a dictatorship on the model of Pinochet in Chile; Yeltsin, to advance his own conception of reform and to assure his own power, is now even further on the way to becoming such a dictator himself.

Yeltsin continues after the carnage in Moscow to promise free parliamentary elections in December and the restoration of democratic government. In the meantime he will rule by decree—democratic dictatorship, some of his supporters called it, forgetting that this was Lenin's phrase. Already Yeltsin has moved to suppress the irreconcilable opposition and their newspapers, and has briefly imposed censorship on the rest of the press. He has forced the chairman of the Constitutional Court to resign by threatening to prosecute him, and has indicated that "treasonous" elements will not be permitted to participate in the December election— the same logic that the Communists used when they took over Eastern Europe. All indications so far are that Yeltsin will decree constitutional terms and an election law to give him a rubber-stamp parliament that he can manipulate as he sees fit. Perhaps his most conscious model is Prime Minister Stolypin, who dissolved the newly created Duma in 1907, decreed a new election law, and obtained a Duma that remained submissive until the 1917 revolution. Indeed, the name for the lower house proposed in Yeltsin's constitutional draft last summer was the "Duma."

Meanwhile, there is still potential trouble in the provinces and republics of the Russian Federation, where a majority of the local councils came out against Yeltsin's suppression of the central parliament. Yeltsin has responded by removing several provincial governors and threatening to dissolve obstreperous provincial assemblies. Thus he is trampling on the basic principles of federalism, at the price of stirring up more resistance that could well take violent forms in the non-Russian minority republics.

Conceivably Yeltsin could be pressured by Western governments into more respect for democratic norms. Unfortunately, this does not appear likely, given his stubborn personality on the one hand, and on the other the uncritical support that Western leaders have so far been expressing for him.

By dissolving the Russian parliament, and outlawing its defenders, admittedly without any constitutional basis, Yeltsin has taken a step of political and economic expediency fraught with great risks for both peace and democracy in his country. For him and his apologists, the end appears to justify the means. This was precisely the original sin of the Communists.

CHAPTER THIRTY-FOUR

YELTSIN IN CONTROL
(OCTOBER 1993)

Yeltsin's violent confrontation with the Russian parliament and its supporters on 3–4 October 1993 set the stage for personal rule legitimized by a new, authoritarian constitution.

After months of adulation of Boris Yeltsin, all through the crises of March–April and September–October, some American leaders and media outlets are beginning to have second thoughts about the Russian president's authoritarian proclivities. But they should not be surprised now at his rule by decree, the suppression of parties and press that he considers extremist, and his attempts to bring local governments to heel. Yeltsin's record of relations with the institutions of representative government shows that his suppression of the Russian parliament and his "temporary" assumption of absolute power were perfectly natural if not inevitable.

Most Western spokesmen still cling to the hope that Yeltsin believes in democracy and that he will abide by his promises of free elections for a new parliament in December and for president in June of next year. This scenario of a Russian Charles de Gaulle, surrendering the personal power that he had obtained in an anti-constitutional coup and submitting to the democratic rules of a new constitution, is the most optimistic. Conceivably, quiet suasion by the United States and other Western governments might nudge Yeltsin in that direction. However, the steps he has taken since putting down the parliamentarians and their extremist supporters cast a pall of doubt over such an outcome.

Even if the promised elections are held on schedule, Yeltsin will be exercising untrammeled power to decree new constitutional terms and election rules. He has already announced that "treasonous" parties and individuals as he defines them will not be allowed to participate, while launching his own semi-official political organization, "Russia's Choice." He has defined the structure of a new parliament, the "Federal Assembly," without waiting for the new constitution. He has decreed a referendum on the constitution for the same date—12 December—that the two houses of the parliament, the "Council of the Federation" and the "State Duma" are to be elected, without yet even deciding on the constitutional text that is to be voted on.

Presumably the new constitution will be some combination of the version that Yeltsin floated last June and the version that his largely appointed constitutional conference recommended in July. The presidential powers in these drafts have clearly been designed to obviate the parliamentary resistance that balked Yeltsin between March and September. Barring any unforeseen intervention, it will be up to Yeltsin himself to determine the constitutional terms to be put before the voters.

Given Yeltsin's control of the media, his ban on troublesome opponents, the preponderance of financial resources on his side, and the limited time for tolerated opponents to organize and campaign, he will win in all probability on the constitution, and his new party will deliver a parliament that will do his bidding. If not, he will be back at odds with the parliament again just as he has been for the past year and a half, except that this time he will have the powers written into the new constitution that he used unconstitutionally against the old parliament—to dissolve the legislative branch and proclaim a state of emergency. Yeltsin waves the banner of Peter the Great, of all people (Stalin's role model, too!), but the more apt precedent for him and his entourage is Prime Minister Stolypin and his tactics of keeping the Duma submissive.

❖   ❖   ❖

Most Western judgments about Yeltsin have been colored by what we might term, paraphrasing the title of Leon Trotsky's famous book about Stalin, the "Yeltsin school of falsification of history." The President and his entourage represent recent Russian history as an either or struggle between Yeltsin-style "democrats" and die-hard "Communist-Fascist" partisans of the old Soviet Union. They ignore all the in-between centrist forces and the reformers who have their reservations about the president. They dismiss the vast (though incomplete) work of reform accomplished under Gorbachev as merely an attempt to shore up the old system, though it was only Gorbachev's reforms that gave Yeltsin his chance to rise to the top. They call the constitution and the parliament remnants of the Brezhnev regime, when of course the old Communist Supreme Soviet was a rubber stamp with no power to oppose anyone, and the parliament that Yeltsin dissolved was the same one that chose him to be its first chairman when it was elected in 1990. They demonize the word "soviet" (which is merely Russian for "council"), to campaign against the present institutions of local self-government by lumping the revolutionary soviets of 1917, the supine soviets of the Communist era, and the recalcitrant soviets of today all together as the same, evil thing. There are Orwellian tones in the justifications we hear of Yeltsin's policies and his personal power-grab: dictatorship is democracy, centralism is federalism, misery is progress, Russian hegemony is national self-determination. Yet one may harbor a suspicion that Yeltsin is the kind of politician who believes his own rationalizations about his enemies, which is even more dangerous.

Thanks to the forty-eight-hour historical perspective of most of the American media, the impression has taken hold that the events of 3 and 4 October in Moscow were an unprovoked uprising of left and right zealots bent on restoring Communism. The parliament was believed to be a "hard-line" Communist holdover and the center of an anti-democratic conspiracy. Yeltsin was faulted only for using excessive force to put down the rebellion, or else for not suppressing his enemies sooner.

In fact the parliament contained perhaps 20 percent Communist ideologues and ultra-nationalists, along with 20 percent unwavering Yeltsinites and 60 percent pragmatists in an unsteady center. But Yeltsin failed to seek consensus with the centrist majority of the parliament, and instead polarized Russian politics with his stubborn defense of presidential prerogative and economic shock therapy. This stance led to the crisis of last March that served as the curtain-raiser to the present imbroglio. Still, the parliament was no monolith, and it could not quite muster the two-thirds vote necessary to impeach the president at that point.

After the April referendum endorsing the President and his policies, the pro-Yeltsin deputies largely boycotted the parliament. The Center crumbled as Yeltsin and Speaker Khasbulatov put the squeeze on it. However, the legislators remaining in the White House on 3 and 4 October did not all belong to the "Red-Brown" extreme. One among them was Rumiantsev, the Social Democratic leader and secretary of the legislative-executive constitutional commission that produced a draft constitution last spring (ignored by Yeltsin, himself the official chairman of the commission, who never attended a meeting).

What of Yeltsin's two main enemies, Rutskoi and Khasbulatov? Yeltsinite propaganda and most of the American media represent them as hard-line conspirators trying to turn the clock back to Soviet times, omitting the fact that these hapless leaders of the resistance in the White House were both creatures of Yeltsin himself, Rutskoi as Yeltsin's choice to run for vice president on the same ticket with him in 1990, Khasbulatov as Yeltsin's choice to succeed him as chairman of the Russian parliament when he moved up to the new presidency. In the course of the parliament's stand-off with Yeltsin over the last year and a half, Khasbulatov acquired the reputation of a power-hungry manipulator, even among centrists, leaving him mainly the nostalgic Communists and the ultra-nationalists on whom to rely when the moment of truth arrived. Rutskoi has been seen as a well-meaning but naive military man who could never reconcile himself to the breakup of the Soviet Union, and who therefore, like Khasbulatov, found sympathy mostly among the "Red-Brown" extremists. There is as yet no evidence that prior to Yeltsin's dissolution of the parliament on 21 September Khasbulatov and Rutskoi had tried to arrange an armed coup against Yeltsin. Apparently they realized that their sole option was to try to hold him to account under the terms of the existing constitution.

The great irony in the events of 3 and 4 October is that the most demonstrative defenders of the principle of constitutionalism—for their own purposes, to be sure—were the extremists of the Left and Right. The proparliament riots were clearly organized by Communist and nationalist die-hards, although it is unclear what they actually expected to accomplish. In such confused and fast-moving crisis situations it is often very difficult to sort out intentions and results, or fix the blame for the first shot when violence is so likely. The tendency is to look back at events and impose more logic on them in retrospect than was really operative, and this is precisely what the Yeltsin camp is doing, perhaps in preparation for a show trial of the alleged conspirators on the eve of the December election. For their part, Rutskoi and Khasbulatov and the nerve-frazzled occupants of the blockaded White House seem to have been momentarily carried away by the belief that the mob who broke through to the building was just like the popular upsurge that defeated the coup of August 1991, and they are guilty at least of imagining on the spot that they were going to overthrow Yeltsin.

The events of 3 October caught Yeltsin's lieutenants by surprise, with their chief closeted at his dacha. They had no assurance that they could count on the military, until a high council of the generals decided early in the morning of 4 October, after the opposition's impulsive attempt to seize the Ostankino television, to go with Yeltsin. Even then, it has been reported, the government trusted only officers to man the tanks brought in to batter the White House into submission.

As the full picture of events has filtered through Yeltsin's censorship, the brief hopes of the parliamentary opposition may not have been so unfounded as they appeared afterwards. Yeltsin's popularity had been falling during the summer, and his decree against the parliament had shaken up defenders of constitutionalism and provincial rights all over the country. Possibly he felt that if he delayed putting the parliament in its place, or again if he allowed it to extend its defiance after the riots of 3 October, his own authority and his ability to rely on the military might evaporate. Thus it is true, as Yeltsin's apologists argue, that in subduing the parliamentarians on 4 October he had no choice, but that meant no choice after he had already decided to assume the powers of a dictator by closing down the parliament.

The potentially most destabilizing problem in Russia now is relations between Moscow and the provinces, in the absence of a real understanding of federalism and its delimitation of powers between the federal government and the states. To the provinces federalism means that they can do anything they want, and override federal laws if they wish. To Yeltsin and his central government it means that they can appoint and control local officials, turning the provinces into mere administrative subdivisions hardly different from their status under the Communists.

The practice that Yeltsin began after the August Putsch of appointing provincial governors plus "personal representatives" to oversee the governors, was initially confirmed by the central parliament but later curbed again. Now Yeltsin is intervening on his own to remove governors who failed to support him during the September-October crisis; to dissolve provincial councils (that awful word "soviet" once more); and to decree the constitutional arrangements and election rules according to which provincial and local governments shall be reconstructed. Not surprisingly, he is being met with resistance. For example, in Karelia (one of the "republics" based on an ethnic minority) politics are generally moderate, but the republic's Supreme Soviet voted to protest Yeltsin's dissolution of the central parliament; then refused to put the question of dissolving itself on the agenda; and finally set new elections for July 1994, long after Yeltsin's deadline.

How Yeltsin may deal with this kind of non-compliance, above all in the non-Russian minority republics, without losing the mystique of power, is anybody's guess. If force is to be considered, it immediately calls up the question of Yeltsin's relationship with the military. Some observers question whether he could depend on the army at all to bring recalcitrant republics and provinces to heel, and suggest that the generals might rebel against him if he tried to use the armed forces in this manner. To avoid such a crisis in dealing with the republics, he would have to work long and patiently through a strictly political process—but this would be out of character.

Nevertheless, we must not overlook Yeltsin's remarkable ability to move swiftly at times of crisis to turn events to his advantage. One such moment was the August Putsch of 1991; another came in March 1993, when he snatched victory from the jaws of defeat by turning a near-impeachment into a television triumph with a crowd of his supporters; and yet another example was his response to the riots of 3 and 4 October. He understands the psychological essence of power, and he knows that you capture the perception of power by appearing to exercise it. When Napoleon Bonaparte seized power in 1799 he is supposed to have said, "The French cannot be ruled—except by me." Yeltsin appears to believe the same of the Russians today.

CHAPTER THIRTY-FIVE

YELTSIN AND DEMOCRACY
(DECEMBER 1993)

Yeltsin's suppression of the Russian parliament invited divergent evaluations of its impact from foreign observers. Looming largest was the factor of personal politics centering on Yeltsin himself.

Events in the Russian Federation under the leadership of Boris Yeltsin have stirred up a measure of controversy within the community of what used to be known as "sovietologists" in the United States. I believe that these disagreements reflect not differences of basic philosophy or factual perception as much as what I would call different "levels of observation." Among these I distinguish three: the legalist; the Realpolitik (in two sub-levels, "hopeful" and "cynical"); and the psychocultural.

The legalist level of observation considers the constitutional and legal aspects of Yeltsin's governance and his relations with the other institutions of authority in Russia. It stresses his step-by-step estrangement from the parliamentary bodies that initially brought him to power and backed his consolidation of leadership; the conflict between the executive decree-making power and the legislative law making power; and the rupture of executive-legislative relations leading to Yeltsin's dissolution of the parliament in September and his suppression of parliamentary resistance in October. It faults Yeltsin for overstepping the bounds of the separation of powers and ultimately carrying out an extra-constitutional coup d'état, thus setting a dangerous precedent for the overthrow of any inconvenient constitution. The result presently is authoritarian rule and a constitutional structure that may prove to be only decorative, given its dependence on the president's will. To invoke an historical analogy, I would suggest the "Napoleon III scenario," where a popularly elected president, at odds with the elected assembly, dissolves the latter by force and assumes dictatorial power. The legalist level of observation characterizes a substantial majority of American academic russianists in history and political science.[1]

The hopeful variant of the Realpolitik level of observation judges Yeltsin's actions as leader as a necessary series of steps to overcome the blockage of his reform program by conservatives in the parliamentary bodies, who made use of what was supposedly a holdover Communist constitution. Ultimately Yeltsin had no alternative other than getting rid of the parliament and the opposition, and introducing a new constitution and a cleaned-up democracy moving rapidly toward the market economy. Hopefully he will return to the role of president under the separation of powers and allow genuine democracy to develop through the new Federal Assembly. This would be the "Charles de Gaulle scenario," where a popular hero, brought to power by a coup d'état, nonetheless abides by his new constitution and presides over the development of a stable democracy.

The hopeful variant of Realpolitik is reflected in the official pronouncements of most Western governments, in most of the American media, and in public statements by a number of eminent American russianists. However, this point of view is uncomfortable with the historical facts and issues adduced by the legalists, and typically glosses them over and even misrepresents them (as with references to the "Brezhnev Constitution" and "Communist holdovers").

The cynical variant of the Realpolitik level of observation acknowledges Yeltsin's movement toward dictatorship as adduced by the legalistic school, but nevertheless considers his rule as the best alternative for an indefinite period to maintain stability in Russia, open the country for Western business activity, and keep it on a cooperative, pro-Western track in its foreign policy. This would be the "Pinochet scenario," where an authoritarian ruler suppresses the destabilizing tendencies permitted by constitutional institutions, presses toward the market economy, and cooperates with the major Western powers in foreign affairs.

The cynical variant of Realpolitik is rarely if ever articulated in public, and is known only third-hand and anecdotally. However, one may presume that many public supporters of the hopeful variant are more sophisticated than they appear about the legal aspects of Yeltsin's rule, and therefore infer that the cynical variant must be fairly widespread, particularly in the American government. If so, part of its cynicism is to assume the garb of the hopeful variant.

The psychocultural level of observation perceives the Yeltsin government in the framework of long-term Russian characteristics that limit the development of democratic government. In this view, the gradual development required for democracy to develop in Russia was disrupted, first by the attempted conservative coup of August 1991, and again by Yeltsin's suppression of the constitutional institutions that had emerged from perestroika. The result was a return to the old psychology of authoritarian rule and popular political apathy. Perhaps this should be called the "Boris II scenario."

The psychocultural level of observation is taken by a number of Western authorities and is favored by many Russian writers, notably Alexander Yakovlev and Alexander Tsipko. Yeltsin's regime, in this view, is moving naturally toward a reassertion of Russian national power and an imperial sphere of interest consonant with the country's historical tradition. Such a development would confound the expectations of both variants of the Realpolitik school.

Now some specific observations of my own. The proposition of Russia's transition to democracy and a market economy requires us to address the question, what is this transition *from*. It is not the end of a "failed Marxist experiment," as much of the media have it, but rather the outcome of a complex historical evolution, of which the genuinely utopian experiment was only an early and very brief phase. The Stalinist and neo-Stalinist regime from the 1930s to the 1980s is best described as a system of postrevolutionary militarized state socialism under the rule of the bureaucratic "New Class," using Marxist-Leninist theory as the obligatory false consciousness to legitimize a highly totalitarian order. This system reached an impasse when it could not accommodate the population's growing sophistication and its consumer demands. The outcome, however, was governed by leadership choices.

Gorbachev, coming to power after the demise of the Communist gerontocracy in 1982–85, attempted to resolve the impasse by working back through the historical evolution of the Soviet regime to try to find better political and economic models. Yeltsin, motivated as he was by the determination to destroy Gorbachev, aimed to undo even more of the revolutionary heritage. Continuing to implement his anti-Gorbachev policies as an independent president, he encountered new opposition in the Russian parliament and in nationalist chagrin over the demise of the Union. To address this opposition he retreated step by step from his democratic commitments, as the legalistic school has shown, until he finally suppressed the opposition altogether. The historical model here is Prime Minister Stolypin and his subordination of the tsarist Duma. Steps by Yeltsin to create a presidentially controlled inner administration distinct from the "government" (i.e., the cabinet and the ministries) recalled both the Communist Party's role and a series of tsarist arrangements.

In nationality relations Yeltsin also retreated from his early commitments once his own power was secure. With respect to the provinces and republics of the Russian Federation he backed away from the promises of local self-government contained in the so-called "Federation Treaty," in favor of a "single administrative hierarchy." With respect to the former union republics, he moved gradually to establish Russian hegemony or a sphere of influence, with emphasis on economic ties and on Russia's peacekeeping role in the former Soviet region under a Russian Monroe Doctrine.

In economics, Yeltsin stuck with his radical reform policies as a foil to use against the Russian parliament. However, the consequences of this utopian program, given the lack of cultural foundations and the necessary legal and institutional infrastructure, have been sharply negative in terms of inflation and falling production and income, with the potential of a social explosion if the trend continues. I anticipate that once Yeltsin has firmed up his political position, can ignore the reactions of foreign governments, and has suppressed those at home who might say "I told you so," he will shift his economic direction and revert to central economic controls, analogously to his turn against democratic government and self-determination (without directly acknowledging these changes).

My own position is a combination of the legalist and psychocultural levels. I recognize the long-term traits of Russian political culture that have ironically reemerged with Yeltsin under the label of democracy. However, with the legalists, I appreciate the role of individual leadership and decisions that may encourage or discourage the evolution of constitutional government and the rule of law. Together with both the legalist and psychocultural approaches, I am pessimistic about the prospects for genuine democracy in Russia in the short run. Yet, considering the possibilities for basic change in a more and more modern country, I share some of the optimism of the hopeful school, but only within the span of a decade or so (unless democratic development is upset, as before, by the nationality problem). By contrast, I believe that the cynical point of view, to the extent that it exists, is destined to be rudely disappointed on all counts.

CHAPTER THIRTY-SIX

THE REVENGE OF RUSSIAN POLITICAL CULTURE (NOVEMBER 1993)

The crisis of October 1993 climaxed a trend back to old Russian habits of authoritarianism and centralism that permitted Yeltsin to impose personal rule and potentially to revert to an imperialistic appeal.

To those in the profession of sovietology who always thought that deep Russian cultural traits were a major factor shaping Soviet Communism, Gorbachev's *perestroika* and the rapid progress toward constitutional government under his leadership came as a perplexing innovation, though not an unwelcome one. Now we know, unfortunately, that these cultural insights were never really invalidated. Noting Yeltsin's recent steps toward presidential dictatorship, we can see that the old Russian habits of authoritarianism, centralism, imperialism, and conformism in belief were never pushed very far below the surface during the last few years of reform.

There is, to be sure, an alternative strand in the Russian tradition, represented since the eighteenth century by the Russian intelligentsia, the class defined by its attachment to culture and ideas (especially Western) and its rejection of the prevailing social order. But the intelligentsia is purist and unstable. Perestroika, for the first time in Russia's history, drew in the intellectuals as a support for the government. Then, growing disillusioned with Gorbachev, many of them rallied to Yeltsin and became apologists for his new pseudodemocracy or for what they perceived to be the lesser evil.

Yeltsin's personality seems tailor-made to fit the expectations for individual authority emanating from Russian political culture. He is bold and impulsive, a fearless gambler, domineering and vindictive. Like the beneficent monarch, he claims to represent the united people against the craven bureaucrats. Given these proclivities and the weakness of so much of the Russian population for a "president-tsar,"[1] the crisis of September–October, when Yeltsin dissolved the Russian parliament, suppressed its supporters, and imposed personal rule, was virtually inevitable.

Since Yeltsin's coup and the futile resistance of the most extreme oppositionists, the traditional Russian style in government has become more and more apparent—the leader decrees and the people conform. The police quickly reverted to their old habits, presumably with assent from above—arrests without cause or warrant, bugging dissidents or beating them up, and running dragnet operations. The latter, aimed particularly at "dark" people from the Caucasus who are blamed for the current crime wave, is a particular form of ethnic cleansing that is unfortunately very popular with the Russian majority.

Regional governments, who behaved very independently after the collapse of Communism, are now being brought into line by Yeltsin-appointed governors and personal representatives, and by Yeltsin-decreed constitutional provisions. Local executive power is to be part of a centrally-controlled "single administrative hierarchy," and provincial legislative bodies will be reduced to no more than fifty members, small enough to be easily manipulated, and curbed by the veto power of the appointed governors besides.

Yeltsin's economic reform program of privatization and free markets would appear to be the antithesis of the Russian statist tradition, tsarist as well as Soviet. Yet even in reform economics, Russian habits are showing up. The economists who authored Yeltsin's program illustrate the penchant among the Russian intelligentsia for embracing utopian Western ideas—now classical economic theory and the Chicago School—and carrying them to extremes in the name of a "radiant future." Furthermore, Yeltsin's method of introducing reform is characteristically Russian—by decree of the autocrat—without thought for the practical financial and legal basis that the West takes for granted.

The chaotic consequences of the Yeltsinites' economic libertarianism underscore the need in the Russian cultural context for some degree of governmental management to keep the economy functioning. Instead, we observe the Russian tendency to plunge into anarchy when the heavy hand of central control is lifted, as it was in 1917.

Beyond all this, the Russian anti-mercantile tradition can already be felt in a growing popular backlash, reflected in the stance of the ill-fated parliament, against the new speculator economy. With his enemies disposed of, one can well imagine Yeltsin using his personal power to reverse the economic reform line as it becomes politically inexpedient and when he no longer needs to please the West. After all, he pushed the free-market reforms primarily as a foil to destroy first Gorbachev and then the Russian parliament, and he may be quite capable of changing his beliefs now that those objectives have been accomplished.

Having seized unlimited power, including a free hand to dictate future constitutional arrangements, Yeltsin seemingly permitted an open democratic process leading to the ratification of the new constitution and the election of new parliamentary bodies. New parties sprang up instantly, though two of them— "Russia's Choice" and the "Party of Russian Unity and Concord"—were officially inspired and led by members of the Yeltsin cabinet, an arrangement that could guarantee Yeltsin's control of the new parliament while maintaining the illusion of a free choice. Furthermore, the electoral process was closed to the banned political organizations and publications of the far Left and the far Right that had most bitterly opposed him up to October. The rest of the political spectrum was hopelessly fractionated among parties that existed, as the Russian say, mostly in the imaginations of their leaders. Yeltsin still tried to remain above the contest as waged by political parties, and avoided explicit identification as leader of his own political forces, preferring to enjoy power as a direct gift from "the people." Touting Peter the Great as the model Russian ruler, he seemed to regard himself as a sort of elected tsar.

It would be surprising, given the origins of this new democracy, if the parliamentary bodies it produced prove to be more than decorative, as some provincial leaders have warned. To the degree that they may become truly independent, however, Russia will be back in the same situation of legislative-executive gridlock that led to the autumn crisis and personal rule.

The near-unanimity of Western leaders and media in swallowing Yeltsin's spurious democratic claims in the face of his crude violations of constitutional processes recalls the pro-Communist fellow-travelling of the 1930s. To be sure, the ideological positions are reversed, but in both cases wish-fulfillment led foreign sympathizers to be taken in by Moscow's propaganda. This time, however, there is one very practical motive for the West. Yeltsin has been willing to be subsidized by Western governments and investors in return for conducting a docile foreign policy. As for the Clinton Administration, for domestic political purposes it has desperately needed to be able to claim one foreign-policy success among its many reverses and tergiversations, and so it persisted in writing blank checks to Yeltsin all through the constitutional crisis of 1993.

Nevertheless, the united front of Western acclaim started to crack after Yeltsin assumed openly dictatorial power and imposed censorship in the course of the September-October crisis. Moreover, Russian independence in foreign policy has already begun to show, as Yeltsin caters to latent nationalist opinion and as the military who saved him in October present their bill. Hence his turn against NATO membership for the East European countries, the threat to veto UN sanctions against Libya, and the assertion of a Russian Monroe Doctrine to keep the peace in the former Soviet realm. A clue to Yeltsin's aspirations is his new identification of himself with the eleventh-century Kievan prince Yaroslav the Great and the "gathering-in of the Russian lands"—a point of Slavic unity that could not have been lost on the Ukrainians and Belorussians. We may expect these hegemonistic tendencies to become more obvious, as geopolitical logic, Russian tradition, and Yeltsin's own deepest instincts impel him to reassert Russian influence in the "near abroad" of ex-Soviet republics, and perhaps in the old East European Bloc and in the Middle East.

Does Yeltsin's consonance with Russian political culture mean that the authoritarian type of rule reestablished in the course of the year 1993 will go on indefinitely? Not necessarily. First of all, Yeltsin's incapacitation or death would be a hazardous point for the new system, as it always is with personalistic regimes where no strong successor has been allowed to develop a real power base or public appeal. His disappearance from the scene could invite real life to spring up in his manipulated constitutional structures, just as the post-Brezhnev succession allowed the old dummy Communist institutions to take on a semblance of reality.

Secondly, Yeltsin's style of rule will not ultimately be compatible with the nontraditional elements in Russian political culture, i.e., the intelligentsia and the millions of educated urban dwellers, whose growing pressure against the Brezhnev system set the stage for reform under Gorbachev. Ironically, it is these people who have most favored Yeltsin, out of fear of backsliding to Communism, while his most natural allies on the nationalist wing, not recognizing their affinity with him beneath their opposing ideological slogans, have been most vocally resisting him. If Yeltsin lasts long enough and if his Great-Russian irredentist proclivities become visible enough, the nationalist elements will no doubt come around to him. Russian authoritarianism and imperialism are challenges that we are not done with.

CHAPTER THIRTY-SEVEN

PROSPECTS FOR DEMOCRACY IN RUSSIA (MAY–JUNE 1994)

In the relative calm following the tumultuous events of 1993 and the imposition of Yeltsin's constitution, it was possible to reflect on different ways of divining Russia's political future. The unique personal factor of Yeltsin's periodic moods of withdrawal put a limit to authoritarianism, and on occasion an evolution in the parliamentary direction, personified by Prime Minister Chernomyrdin, seemed possible.

Since the collapse of the Communist Party and the Soviet Union in 1991, commentators on Russian politics have ranged from naive optimism to dark pessimism about the prospects for democratic political life in that troubled country. Inevitably, judgments have fluctuated with the unfolding of events and the rise and decline of particular personalities. Many observers, hopeful about the outlook for democracy when President Boris Yeltsin dominated the scene in 1992 and 1993, turned pessimistic about Russian politics after he dissolved and shelled the parliament in the fall of 1993 and went on to impose a constitution with authoritarian presidential prerogatives. The following months suggested a more optimistic alternative from the democratic standpoint, until the Chechnya crisis of late 1994 and early 1995 drove a new wedge between the Russian government on the one hand and Russian public opinion together with foreign well-wishers on the other.

During these tumultuous months, just as in August 1991, Yeltsin acted with an intuitive sense of the nature of power—that power lies in the eye of the beholder, and that it is won, as Lenin said, by picking it up off the streets and exercising it in a way for all to see. However, he still needed to dispose of his challengers in the existing parliament, and on September 21, after many hints of resolute new action, he reactivated his suspended March coup and declared the parliament dissolved.

Dissolution of the parliament was no surprise: One merely needed to project the short-run trend. But when Yeltsin shelled the parliament into submission and decreed his own authoritarian constitution, Russians of all political stripes were deeply shocked and aggrieved by these events. In the outside world the reality of authoritarianism represented by Yeltsin and his entourage began to overtake the democratic faith in Russia's president. The danger of despotism loomed large: Suppression of the parliament recalled Lenin's dissolution of the democratically elected Constituent Assembly in 1918. It was widely expected that Yeltsin would rig the elections he set for 12 December and achieve an easily manipulable parliament, just as Stolypin did after his coup of June 1907 against the original Duma. Everything seemed to fit the Russian pattern of authoritarian backsliding by radical reformers.

However, events continued to confound predictions. Ever since he arrived on the Moscow scene, the Russian president has exhibited a mercurial temperament, with near-manic episodes separated by periodic depression and withdrawal from the political fray, as occurred after the August 1991 coup, and again after the October 1993 crisis. Yeltsin distanced himself from the election campaign and failed to identify himself with "Russia's Choice," even though it was the party explicitly formed by his supporters to press on with free-market reform. He was unable to prevent the reform camp from splintering into several rival lists.

Except for the claimed percentage of turnout to legitimize the constitutional referendum, the actual elections proceeded with remarkable honesty, as attested by the outcome, giving Yeltsin a legislative body even less manipulable than the one he had suppressed. So—no more Napoleon III, despite the authoritarian reflexes of some Yeltsinites who called for a "benign dictatorship" or "a plan to suspend democratic procedures for a time."[1] However, democratic futures in the Russian political stock market tumbled with the likelihood of a radical right threat such as Zhirinovsky represented, and of a violent new confrontation between the executive and legislative branches of government.

In fact, none of these dire forebodings came to pass immediately, as individual behavior again foiled all straightline calculations. First, Zhirinovsky proceeded to self-destruct. Secondly, Yeltsin, buffeted by the election, remained in a prolonged state of withdrawal, "a politician who is physically and politically exhausted," in the words of analyst Alexander Rahr.[2] He seemed able to act only out of pique, as when he refused to meet Richard Nixon after the former U.S. president, serving as President Clinton's unofficial envoy, had conferred beforehand with Russian oppositionists.

Meanwhile a third personality emerged to steer events, namely Prime Minister Chernomyrdin. Chernomyrdin had proven himself a politician of uncommon adroitness during all the kaleidoscopic events of 1993, going along with Yeltsin's maneuvers, including the dissolution of the parliament, but remaining aloof from the economic reform program and maintaining his acceptability to the opposition. With the cabinet reshuffle of January 1994, eliminating the ardent free-marketeers Gaidar and Boris Fyodorov, Chernomyrdin became the effective head of the government and the only leader acceptable to a wide enough political spectrum to support stable but representative rule. *The New York Times* reported on 25 January, "It is Mr. Chernomyrdin who is calling most of the shots. Mr. Yeltsin is said by associates to have sunk into one of his post-crisis periods of lassitude and even depression, doing little and saying even less."[3] A little later, *Nezavisimaya Gazeta* headlined, "Yeltsin issues orders, Chernomyrdin administers the country," and attributed to a visiting American congressman the appraisal of Chernomyrdin as a potential future president: "A careful pragmatist, attentive to signals from the West, who at the same time is able to get along with the opposition and conciliate the Communists and national-patriots, he impresses Americans with his predictability."[4] By March, Chernomyrdin had actually passed Yeltsin in the pollsters' influence ratings, thereby provoking an explosive confrontation with his chief.[5]

With Yeltsin's eclipse and the rise of Chernomyrdin as the country's de facto leader, the possibility appeared that Russia might revert from its dangerous presidential structure of government to the parliamentary republic on the German or Italian model that the old Soviet constitution pretended to embody. There is a historical parallel for this sort of unplanned development, in the early years of the Third French Republic, when hopes for a monarchical restoration or a strong presidency foundered on the squabbles of their proponents and gave way to the parliamentary republic and cabinet government. The outcome of this process in Russia, however, depended on the balance of influence between Chernomyrdin and Yeltsin, and the inclination of the president to try to impose his authority again.

How far Yeltsin had slipped, and how much the October events were held against him, was demonstrated by the new parliament's vote in February 1994 to approve an amnesty for all involved both in the August 1991 putsch and in the October 1993 clashes. Yeltsin or aides speaking for him—tried to overrule the amnesty, but in vain, thereby revealing that real power was slipping from their hands. Yeltsin's orders were ignored. The prosecutor-general whom he had just installed in October— the very same Alexei Kazannik who had given up his Supreme Soviet seat to Yeltsin in 1989—resigned rather than block the amnesty as Yeltsin directed him to do.

Overall, the amnesty appears to have eased political tensions in all quarters. It ended for the time being the authoritarian threat represented by Yeltsin during the whole previous year. Yeltsin beat a retreat with the statement, "At present I do not see any real danger for civic accord."[6] The anti-Yeltsin reformer Sergei Shakhrai described the amnesty as "an act of reconciliation" that gave the country a "respite," evoking a general "sigh of relief," and saved Chernomyrdin's government from a parliamentary revolt.[7] Furthermore, by freeing the popular Rutskoi to pursue his announced presidential ambitions once again, the amnesty seemed to have allowed into play a more reasonable alternative to Zhirinovsky to rally the protest vote. Here again we have the unpredictable personal factor.

In March and April the elections were held that Yeltsin had required to form new local governments. Evincing the literalism of the not-too-well-educated, Yeltsin satisfied himself that he had finally liquidated the Soviet system by abolishing the old local councils, i.e. "soviets," an ironic exercise of old-style Russian centralism against bodies that had actually begun to function more democratically and autonomously under the Gorbachev reforms. Popular apathy and cynicism had now become the rule, with turnouts in the new elections around 25 percent and results favoring the Communist and Agrarian conservatives. However, evolving in the social-democratic direction as in East-Central Europe (to the disgust of the hard-line Communist splinter groups), the old Left was less of a threat to democratic stability than the radical nationalists. Moreover, political resistance to Yeltsin on the part of many regions in the Russian Federation was a plus for democracy as well as federalism, at least for the time being. Many of the old *nomenklatura* proved surprisingly adept at recovering their status while playing by the new democratic and free-market rules. Paradoxically, they may turn out to be more of a stabilizing factor for constitutional government than the huge bloc of non-voters, especially among younger age groups, who could upset the whole picture if their anger drove them to come out for the ultra-Right.

Chernomyrdin's preeminence in the winter and spring of 1994 pointed to a curb on presidential authority and a strengthening of representative government. But the hazards of short-run projection were underscored by Yeltsin's return to a more vigorous role in May, following his late-April push for a nebulous "agreement on social concord" to curb political infighting. What may have been the Yeltsinites' motive surfaced afterwards, when the commission investigating the December referendum confirmed the worst opposition suspicions, that the turnout actually failed to reach the 50 percent required to make ratification of the constitution valid.[8] The Yeltsin team was ready with its response, that the failure would make no difference, and they now had the civic accord to argue against any oppositional thought of invalidating the post-December regime. In any case, so fatigued were all parties over constitutional wrangles that they let the new document stand.

Next, needing an enemy as always in order to function effectively, Yeltsin turned against the prime minister who had threatened his leadership. On June 1 Chernomyrdin was sent on "vacation," to the accompaniment of rumors that he might be replaced, and the way was opened for Yeltsin to take the initiative and defy the parliament with controversial decrees to fight crime (searches without warrant and preventive detention) and resume the free-market reforms (cash privatization and concessions to foreign banks and businesses). Once again Yeltsin succeeded in enhancing his own power psychologically simply by acting powerfully. He was back in action as "the Yeltsin of 1991," reported *Sevodnya.*[9] "One thing is obvious," said *Moscow News.* "The President has deliberately seized the initiative from Chernomyrdin. In effect, the President has demonstrated who is the master of the house."[10] Under this pressure Chernomyrdin, flexible politician that he was, swung back in Yeltsin's direction, risking his parliamentary support, and for the time being suspended his attachment to middle-of-the-road economics.

The contest between Yeltsin and Chernomyrdin in the spring and summer of 1994 was possible only because the Gorbachev-Yeltsin constitutional design incorporates the French model of strong president plus prime minister. This dualism has allowed a unique oscillation to develop within the political space afforded by the moderate revolutionary revival. At one pole are more authoritarian politics based on presidential powers and a commitment to free-market economics—the Latin American, Pinochet model. At the other pole lies more genuinely representative government incorporating an economic compromise between statism and private enterprise—a social-democratic model, perhaps. What overall direction this tension will produce is hard to say; the outcome depends on the unpredictable personal element of Yeltsin's health and moods.

Broader factors working against the more constitutional outcome are thoroughly familiar—apathy and cynicism among a population buffeted by the storms of economic change; unrequited national chagrin over the loss of empire and superpower status, vented in the Chechnya gambit; the power drives of authoritarian egos, coupled with the dearth of democratic leaders at the national level who are both capable and popular; the weakness of the party system as contrasted with East-Central Europe; the inter ests and habits of the old bureaucratic class, even if they may have been born again politically; the ingrained expectations of old Russian political culture, that leaders will command and the masses will submit.

Nevertheless, the historical pattern of moderate revolutionary revival points ultimately to the more democratic alternative, while the realities of the modern economy will not permit dispensing with the state (despite the international vogue of privatization that the collapse of Communism has triggered). Serious destabilization of these prospects is most likely from the radical nationalist quarter, if fueled by the "social explosion" of mass unemployment—the Weimar scenario. But again, the fact that Russia is at the end of its revolutionary process, not in the middle, suggests that moderation will prevail.

Chapter Thirty-Eight

Russia's Road to OZ
(March 1995)

A consideration of reform efforts in Russia since 1991, and their questionable results, prompts reflection about the contradiction between utopian ideology and the real requirements of economic success in a modern society.

The profession that used to be known as sovietology has been torn apart by debates over who failed to predict the collapse of Communism, and why. But a greater failure of prediction, by any lights, was Russia's slide into chaos, crime, and corruption under its post-Communist leadership. This misunderstanding stems from the same fallacious assumptions that have been steering Russia's reform efforts into that morass ever since the breakup of the USSR and the advent of Boris Yeltsin's leadership.

Reform in Russia has been inspired less by practical considerations than by ideology. It was both a reaction against whatever the Soviet regime professed to stand for, and an attempt to implement an idealized free-market image of Western society. However, the free-market model, the false consciousness of capitalism, is not adequate to describe Western reality, let alone guide a society emerging from the straitjacket of the Communist past. This contradiction between the theory that has inspired reform and the actual nature of modern society—particularly the peculiar kind of modern society that was the Soviet system—lies at the root of Russia's troubles of the 1990s.

Mesmerized by a utopian vision of capitalist society, Russia's reformers have shrugged off the country's past accomplishments, spotty as these may have been, in such key elements of modernization as industrialization, education, and technology. They have overlooked the parallel evolution—some have said "convergence"—of both Communist and Western societies towards bureaucratic organization and concentrated economic power. They have plunged into disruptive institutional rearrangements without first addressing the need for the legal, financial, and policy infrastructure that underlies the Western economy, not to mention the decades of struggle in the West to remedy the failings and injustices of capitalism. They have perpetrated deep and damaging contradictions among the various elements of their attempted reforms. They have inadvertently degraded their own society by facilitating crime, corruption, extremes of speculative wealth and mass impoverishment, and accelerated environmental deterioration, with consequences that may take decades to rectify. They are wasting the unique opportunity that their escape from totalitarianism has afforded them, to fashion a social system combining freedom, justice, and material progress.

The Utopian Program in Russia

How did reform in Russia come to be guided by a utopian plan that had little reference to Western reality and none to the Soviet past? What led the radical reformers to embrace a new false certainty when they had barely escaped from the false consciousness of Marxism-Leninism? The reasons are more emotional than logical.

Reform in Russia has been called a "revolution," both by Gorbachev and by his successors. This is an exaggeration; the reform era was not so much a new revolution as it was the closing phase of the original one that began in 1917, the phase of the moderate revolutionary revival. After a long postrevolutionary dictatorship, the country was returning to the democratic, constitutional hopes that arose in 1905 and in 1917 before violence and extremism overwhelmed the moderate reformers. Yet there was no consensus in Russia about this reversion to old reference points. Gorbachev wanted to preserve the "socialist choice" of 1917–18, while Yeltsin repudiated everything smacking of the Communist era and harked back to the semi-authoritarian structure of tsarism between 1905 and 1917.

In undertaking to dismantle the totalitarian system, Gorbachev worked his way back through Soviet history to attack the military-style planned economy and the "command-administrative system" in the name of the NEP model of market socialism. He gingerly relaxed state controls over those sectors—retail trade, services, agriculture—where nationalization and command methods had been most inappropriate to begin with. However, under contemporary Soviet conditions of centralism and superindustrialism these reforms were far more difficult to accomplish than in the 1920s without risking deep economic disruption. As everyone in Russia was soon saying, *perestroika* broke up the old economic guidance mechanism without putting anything in its place. The fundamental fallacy was to suppose that the market could be invoked out of nothing as an instrument for the transition to itself.

Nevertheless, in 1989 and 1990, under the influence of Western ideology and the Communist collapse in Eastern Europe, Soviet economic thinking underwent a paradigm shift. The pursuit of market socialism, barely underway, was supplanted by the conviction that only a purely private, capitalist market economy could rescue the Soviet Union from its economic difficulties. This was the presumption underlying the "five hundred days" plan of 1990. As one rereads this proposal, one is struck by its ambition to combine emergency economic stabilization with radical change: "The program sets the task of taking everything possible away from the state and giving it to the people. . . . The right to property is realized through destatization and privatization, through the transfer of state property to citizens."[1] As an attempt to reconstruct the Soviet economy overnight in line with an abstract theory, the five hundred days plan was a manifesto of Bolshevism in reverse.

As Russia entered the Yeltsin phase of reform, it was driven all the more by ideology, both the negative reaction against anything associated with the Stalinist model, including socialism and planning, and the positive attraction of Western free-market capitalism. But the reformers failed to grasp that these ideologies neither described nor guided their respective systems, serving rather to obfuscate and legitimize them. If anything, Yeltsin's people were more genuinely devoted to their ideology than their Communist predecessors had ever been, except for the "heroic" period of the early Soviet years. Rejecting everything that happened since 1917 as a historical wrong turn, the Yeltsinites remind one of the anarchists of 1917–18 who wanted to tear up the tainted tsarist railroad tracks and start over again. Railing against a demonized image of the Soviet regime on the basis of an idealized image of the West, the reformers threw away the tools of planning and control that might have helped them deal with the problems they had inherited from the past.

The troubles of perestroika under Gorbachev were serious enough, but minor compared with the crisis brought on by the Yeltsin phase of reform. Here political events and the interaction of personalities became crucial, a point neglected by theories of an inevitable post-Communist transition. Yeltsin was clearly driven to settle scores with Gorbachev after their falling out in 1987. Taking advantage of Gorbachev's steps toward democratization in 1989–90, he put himself at the head of the radical democratic movement, won the leadership of the Russian Republic, and embraced those policies that were most calculated to embarrass and discredit his rival, specifically the radical free-market alternative in economics and self-determination in nationality relations.

Far from being a natural process of "transition" as it has been so widely represented, the Yeltsinite project of recreating capitalism was entirely without historical precedent. It was a deliberate attempt, by state command, to unscramble eggs, ignoring both the modern limitations of the market system and Russia's unreadiness for it. Yet the West connived in Yeltsin's pursuit of the free-market chimera, offering promises of aid and investment in return for radical reforms that would open up Russian markets and investment opportunities to Western capital.

Yeltsin's radical approach had precedents in the Russian intellectual tradition. It was a new manifestation of the old habit of political utopianism, the temptation to embrace ideal solutions without regard to the practical consequences. The program advanced by Yeltsin's deputy Gaidar was a form of super-Westernism, distrusting everything Russian and naively adopting the foreign model—even if it had to be imposed by old Russian command methods. However, like past Russian reforms copied from the West, the Yeltsin-Gaidar program rested on a serious misunderstanding of the Western context. Capitalism in the West was built over the course of centuries by capitalists pursuing their own profit; in Russia the reformers aimed to recreate capitalism overnight by an act of state policy, while they overlooked the century and a half of efforts in the West to address the defects and injustices of capitalism.

In their new attachment to the free-market ideal, the Russian reformers succumbed to the basic fallacy in Anglo-American economics, inherited from Adam Smith, that the pursuit of individual advantages necessarily yields in the aggregate the maximum community advantage. This error led them to minimize the role of the state in expressing a democratically-derived common interest and taking care of those "externalities" such as health, safety and environmental quality that are beyond the scope of the individual enterprise. Idealizing the capitalist market, the reformers overlooked both its short-term and long-term weaknesses—cyclical instability and structural unemployment on the one hand, corporate concentration and market manipulation on the other, problems that require continuous state intervention and management in order to make the market function as it is supposed to.

Today's utopians have unwittingly subscribed to Lenin's uncompromising formulation: between capitalism and socialism, "There is no third way." They assert, "You cannot jump over a chasm in two leaps," an argument that illustrates the fallacy of misplaced concreteness, i.e., describing a complex social situation with a physical metaphor, and then deducing answers from the physical properties of the metaphor.

The practical question is not which ideal system to choose and how to jump there, but how and how much the existing social system should be modified and what the side effects might be. In real life there are innumerable policy positions between Smithian laissez-faire capitalism and Stalinist barracks socialism. The challenge is to work out the best intermediate position for a particular country. Russia's circumstances, above all the challenge of escaping the burden of the Soviet past, do not necessarily call for the same policies that Western countries follow, let alone what Western ideology prescribes.

Defenders of the free-market project commonly assert that democratic government must rest on the market and private property, and that the

capitalist economy assures democracy. It follows that to consolidate democracy in the former Communist countries, the socialist economy had
to be broken up and converted to capitalism as rapidly as possible, to
create a new middle class and make the reforms irreversible. But the
premise is historically questionable, as well as the conclusion. Max Weber,
so fashionable today, actually wrote, "It is absolutely ridiculous to ascribe
to the high capitalism which is today being imported into Russia [this in
1906] . . . any elective affinity with 'democracy' let alone with 'liberty'."[2]
True, early capitalism, small-scale and individualist, was associated with
the rise of liberal government in Britain and America and with the principles of the French Revolution. In most of Europe, however, democratization of the political process proceeded only with the rise of the working
class and the critics of capitalism. In more recent history, there are ample
instances, from Mussolini's Italy to Pinochet's Chile, where capitalism
not only did not prevent the overthrow of democracy but connived in
it. Some measure of market freedom may be a necessary condition of
democracy, but it is not a sufficient one. The real question, for the West
as for the ex-Communists, is how to adapt democracy to the realities
of a society based on large organizations, by democratizing bureaucratic
structures rather than trying to break them up (as in Russia and in the
public sector in the West) or ignoring their implications (as in the private
sector in the West).

The Consequences of Utopianism

Like the other ex-Communist countries, Russia has been guided since
1991 by a combination of fallacies. They include the simplistic perception
of a Western model that never (or hardly ever) existed; systematic denigration of the public powers and national resources inherited from the
Soviet regime; and the urge to extirpate the past in the name of a myth.
These errors have torn the country apart economically as well as politically, creating a situation distinctly more serious than Brezhnev's era of
stagnation despite superficial appearances of Western-style glitz in the
major cities. Retrogression is disguised as progress. When and in what
form the country may regain a measure of stability and decent living
conditions for the mass of the population still remains to be seen.

The Gorbachev reforms are widely faulted, but for contradictory reasons: They went too far, too fast, or they did not go far enough, fast
enough. Gorbachev's regime certainly made economic mistakes—wage
increases without productivity increases, generating "inflationary over-
hang"; naive trust in managers who had no sensitivity to market stimuli;
and premature dismantling of the planning and controls that might have

guided more constructive reform, including conversion of the military-industrial complex. Russia would have done better following the Chinese path of market reform at the bottom while retaining planning at the top. However, reform in the Yeltsin phase, inspired by utopian ideology, has proved to be far more disruptive and confrontational.

With the decree powers voted to it by the Russian parliament in November 1991, the Yeltsin government undertook radical economic reconstruction along three principal lines—market liberalization, macroeconomic stabilization, and privatization. Marketization, on the NEP model, had already been carried to excess in the Gorbachev era in the application of the profit-and-loss principle to inappropriate areas, even to cultural and scientific institutions. But the critical step was the decision by the Yeltsin government in January 1992 to free most prices and loosen foreign exchange controls. A surge in prices was the inevitable result, launching one of history's classic inflations, evoking an orgy of speculation and white-collar crime, and devastating a large part of the Russian population economically. Prices rose so fast that they failed to stimulate domestic production and investment, while foreign imports undercut existing employment in consumer goods. Nevertheless, the Yeltsin government has continued to put marketization at the forefront of its program, even though the resulting chaos and criminality have more than offset any benefits that the free market might have offered in the encouragement of initiative and efficiency. Marshall Goldman writes, "These leaders all seem to have forgotten that, as a minimum, a successful reform must make the life of the average consumer better."[3]

Macroeconomic stabilization, in other words the shock therapy of restricting the money supply to fight inflation, has not merely failed in Russia—it has never been systematically applied, and for good reason. Shock therapy is a paradoxical treatment, aiming to cure an ailing economy by making it sicker. It proposes to liquidate "inefficient" firms through credit starvation and bankruptcy, but a whole country cannot go into bankruptcy and liquidate itself. While the shock prescription is orthodox Western medicine for the Third World, no developed country has voluntarily submitted to it.

Though shock therapy was dear to the hearts of Russia's new Western advisors, it was not really called for until the 1992 price reforms unleashed the inflationary storm. But from this point on, parliamentary resistance to Yeltsin, and the general fear of unemployment and a "social explosion," stymied the serious imposition of monetary restraints. The government deficit was financed not by borrowing but by unrestricted currency emission—just printing the money--while tax revenue remained in limbo between impossible demands and problematical collection. The inflationary surge has continued right down to the present, with all its deleterious consequences for public morale and the productive economy. Confounding the utopians, the goal of market liberalization hopelessly undercut the parallel goal of financial stabilization.

Privatization, the third component of reform, has achieved a mixed record. The Gorbachev regime, wedded to the "socialist choice," moved slowly here, acting mainly to ease restraints on new, small-scale private enterprise. By contrast, the Yeltsin regime abandoned the distinction between new enterprise and existing large-scale entities. It made the conversion of state property into private enterprises an ideological imperative, carried to extremes (airports and museums, for instance) undreamed of in the West. The reformers never realistically addressed the problems of what a state-initiated system of private ownership would ultimately look like, how they would deal with existing monopolies and conglomerates, who would take title to state property, and how it would be paid for, if at all.

Privatization has naturally proceeded furthest and most successfully in the sectors of small enterprise, housing, and direct consumer services where nationalization was least appropriate to begin with. In agriculture, the campaign to break up the collectives has achieved only a modest degree of individual farming, at the price of much disruption and declining output; turning the *kolkhozy* into genuine cooperatives supporting expanded private plots would have made much more sense. Meanwhile, contemporary capitalism in the West is rapidly socializing formerly independent business activity.

As to large-scale enterprise in Russia, the only way to privatize it was to give it away. The voucher method of distributing shares to employees and to the public seemed most democratic and politically palatable, though it highlighted the contradiction between the utopian eighteenth-century ideal of a democracy of smallholders and the twentieth-century reality of large authoritarian organizations. Inevitably, a large proportion of the vouchers issued to the public ended up in the hands of speculators. Employee shares, by contrast, harked back to old syndicalist ideas of workers' control, not heard since the Workers' Opposition of 1920–21. Finally, large blocks of shares were left in the hands of the state, causing Russia's supposedly private economy to look more like the French or Italian economic structures than the German or American. By most accounts, the chief gainers in privatization have been the old managers and officials, the nomenklatura, taking over as private fiefdoms the entities that they formerly directed as state bureaucrats. Marshall Goldman calls it "grabitization."[4]

Though the reforms of marketization, stabilization, and privatization have been justified as the answer both to pre-Gorbachevian stagnation and to Gorbachevian confusion, their effect on Russian economic performance has been little short of disastrous, recorded economic activity falling by 1993 to perhaps one-half of the level of the 1980s.[5] Reform advocates blame this collapse on the failings of the prereform system, just as the Communists habitually blamed "survivals of capitalism" for their troubles. Russia, it is suggested, had to go through the phase of "Wild West capitalism"—though this formula ignored Russia's accomplishment of primary capital accumulation under pre-Communist as well as Communist auspices. Gaidar went further, to suggest that economic disruption was the necessary price for quickly exploiting the window of opportunity to extirpate the *nomenklatura* as a ruling class and make the reforms irreversible. This was precisely the logic, in reverse, of the Bolshevik radicals like Bukharin who attempted to justify the economic disaster of War Communism between 1918 and 1921.

The ultimate irony of utopian reform, trying to implement an unreal image of the First World, has been to turn Russia into a Third-World country, the opposite of what the theorists of transformation expected. This means speculative capitalism, grafted onto an impoverished society to extract natural resources and exploit cheap labor, a kind of economy marked by colossal theft, speculation, and luxury imports. Solzhenytsin describes it as "fraught with unproductive, savage, and repulsive forms of behavior, the plunder of the nation's wealth, the likes of which the West has not known."[6] With widening inequality and endemic corruption, Russia is headed for the model not of Germany but of Brazil, or perhaps of a low-level Arab sheikdom where most of the population lives on handouts financed by the export of natural resources.

Kto vinovat? Chto delat?

Who is to blame? What is to be done? These are Russians' eternal questions about their destiny, today as much as in the past.

The blame for Russia's current distress lies first of all with the utopian image of the free-market economy touted by Western theorists. Secondly, there is the traditional Russian penchant for extreme and simplistic solutions. Thirdly, there is the equally ideological rejection of everything associated with the Soviet past. On top of all this came the divisive leadership politics of the post-totalitarian succession—first, Gorbachev's quest for an alternative to the Communist bureaucracy, and then Yeltsin's embrace of the radical free-market program in order to mark himself off from Gorbachev. Western advice and promises of aid only confirmed the Yeltsin regime in its radical commitments.

In a population without much internalized self-discipline and a tendency to see the market as an opportunity for speculation rather than

production, the sudden removal of economic controls caused a catastrophic lapse into crime and corruption. The "social safety net" and the
"social market" are more fiction than fact. The democratic enthusiasm of
1991 is gone, replaced by cynicism and apathy. The Brezhnev era begins
to look good in contrast.

Free-market reform has not strengthened democracy in Russia. On the
contrary, by stimulating political reactions against the Yeltsin regime, it
has provoked the latter into more and more authoritarian methods of
rule. Russia is experiencing the Pinochet scenario by degrees, as it moves
backwards politically towards dictatorship in order to support the ideological commitment to capitalism.

To find a way out of its current crisis Russia needs to de-ideologize its
thinking and analyze its problems and resources without illusion, whether
Westernist or nativist. It has to confront its limitations in experience and
cultural background, and the ghastly lapse into anarchy and criminality
that utopian reform efforts have allowed. Clearing away the damage done
by ideological mythology would require, among other things, that the
government stop artificial privatization of existing state entities; reassert
control over foreign trade and the revenue from the export of natural
resources; restore economic planning in its indirect form and accelerate
conversion in the military-industrial complex, rather than contemplate
bankruptcies and unemployment (or arms sales abroad); temporarily re-
control basic prices; protect industry and agriculture from foreign competition in order to revive domestic production and employment; recognize regional interdependence among the former Soviet republics without
imposing coercive unity on the one hand or abetting particularistic impoverishment on the other. All these steps, unfortunately, defy the model
of free-market reform demanded by Western governments and financial
institutions as the price of aid and credits. Nevertheless, Russia needs to
define its own destiny and not let it be imposed by outside ideologists.

A remedy for Russia that combines democratic values with recognition
of modern social realities points logically to some form of compromise
solution, including the politics of federalism and a mixed economy. In
essence this means the direction that perestroika was moving in up to
1990, before opposition on the left and on the right disrupted its progress.
Whether the necessary political forces could be mustered in the near term
to support such an approach remains to be seen, but it would clearly
be more compatible with Russian democracy than the obsession with
unfettered capitalism that has dominated Russian reform since perestroika was abandoned. Still, it will take a long time to undo the political
as well as economic damage inflicted on Russia by the Yeltsin regime just
as the country was coming out of the long shadow of totalitarianism.

PART SIX

REFLECTIONS

CHAPTER THIRTY-NINE

AMERICAN SOVIET STUDIES AND THE GRAND SURPRISE OF 1991 (1996)

By 1995, despite its self-inflicted troubles, post-Communist Russia had stabilized enough for a retrospective review of outsiders' understanding of the country's transformation.

Was sovietology as it was pursued in the United States invalidated because it failed to predict the collapse of Communism? This proposition has come to be accepted even among people who used to practice that occult art themselves but have since 1991 been at pains to disown it. However, the question assumes too much. We have to pick it apart and put to ourselves a series of more specific queries in order to grasp the impact of 1991 on the study of Russian/Soviet affairs. What was "sovietology"? What, in actuality, was "Communism," and what do we mean by its "collapse"? Finally, was there a failure of prediction that was out of line with other surprises in human affairs?

The conventional wisdom, expressed by most observers in Western governments and media as well as a few senior sovietologists themselves, is that Communism was a "utopian experiment," based on the insidious theory of Marxism-Leninism, defying human nature, but cruelly foisted upon hapless populations until at length the Soviet empire proved incapable of keeping up in the global competition for power. Ideological commitment to their elusive goal, it is said, drove the Communist leaders to erect the system of totalitarianism with all its horrors, paralleling (or perhaps copied by) the totalitarianism of a rightist utopia in Central Europe. This is a thesis of the doctrinal generation of totalitarianism, implying a sort of ideological determinism according to which evil results are due simply to evil ideas, independently of the circumstances. The resulting system, therefore, could not be altered in its "essence"; it could only be overthrown from without, or—a possibility that no one expected—it could break down internally and be replaced by something altogether different. Gorbachev's *perestroika*, in this reasoning, was a futile attempt to salvage the Communist system without giving up its putative essence, whereas the Yeltsin regime, heir to the collapse, is presumed to represent a wholly new departure.

This picture, for all its prevalence, does not withstand close scrutiny. The Soviet record since the revolution manifests a profound transformation, proceeding through a series of markedly different stages and reflecting the traditions and conditions of the Russian scene as well as the ambitions, obsessions, and usually misbegotten choices by successive political leaders. Generally speaking, the more closely one looks into the details of any social system and its development, the less accurately do "models" such as totalitarianism fit the facts or tell us something we could not observe directly. This is not to say that Soviet reality did not approach the totalitarian model, but the theory did not allow for either the complex development or the dissolution of the totalitarian state. Instead, as some of its critics have contended, the totalitarian model became an emotional rallying point for moralistic anti-Sovietism in the later Cold War era. Westerners who questioned it on scholarly grounds ran the risk of political denunciation—and still do.

The so-called "collapse" of Communism is another formula that needs to be reexamined. "Collapse" is a facile popular image of what was actually a complex, step-by-step, and still incomplete process of change in the society or societies of the Soviet Union. Moreover, it obscures the elements of continuity in the successor regimes and their problems.

The key to this experience of transition was a sequence of events at the political center, inherently unpredictable, that eviscerated the authority and legitimacy of the Communist Party dictatorship. Democratization and decentralization, set in motion by Gorbachev in 1988–89, quickly became irreversible. By the time of its Twenty-Eighth Congress in 1990, more than a year before its debacle in the August Putsch, the party had become a hollow shell. By the last months of the Soviet Union, governance was arguably less personalistic than it was to become later on in the majority of the successor states, including Russia. What came nearest to an abrupt collapse was the ideological rationale of official Marxism-Leninism, but this had long since become a mere liturgical façade, believed in by none but the few who now make up the unregenerate Communist splinter parties. (Brezhnev is reported to have told his brother that faith in the doctrine was only for the gullible masses.[1]) Russian nationalism and great-power pride was the real ideology of the Communists, and this mentality persists virtually unabated along much of the political spectrum in Russia.

The command economy and the principles of state socialism held on a little longer, while Gorbachev's attempts at reform and reinvigoration undermined the actual performance of the system. Yeltsin, as president of the Russian Republic in opposition to Gorbachev from mid-1990 on, espoused a more drastic break with the economic past, and put it into effect following the dissolution of the Soviet Union. However, this economic change was not so much a "collapse" as it was the introduction of new principles from above by political command—an old story in Russia.

Serious economic breakdown was a characteristic not of Communism but of the system that replaced it.

Combining both the spontaneity of the political changeover and the directed character of the economic transition was the crisis of the Soviet nationalities and the liquidation of the Union. The latter event has been represented by the Yeltsin government as Russia's assertion of independence, along with the other republics, against an antinational Soviet dictatorship. This is absurd: The Soviet Union always was a revived version of the Russian Empire, and Russia was its core. It is more accurate to think of the breakup of the Union as a process of decolonization, driven by the minorities' assertion of autonomy as soon as Moscow began to democratize. Yeltsin's alternative Russian government in Moscow simply endorsed and accelerated this movement in order to strike against Gorbachev's more slowly reforming regime. De facto independence of the colonies and formal dissolution of the Russian Empire came easily once the August Coup had crippled the Union government. But within his Russian jurisdiction, Yeltsin has shown no sympathy toward the separatist aspirations of lesser national minorities.

It is a metaphorical excess to term the events of 1991 a "revolution," even if this notion seems to preserve the purity of the totalitarian model, that is, a system that remained solid until abruptly overthrown. There was no sudden, violent breakdown in the nationwide structure of power comparable to 1917. All of the elements of the so-called collapse of Communism started gradually, defying the totalitarian model, and none have yet been completed, which defies the simplistic image of a transition to market democracy.

Democratic politics have not scored any net progress in the former Soviet Union since the Communist Party surrendered its monopoly in 1990. Under Yeltsin, Russia moved step-by-step back to personalistic authoritarianism, particularly after the coup from above of September–October 1993 gave the President the power to ignore the legislative branch at his pleasure. At the same time, prodded by Russian nationalists, Yeltsin's government undertook to restore its hegemony over the former imperial space, in a horizontal mode of bilateral ties outside the Russian Federation and in a mode of vertical subordination within it. This is a process that economic, cultural, ethnic, and strategic realities make very logical, if not inevitable. Finally, the economy, if it could be brought out of its state of chaos and criminality, might remain more durably reformed than other aspects of Russian life, but this is not a facet of the Communist collapse so much as a product of governmental initiatives taken before as well as after the political overturn. Overall, Russia is still Russia, with its problems and obsessions rooted partly in the Communist past, partly in a political culture that is much older, and partly in the unique series of events that undid the old system of government.

❖   ❖   ❖

Analyzed into its elements, the so-called collapse of Communism be-comes a large order for any effort at prediction. Exact forecasting of polit-ical events in an inherently uncertain world is beyond the claims of any social science, excepting only quasi-religious doctrines such as Marxism (which despite its pretensions could not even predict the Russian Revolu-tion). Nevertheless, when we consider the specific elements that went into the transformation of the Soviet/Russian realm between 1985 and 1991, it is in fact remarkable how much broad awareness had been developed by sovietological research regarding the changes, stresses, and weaknesses that already marked the Soviet Union.

Signs of an impending crisis were perhaps clearest to Western econo-mists. It was obvious to them that the methods of the command econ-omy, no doubt effective as one alternative approach to extensive development, had become counterproductive when resource limits and foreign technological advantages imposed on the Soviets the need to shift to intensive development. A steady decline in the rate of economic growth between the 1960s and the 1980s made it impossible to reconcile the demands of consumers, investment, and the military, while the require-ments of the information society collided with Russian habits of official secrecy, and the gray economy corrupted the whole society. These prob-lems, of course, were equally obvious to Soviet reformers, the people who, under Gorbachev, initiated the disruptive efforts to decentralize and marketize the economy that in turn set the stage for real economic crisis under Yeltsin.

Sovietologists and social historians were long aware of the truly dialec-tical contradiction between the social modernization promoted by the Soviet regime, and the rigid and dysfunctional behavior of the regime itself. This is the typical recipe for revolution. An urbanized and educated populace with rising expectations pressed for material improvements and personal freedom, while the frustrations imposed by party controls un-dermined national morale. Soviet critics, up to the very top, themselves highlighted weaknesses in incentives and income fairness.

Soviet studies have been frequently faulted for neglecting the non-Russian minorities, yet in this area too an impending crisis had long been evident to specialists. Soviet propaganda about the "rapprochement" if not "merger" of nationalities was singularly unconvincing. Despite a con-siderable degree of ethnic mixing through internal migration and inter-marriage, it was clear that the façade of unity was maintained only by the secret police, and that any degree of democratization at the center would be a signal to the forces of national autonomy on the periphery. As I wrote on the eve of Gorbachev's accession to power, "In the minority regions particularly, there is reason for [the rulers'] anxiety if political liberalization should signal the opportunity to resist control from Moscow."[2]

Historians and political scientists also saw signs of inevitable change, even if its eventual depth took them by surprise. For one thing, analyses of generational differences in the Soviet leadership pointed to a major break when the cadre of Stalinist conservatives, growing old in office from the time of the purges of the 1930s, finally fell by the wayside. Political scientists noted the erosion of totalitarian discipline and ideological authority, and the formation of interest group politics and enclaves of professional autonomy beneath the skin of party conformity. For this insight, incidentally, sovietology was roundly denounced by some of the same defenders of the totalitarian model who subsequently faulted the alleged failures of sovietological prediction.

Taken as a whole, the work of Western slavists and sovietologists in their various disciplines was remarkably accurate and insightful in defining the elements of the crisis that overtook the Soviet Union. Their judgments went as far as any social science scholarship could responsibly go without resorting to wild guesswork. What could not be accurately foreseen, in the nature of the matter, was how these elements of crisis would play out at the political level where the decisions of leading personalities and the effects of chance events could be decisive. On this plane, contingencies and indeterminacies among alternative lines of development can never be ruled out. Above all, the August Putsch of 1991, widely anticipated and hardly surprising in its conservative intent, had totally unpredictable consequences, first in its ignominious failure, and second in the ultimately fatal destabilization of the government that it had unsuccessfully tried to overthrow.

As reforms unfolded and crises sharpened in the USSR between 1985 and 1991, Western scholarship was in most respects closely attuned to the new developments. Again, economics—the most concrete of the social sciences—was most accurate and perspicacious about Soviet needs and shortcomings, more so than the Soviet leadership itself. Studies of culture and the media tracked Gorbachev's introduction of *glasnost*, and had little difficulty anticipating its impact. In politics and particularly in foreign policy matters, sovietology fell behind events, reluctant as it was to take Gorbachev's "New Thinking" seriously enough, soon enough. If the profession had a general fault, it was not lack of insight but excessive caution, perhaps reflecting the continuing influence of prominent exponents of the totalitarian model who insisted that the Communist system could never seriously change from within. Notions that democratization and accommodation with the West could really be underway under perestroika were widely dismissed as 'Gorbymania.'

In nationality matters, events bore out the reality of change under perestroika, as local nationalists seized the opportunities offered by loosening at the center, and Russian conservatives reacted against threats to the integrity of the empire. Mark Beissinger and Lubomir Hajda are among those who have faulted Soviet studies for neglecting the nationalities, but their own work refutes the charge: "There is a nationalities component to every facet of Soviet politics. . . . The most likely outcome, short of a revision of *glasnost,* is sustained crisis. . . . In an era of reform, the nationalities problem presents Soviet leaders with their most serious challenge, one that virtually guarantees that Soviet political evolution will be neither smooth nor simple."[3] Gorbachev was caught in the middle, and responded erratically, while Yeltsin's decision to play the nationality card against him was highly predictable if one considered the personal animosity between the two. Truly surprising, on the other hand, was Soviet tolerance of the Communist debacle in Eastern Europe. Here we have a series of events that in some cases, above all in East Germany and Czechoslovakia, really did amount to a "collapse." Undoubtedly it was impressions of 1989 in the former Soviet bloc that lent the sense of "collapse" to events in the Soviet Union itself in 1991.

In my own conceptualization of developments since 1985 I use the perspective of revolution as a long-term process that comes to a close in the moderate revolutionary revival, with a return to some point of departure in between early revolutionary radicalism and the Old Regime.[4] (One might conceive of Gorbachev as representing a leftist alternative, and Yeltsin a rightist one.) The period of this revolutionary endgame is unstable and unpredictable, until a functioning constitutional government is finally arrived at. I have found the moderate revolutionary revival a useful concept for relating both the Gorbachev and Yeltsin periods to what went before, and for anticipating some of the changes and struggles that the most recent years have witnessed.

❖   ❖   ❖

Notwithstanding its impressive record of achievement, American sovietology went into a state of shock after the political earthquakes of 1989 and 1991. Numerous high-profile commentators—some within the profession, more outside it—seized on these events to denounce the entire practice of sovietology as worthless because it had "failed to predict" the unpredictable demise of Communist rule. Many practitioners in the field, swamped by media amplification of the anti-sovietological view, succumbed to the mood of professional breast-beating.

As I have noted, the actual crises of 1989 and 1991, governed as they were by personalities and contingencies, could not have been closely predicted from any model or precedent. Historians should be able to understand this truth better than those social scientists who try too hard to make events appear to be law-governed. What happened was just as surprising to all the political actors in the Soviet Union and Eastern Europe as it was to observers in the outside world. But this does not rule out the role of expertise in attempting to comprehend the background and consequences of the upheaval.

Intellectually in retreat since 1991, sovietology has been guilty of much more serious errors both of commission and of omission in addressing events since that turning point, when the new orthodoxy of "transitional studies" took hold in Western work on the former Soviet bloc. In this framework it was assumed beyond rational demonstration that democratic government and market economics would be the uniform outcome, subject only to debate about the best path and pace to this end. The process was not thought essentially different from comparable experiences in southern Europe, Latin America, and elsewhere in the Third World. Russian and Central European policy-makers who were most closely attuned to Western theory acted according to the premises of this school, and often appeared to validate the theory. Yet in detail the policies prescribed by transitology, intentionally undertaken to realize a predicted outcome, have been quite confounded by events.

In economics, the Russian disciples of the transitology school attempted to apply simultaneously the shock therapy of monetary austerity and the institutional reorganization of state socialism into private capitalism, presumably following the experience of Latin America and Central Europe. The financial outcome was the opposite of intention and prediction—runaway inflation, extinction of investment, plummeting of production, and mass impoverishment—in short, true collapse. Haste in trying to change the economic power structure, without first providing the necessary legal and financial framework, reminded one of the impetuosity of the Bolsheviks in the original extremist phase of the revolution. In behavioral terms, the outcome was predatory speculation and the metastasis of criminality, while the old "New Class" of the Communist *nomenklatura* turned itself into a phalanx of self-aggrandizing entrepreneurs. None of this was foreseen, obviously, or Western advice would no doubt have steered the reforms quite differently.

Transitology was equally defied by political developments. Taking account neither of the personal factor nor of Russian political culture, it failed to foresee the subversion of fragile new democratic institutions by supposedly democratic leaders in the successor republics. It pinned its democratic hopes and expectations on the personality and pronouncements of Yeltsin so uncritically that the unfolding of his authoritarian instincts and his break with the legislative branch of government in 1993 prompted some of his Western apologists to the patent falsification of the history of these events. No one seems to have expected the survival of the nomenklatura as a social force in enterprise administration and local government. The Yeltsin regime evoked illusions of democratic and capitalistic wish-fulfillment mirroring the self-deception of fellow travelers on the opposite end of the political spectrum in the 1930s.

Nationality studies, entranced by the seeming victories of self-determination in 1989 and 1991, failed to anticipate the ongoing curse of interethnic conflict as well as the economic and security pressures for reintegration in the CIS. Missed almost completely, until it became obvious, was the consolidation of political power in most of the former Soviet republics and many Russian regions by former Communist officials, now turned nationalist but still operating in the old authoritarian manner. The success of reform Communism in Eastern Europe was equally unanticipated and underappreciated. The force of Russian nationalism and chagrin over the dissolution of the empire were particularly underestimated until the startling showing of Zhirinovsky and his "Liberal Democratic" party in the elections of December 1993. In sum, Western sovietology—by now post-sovietology—shamed by its alleged failure to predict the Communist collapse, has in the main allowed itself to be seduced by the democratic and nationalist claims of the successor regimes, while putting its critical predictive powers on ice.

Since 1992 American sovietology, or rather the hastily renamed field of "Russian, East European, and Eurasian studies," has been caught in a mood of pessimistic soul-searching. It has lost confidence in the merit of its analyses. It has lost the sense of a unifying context that had been provided by the geographic compass of Communist regimes. It has seen financial support for training, research, and publications begin to dry up; presumably we no longer need to "know our enemy." Practitioners of Soviet studies, losing their sense of relevance, have begun to rejoin the mainstreams of their respective disciplines (usually theoretical, statistical, and parochially American), and they may fail to replicate their expertise on the area. All this at a time when the actual needs, opportunities, and talent for study of the former Communist realm were never more compelling. The slavist profession in the United States is running on the oil left in the pipeline.

Confronted by such professionally disconcerting conditions and events, American post-sovietology is in danger of embracing new simplicities that may render its analytical and predictive powers less effective than they actually were before perestroika. Some of the deceptively universalistic tendencies in political science have already been noted. History of the area is being carried away by the mainstream fashions of social history and gender studies at the expense of the political history of the Communist regimes now documented by newly accessible archives. Economics, once the star discipline in sovietology, has dismissed the planned economy as a synonym for Stalinism, and has lapsed into simplistic mainstream assumptions that the post-Communist economies are almost "normal," or if not should be made so by shock therapy.[5]

Under the circumstances, within the American scholarly community as well as in the target region, do post-Soviet studies have any future? If they do, the outcome depends on intellectual effort and serious self-criticism, though not the kind of breast-beating that has been so fashionable since the end of the Communist regimes in Europe.

Firstly, post-sovietology needs to recognize the path it took to post-Soviet error. It was too skeptical of Gorbachev and too trusting of Yeltsin, too reserved about the possibility and progress of reform under Communist aegis, too uncritical of reform in its radical, post-Communist version. Like much of sovietology in the old days, it read the successor regimes too literally: Gorbachev was still a Communist and therefore he could not really change; Yeltsin was an anti-Communist (notwithstanding his identical background) and therefore his every action had to be legitimate.

Secondly, post-sovietology must emphasize that the Communist background is still relevant. To be sure, Communism has passed from the purview of the present-minded disciplines to the historical. Nevertheless, it still gives a unity of experience and circumstance to all the countries of the former Soviet bloc, however diverse their post-Communist lines of development may be.

Thirdly, post-sovietology should be chary of simplistic or rigid paradigms. This was the most obvious drawback in pre-collapse sovietology, with its partiality to glib formulas such as totalitarianism or pat explanations such as Marxist ideology. Now new catch-phrases have taken over— transitions to democracy, market economy, national self-determination—without enough critical reflection about their meaning and their relationship to actual events. Though sovietology's effort to be value-neutral in the spirit of modern social science has been denigrated by ex-Cold Warriors, post-sovietology needs to hew again to this standard at least to the extent that it distinguishes between wish and reality.

Finally, area specialists in their respective disciplines must keep their common area studies identity intact so that they can continue to learn from each other as they have in the past. Someone needs to understand the singularities of the region as a whole, not to mention individual countries, as against the global generalities propounded by the traditional academic fields. Otherwise, expertise on the region will sink out of sight into the respective disciplinary mainstreams, leaving afloat only the earliest pieces of Russian and East European studies, namely a little language work and antiquarian history. This would be a sad conclusion to one of the most exciting facets of American scholarly accomplishment in this century.

CONCLUSION

Russia's transformation was a unique episode in history, a many-stranded process not easily reducible to simple formulas like "transition to market democracy." It was historic in every sense, as a momentous event governed by contingencies and personalities that made it hard either to predict or to explain. It was history as it unfolds from moment to moment, when even the historical actors themselves do not know what is coming next or how they are going to respond to new situations. It challenges the rationalist fallacy of retrospective determinism, which presumes that things had to happen the way they did, because the mind balks at the thought that matters could have turned out very differently if the crucial accidents had gone another way.

Though Russia's transformation was unpredictable in detail, the anticipation of great change was possible in an incremental fashion. At each step in the process the next development was fairly obvious, from the contradictions of the Old Regime, through the measures of reform that Gorbachev found himself pressed to take, to the forces—reformist, conservative, and minority separatist—that undermined perestroika, followed by the collapse of the shell of Communist authority and the search for some workable combination of freedom and order. What was less governed by logic, and hence less predictable, was the choices and actions of decisive personalities, above all Gorbachev and Yeltsin, as they sought avenues both of societal reform and of personal vindication. In particular, Gorbachev's backing away from reform in 1990–91 and the radicalness of Yeltsin's subsequent reform efforts could not have been anticipated. The August Coup could be seen coming, but not its denouement with the delegitimization of the whole Soviet system. If there was any widespread failure of prediction where prediction was possible, it was in foreseeing the consequences of Yeltsin's political and economic decisions, and the grim conditions under which Russia's experiment in post-Communist democracy has had to operate.

In the aftermath of perestroika and the power struggles under Yeltsin, Russia has become politically exhausted. In combination, the Communist success in the parliamentary elections of December 1995 and Yeltsin's victory in the presidential election of June–July 1996 left the country in an impasse, unwilling either to go back to Communism or to support the consummation of free-market reform. Does this mean that Russia's transformation is now complete? That is unlikely.

Russia still suffers deep, unresolved contradictions in its incomplete course of post-Communist reform. There is the contradiction between new democratic institutions and an old authoritarian political culture (in the minds of both rulers and ruled). There is the contradiction between ideology and reality in the economic realm, with the challenge of a depressed and degraded economy. There is the contradiction between the principle of national self-determination in the former Soviet Union and Communist bloc, and Russian imperial reflexes and great-power nostalgia—the Weimar complex, as it were. These contradictions are bound to drive further changes along until Russia's post-Communist transition can be considered complete. How the country will emerge from the rubble, and how long this will take, is a new challenge to the art of political prediction.

ENDNOTES

Chapter 1

1. *The Mind of Napoleon: A Selection from his Written and Spoken Words*, J. Christopher Herold, ed. (New York: Columbia University Press, 1956), 64.

2. Trotsky, Speech to the Central Control Commission, June 1927, in Leon Trotsky, *The Stalin School of Falsification* (New York: Pioneer Publishers, 1937), 143. N. V. Ustrialov was a conservative Russian economist who advocated cooperation with the Communists under the New Economic Policy after 1921.

3. Crane Brinton, *The Anatomy of Revolution* (New York: Prentice-Hall, 1938, 1952). See also Henri Sée, *Evolution et Révolution* (Paris, Flammarion, 1929); Pitirim Sorokin, *The Sociology of Revolution* (Philadelphia: Lippincott, 1925).

4. Alexander Yakovlev, "The Great French Revolution and the Present Day," *Sovetskaya Kultura*, 15 July 1989.

5. M. S. Gorbachev, Speech at a meeting with representatives of the country's miners, 3 Apr. 1991.

6. Yakovlev, "The Great French Revolution and the Present Day."

7. Cf. Robert V. Daniels, *Russia— The Roots of Confrontation* (Cambridge, Mass.: Harvard University Press, 1985), 363.

8. Cf. Robert V. Daniels, "The Revival of the Russian Revolutionary," *Rinascita*, 14 Feb. 1987; English text published as chapter 7, "The Revolutionary Legacy," in Robert V. Daniels, *Is Russia Reformable?* (Boulder, Colo.: Westview Press, 1988), 128–29.

9. See M. S. Gorbachev, Report to the Nineteenth Party Conference, 28 June 1988.

10. Yakovlev, "The Great French Revolution."

11. M. S. Gorbachev, Political Report of the CPSU Central Committee to the 28th CPSU Congress, 2 July 1990.

Chapter 2

1. In fact, Rusakov became head of that department in the spring of 1968 and served as a member of the Secretariat from 1977 to 1986.

2. Carl Linden, *Khrushchev and the Soviet Leadership* (Baltimore: Johns Hopkins University Press, 1966).

3. John Kenneth Galbraith, *The New Industrial State* (New York: Harcourt, Brace, 1967).

Chapter 3

1. See *Interest Groups in Soviet Politics*, H. Gordon Skilling and Franklin Griffiths, eds. (Princeton: Princeton University Press, 1970).

2. See, for example, Victor A. Thompson, *Modern Organization: A General Theory* (New York: Knopf, 1961).

Chapter 4

1. *Die Presse* (Vienna), 28 May 1977.
2. Myron Rush, *Political Succession in the USSR* (New York: Columbia University Press, 1965), 209–10.
3. Michel Tatu, *Power in the Kremlin: From Khrushchev to Kosygin* (New York: Viking, 1968), 403–4, 408-9.

Chapter 5

1. T. Harry Rigby, "Politics in the Mono-Organizational Society," in *Authoritarian Politics in Communist Europe*, Andrew Janos, ed. (Berkeley: University of California Press, 1976).
2. Marx, *Capital*, vol. 1 (New York: Modern Library), 837.
3. Alec Nove, "Socialism, Centralised Planning, and the One-Party State," in *Authority, Power, and Policy in the USSR*, T. H. Rigby, Archie Brown, and Peter Reddaway, eds. (New York: St. Martin's Press, 1980).
4. T. H. Rigby, "A Conceptual Approach to Authority, Power, and Policy in the Soviet Union," in *Authority, Power*, 19.
5. Jerry F. Hough, *How the Soviet Union is Governed* (Cambridge, Mass.: Harvard University Press, 1978), 530–34, 550–51.
6. Roy A. Medvedev, *On Stalin and Stalinism* (Oxford: Oxford University Press, 1979), 178–79.
7. Rigby, "Conceptual Approach," 11–19.
8. Darrell P. Hammer, "Inside the Ministry of Culture: Cultural Policy in the Soviet Union," in *Public Policy and Administration in the Soviet Union*, Gordon B. Smith, ed. (New York: Praeger, 1980), 54.

Chapter 8

1. Marc D. Zlotnik, "Chernenko's Platform," *Problems of Communism*, 31, no. 6 (Nov.–Dec., 1982): 74–75.

Chapter 11

1. *Histoire mondiale des socialismes*, Jean Elleinstein et al., eds. (Paris: A. Colin, 1984).
2. Edward L. Keenan, "Muscovite Political Folkways," *The Russian Review*, 45, no. 2 (Apr. 1986): 115–81.

3. Valery Chalidze, "One-Party Democracy," in *SSSR: Vnutrennie Protivorechiya*, Valery Chalidze, ed. (Benson, Vt.: Chalidze Publications, no. 19, 1987): 18–29.

Chapter 12

1. Nina Andreyeva, "I cannot forego principles," *Sovetskaya Rossiya*, 13 Mar. 1988. The letter was clearly inspired by the Ligachev faction, and seemed to presage a reversal of Gorbachev's reforms.

Chapter 13

1. Press conference of M. S. Gorbachev, 1 June 1988, *Pravda*, 2 June 1988.
2. Ronald Reagan, Remarks to Members of the Royal Institute of International Affairs, London, 3 June 1988, *Papers of the Presidents of the United States*: Ronald Reagan, 1988 (Washington: GPO, 1990), 718.
3. Interview with O. N. Bykov, *Izvestia*, 7 May 1988.
4. Mikhail S. Gorbachev, *Perestroika: New Thinking for our Country and the World* (New York: Harper & Row, 1987).
5. Fyodor Burlatsky, "Brushstrokes in a Political Portrait," *Literaturnaya Gazeta*, 24 Feb. 1988, 14.
6. Resolution of the Nineteenth Conference of the CPSU, "On Glasnost," *Pravda*, 5 July 1988.
7. M. S. Gorbachev, Concluding Speech to the Nineteenth Party Conference, 1 June 1988.
8. Jack Gray, "Conclusions," in *Political Culture and Political Change in Communist States*, Archie Brown and Jack Gray, eds. (New York: Holmes & Meier, 1977), 260.

Chapter 14

1. V. Rubanov, "From the 'Cult of Secrecy' to the Information Culture," *Kommunist*, no. 13 (Sept. 1988): 24–36.
2. V. A. Medvedev, "An Up-to-date Conception of Socialism," Speech at an International Scholarly Conference, 4 Oct. 1988, *Pravda*, 5 Oct. 1988.
3. Robert M. Slusser, *Stalin in October: The Man Who Missed the Revolution* (Baltimore: Johns Hopkins University Press, 1987).
4. The reference is to the imposition of martial law in Poland in 1981.

Chapter 16

1. Dawn Mann and Elizabeth Teague ("Gorbachev's Green Revolution," *Radio Liberty Reports*, 31 Mar. 1989, 1–2) report that Soviet television film of the Central Committee's

session held on 15 March to elect the party's 100 members to the People's Congress showed prospective as well as de jure members of the Central Committee casting ballots.

2. For complete data for all central committees since 1952, see Robert V. Daniels, *Is Russia Reformable?* (Boulder, Colo.: Westview Press, 1988), 94.

Chapter 17

1. David Remnick, "Soviet Slavic Republics Holding Key Elections," *The Washington Post*, 4 Mar. 1990.

Chapter 18

1. Lilia Shevtsova, "Opposition: A New Word in Our Political Vocabulary," *Izvestia*, 22 Feb. 1990.

2. *Ogonyok*, no. 8 (Mar. 1990): 5; *Literaturnaya Gazeta*, 14 Feb. 1990. The "Black Hundreds" were violent ultra-rightist groups before the revolution.

3. Alexander Yakovlev, Speech to the Supreme Soviet, 27 Feb. 1990.

4. V. M. Mishin, Speech at the Central Committee Plenum, 11 Mar. 1990.

5. Yegor Ligachev, Interview with *Selskaya Zhizn*, 4 Apr. 1990.

6. Alexander Tsipko, Quoted in Radio Liberty *Report on the USSR* 2, no. 13 (30 Mar. 1990): 2.

7. Yegor Ligachev, Television interview, "Vremya," 21 May 1990.

Chapter 19

1. Giulietto Chiesa, *Transizione alla democrazia: La nascita delle forze politiche in Urss* (Rome: Lucarini Editore, 1990), 83–86 [English edition, *Transition to Democracy: Political Change in the Soviet Union, 1987–1991* (Hanover, N.H.: University Press of New England, 1993), 60–63].

Chapter 20

1. A. Migranyan, "An Indissoluble Union? On the Prospects of the Soviet State System," *Izvestia*, 20 Sept. 1990.

2. Migranyan, "An Indissoluble Union."

3. *The Washington Post*, 18 Nov. 1990.

Chapter 21

1. M. S. Gorbachev, Speech to the Supreme Soviet, 16 Nov. 1990.

2. Yuri Levada, Interview in *Moscow News*, 9 Dec. 1990.

3. Galina Starovoitova, Quoted in *Moscow News*, 23 Dec. 1990.

Chapter 22

1. Engels to Vera Zasulich, 23 Apr. 1885, in Karl Marx and Friedrich Engels, *Selected Correspondence, 1846–1895* (New York: International Publishers, 1942), 437–38.

2. *Literaturnaya Gazeta*, 23 Jan. 1991.

Chapter 23

1. Mikhail S. Gorbachev, *The August Coup: The Truth and the Lessons* (New York: HarperCollins, 1991).

2. Text in Gorbachev, *August Coup*, appendix C, 97–127.

3. Gorbachev, *August Coup*, 47.

4. Michel Tatu, *Mikhail Gorbachev: The Origins of Perestroika* (New York: Columbia University Press, 1991), vii.

5. Tatu, *Gorbachev*, 149–50.

6. Giulietto Chiesa, *Cronaca del golpe rosso* (Milano: Baldini & Castaldo, 1991), 18.

7. Chiesa, *Cronaca*, 24.

8. Chiesa, *Cronaca*, 229–30.

9. John Morrison, *Boris Yeltsin: From Bolshevik to Democrat* (New York: Dutton, 1991), 291.

10. Morrison, *Yeltsin*, 274.

11. Morrison, *Yeltsin*, 289–90.

12. Vladimir Bukovsky, "Born Again and Again," *The New Republic* (10 Sept. 1990), quoted in Morrison, *Yeltsin*, 22.

13. Morrison, *Yeltsin*, 25.

14. Anatoly Sobchak, *For a New Russia: The Mayor of St. Petersburg's Own Story of the Struggle for Justice and Democracy* (New York: The Free Press, 1992), 158.

15. Sobchak, *New Russia*, 160.

16. Sobchak, *New Russia*, 141.

17. Chiesa, *Cronaca*, 10.

18. Sobchak, *New Russia*, 175.

Chapter 24

1. Alfred G. Meyer, *Marxism: The Unity of Theory and Practice* (Cambridge, Mass.: Harvard University Press, 1958).

2. Milovan Djilas, *The New Class: An Analysis of the Communist System* (New York: Praeger, 1957); James Burnham, *The Managerial Revolution* (New York: John Day, 1941).

3. Alexander Yakovlev, *The Fate of Marxism in Russia* (New Haven: Yale University Press, 1993), 102.

4. Yakovlev, *Fate of Marxism*, 51–52, 65.

5. Yakovlev, *Fate of Marxism*, 73.

6. Yakovlev, *Fate of Marxism*, 109, 118–19.

7. Alexander Yakovlev, Answers to questions from Young Communists, 4 July 1990, *Komsomolskaya Pravda*, 10 July 1990.

8. Alexander Yakovlev, "Bolshevism as a Phenomenon" (lecture at Harvard University, 17 Nov. 1991), in *Fate of Marxism*, appendix 2, 191–96.

9. Alexander Yakovlev, "The Great French Revolution and the Present Day," *Sovetskaya Kultura*, 15 July 1989.

Chapter 25

1. Draft Treaty on the Union of Sovereign Republics, *Pravda* and *Izvestia*, 9 Mar. 1991.

2. M. S. Gorbachev, Report to the Supreme Soviet, 16 Nov. 1990.

3. Appeal to the Soviet People by the State Committee on the State of Emergency in the USSR, *Pravda* and *Izvestia*, 20 August 1991.

4. Text in *The New York Times*, 26 Dec. 1991.

5. *Newsweek*, 30 Dec. 1991, 21; John Morrison, *Boris Yeltsin: From Bolshevik to Democrat* (New York: Dutton, 1991), 290.

Chapter 26

1. Hannah Arendt, *The Origins of Totalitarianism* (New York: Harcourt, Brace & World, 1951).

2. See Moshe Lewin, *The Gorbachev Phenomenon: A Historical Interpretation* (Berkeley: University of California Press, 1988); J. Arch Getty, *The Origins of the Great Purges* (Cambridge, Eng.: Cambridge University Press, 1985).

Chapter 27

1. *Delo Petrashevtsev* (Moscow and Leningrad: Academy of Sciences Press, 1937–51) 1, 522.

2. So known from the collection of essays by that name published in 1909; English translation, *Landmarks: A Collection of Essays on the Russian Intelligentsia*, Boris Shragin and Albert Todd, eds. (New York: Karz Howard, 1977).

3. See Nikolai Berdiaev, *The Origins of Russian Communism* (Boston: Beacon Press, 1962).

4. Nina Andreyeva, "I Cannot Forego Principles," *Sovetskaya Rossiya*, 13 Mar. 1988.

5. Resolution no. 1 of the State Committee on the State of Emergency in the USSR, *Pravda* and *Izvestia*, 20 Aug. 1991.

6. The reference is to General Augusto Pinochet, dictator of Chile from 1973 to 1989, and his suppression of the Left in favor of a free-market program.

Chapter 28

1. Quoted in *The Montreal Gazette*, 21 June 1992.

2. Lyudmila Telen, "Revolution without an End," *Moscow News*, 7 June 1992.

3. Quoted in *The Washington Post*, 27 Dec. 1991.

4. Quoted by Serge Schmemann, *The New York Times*, 12 June 1992.

5. Oleg Saveliev, "Confidence in Russian Leaders is Falling," *Nezavisimaya Gazeta*, 30 May 1992.

Chapter 30

1. Georgi Sakhnazarov, "A Centrist Alliance will Save Russia," *L'Unità*, 24 Feb. 1993.

2. Charles de Gaulle, press conference in 1964, quoted in Henri Astier, "The Unmasking of the President," *Times Literary Supplement*, 5 Feb. 1993, 6.

3. *Moscow News*, 19 July 1992.

4. Sakhnazarov, "Centrist Alliance."

Chapter 31

1. Quoted, e.g., in Fred Barnes, "Bill and Boris," *The New Republic* (26 Apr. 1993): 12.

Chapter 32

1. Arkady Volsky, in *Megalopolis-Express*, 21 April 1993.

2. B. N. Yeltsin, Speech to the Russian Federation Council of Ministers, 29 Apr. 1993.

3. Oleg Rumiantsev, Quoted in *Nezavisimaya Gazeta*, 20 May 1993.

4. Georgi Shakhnazarov, "A Straitjacket of a New Cut," *Nezavisimaya Gazeta*, 20 May 1993.

Chapter 36

1. *Nezavisimaya Gazeta*, 13 Oct. 1993.

Chapter 37

1. Quoted in Margaret Shapiro, "New Parliament—Same Yeltsin Headache," *The Washington Post*, 19 Dec. 1994.

2. Alexander Rahr, "Russia: A Troubled Future," *RFE/RL Research* 3, no. 24 (17 June 1994): 5.

3. Steven Erlanger, "Russian Premier's Star is Rising Fast," *The New York Times*, 26 Jan. 1994.

4. "Who, in the Opinion of the Americans, Will Become the New President of Russia?" *Nezavisimaya Gazeta*, 12 Apr. 1994.

5. *Nezavisimaya Gazeta*, 3 Mar. 1994.

6. Quoted in *The New York Times*, 2 Mar. 1994.

7. Interview of Shakhrai in *Komsomolskaya Pravda*, 10 Mar. 1994. Shakhrai later returned to work for Yeltsin.

8. See James Douglas, report to the International Foundation for Electoral Systems, Mar. 1994.

9. Lev Bruni, "The President's Old New Style," *Sevodnya*, 11 June 1994.

10. Lyudmila Telen, "Yeltsin on the Offensive," *Moscow News*, 24 June 1994.

Chapter 38

1. S. Shatalin et al., "Man, Freedom, and the Market (Outline of the program for changing over to the market)," *Izvestia*, 4 Sept. 1990.

2. Max Weber, "Bourgeois Democracy in Russia," in *The Russian Revolutions* (Ithaca: Cornell University Press, 1995), 109.

3. Marshall Goldman, *Lost Opportunity: Why Economic Reforms in Russia Have Not Worked* (New York: Norton, 1994), 255.

4. Marshall Goldman, "Comrade Godfather," *The Washington Post*, 12 Feb. 1995.

5. To some extent this collapse was offset by the upsurge in private and illegal activity that never came to the attention of the statisticians and the tax collectors. Post-Soviet figures may understate economic performance as much as Soviet figures exaggerated it.

6. Alexander Solzhenitsin, "To Tame Savage Capitalism," *The New York Times*, 28 Nov. 1993.

Chapter 39

1. Luba Brezhneva, *The World I Left Behind: Pieces of a Past* (New York: Random House, 1995), 162.

2. Robert V. Daniels, *Russia—the Roots of Confrontation* (Cambridge, Mass.: Harvard University Press, 1985), 365.

3. Mark Beissinger and Lubomir Hajda, "Nationalism and Reform in Soviet Politics," in *The Nationalities Factor in Soviet Politics and Society*, Hajda and Beissinger, eds. (Boulder, Colo.: Westview Press, 1990), 305, 320.

4. See Daniels, *Russia—The Roots of Confrontation*, 363–64; Daniels, *Is Russia Reform-able* (Boulder, Colo.: Westview Press, 1988), 127–32; chapter 1 above.

5. See James R. Millar, "Rethinking Soviet Economic Studies," Ford Foundation Workshop Series, "Rethinking Soviet Studies" (Washington, D. C.: Kennan Institute, 23 Oct. 1992).

INDEX